Our Own Language:
An Irish Initiative

Multilingual Matters

Please contact us for the latest book information:
Multilingual Matters,
Bank House, 8a Hill Road,
Clevedon, Avon BS21 7HH,
England

MULTILINGUAL MATTERS 66
Series Editor: Derrick Sharp

Our Own Language: An Irish Initiative

Gabrielle Maguire

MULTILINGUAL MATTERS LTD
Clevedon • Philadelphia • Adelaide

do
Phádraig ó Brannduibh,
cara dílís

Library of Congress Cataloging in Publication Data

Maguire, Gabrielle
Our Own Language: An Irish Initiative/Gabrielle Maguire
p. cm. (Multilingual Matters: 66)
Includes bibliographic references and index.
1. Irish language — Social aspects — Northern Ireland — Belfast.
I. Title. II. Series: Multilingual Matters (Series): 66.
PB1298.B45M34   1990
306.4'4'0899162   dc20

British Library Cataloguing in Publication Data

Maguire, Gabrielle
Our Own Language: An Irish Initiative (Multilingual Matters: 66)
1. Belfast. Irish language. Sociolinguistic aspects.
I. Title
491.62

ISBN 1-85359-096-7
ISBN 1-85359-095-9 (Pbk)

Multilingual Matters Ltd

UK: Bank House, 8a Hill Road, Clevedon, Avon BS21 7HH, England.
USA: 1900 Frost Road, Suite 101, Bristol, PA 19007, USA.
Australia: P.O. Box 6025, 83 Gilles Street, Adelaide, SA 5000, Australia.

Index compiled by Meg Davies (Society of Indexers).
Typeset by Editorial Enterprises, Torquay.
Printed and bound in Great Britain by the Longdunn Press, Bristol.

Contents

The story of the Shaw's Road Community and school as a natural
progression in the evolution of consciousness and achievement.
The growth of a school-centred sociolinguistic network expanding
beyond Shaw's Road.

A socio-economic description of families from outside the Shaw's
Road Community whose children attend the school.

An examination of considerations influencing parents' decisions to
send their children to the Irish-medium primary school at Shaw's
Road.

An analysis of the language shift towards bilingualism occurring
in the homes of pupils drawn from outside the Shaw's Road
Community.

An examination of those language shift patterns, in domains
outside the home, which are characteristic of non-Shaw's Road
families of Bunscoil pupils.

Parents' contact with traditional rural Gaeltachts is probed along
with their attitudes towards the variety of Irish in common usage
in Belfast.

An insight is provided into how Community children view the role
of Irish in their lives. This information draws on lengthy, in-depth
discussions together with the author's observations.

A description of the principal linguistic trends distinguishing the
variety of Irish which is developing among Community children
and indeed is in popular use in Belfast.

Introduction

General Orientation

This book tells the story of a bilingual community in Belfast. It had its origin in a PhD thesis which was commenced in 1982 and completed in the autumn of 1986, at the Queen's University of Belfast. The subject of the study was a community of eleven families who, during the 1960s, determined to raise their children through Irish in a favourable, supportive environment. At a first glance, this goal may seem reasonable and unremarkable. It can be better appreciated in light of the fact that none of these couples were native speakers of Irish. Rather, they had all taken steps to become competent speakers as young adults.

Indeed, any project aimed at rebuilding the status and functional value of what is perceived as 'our own language' could be further appreciated within a broader context. Within a global framework, where multinational industries postulate uniformity, peoples who protest the authenticity of their cultural identity become an endangered species. Mass media and mass marketing share a common interest in moulding a culturally homogeneous target population, embracing as wide a territory as possible. Under the impact of these commercial forces ordinary peoples become submerged in value systems which do not take cognisance of distinctive identities. The object of reaching a wide target population which has been trained to respond to these commercial forces makes financial sense. However, cultural diversity can only hope to hover on the periphery of this type of model. Accordingly, the preservation of cultural distinctiveness becomes an uphill struggle, posing an awesome challenge.

This book tells of a community in Belfast which accepted the challenge. These people resolved not only to learn Irish but to become active, competent bilinguals and to rear their children as confident Irish speakers whose view of the world would be perceived from their own culturally unique perspective. Furthermore, they set about generating a wider awareness, in surrounding neighbourhoods, of the relevance of the Irish language in today's urban scene. In addition to the vast economic pressures which discourage such a venture, the reality of pursuing these goals lacked the advantage of a favourable social, historical and political framework.

Irish enjoys no official status in the six north eastern counties of Ireland and the promotion of the language has depended largely on the work of independent cultural groups and organisations. Until the early part of the twentieth century Irish survived as a native language in four of those six counties — Tyrone, Antrim, Armagh and Derry. Indeed, in parts of Tyrone, native speakers could still be found in the 1950s. However, any opportunity for being raised in an Irish-speaking (or bilingual) environment in Northern Ireland was eradicated as these Irish-speaking pockets disappeared. The young couples who determined to restore some of its former vigour to the language, by acquiring it and developing it as the family and community language, realised that this could not be achieved satisfactorily if they were dispersed throughout Belfast. They had to establish an Irish-speaking nucleus wherein social interaction could be carried out through Irish.

Participants in the enterprise set about securing a site and building their houses, with a view to constructing an Irish-speaking urban enclave wherein the Community children could find it 'natural' to communicate through Irish. Their acquisition of English was ensured by exposure to the media and by interaction with non-Irish speakers from outside the Community. The conditions wherein Irish could be used had to be created and nurtured.

Community members were motivated by the recognition that the creation of a socially cohesive speech community was necessary if they were to have any chance of bringing up Irish-speaking families in Belfast. This project proved successful. Not only did the Community of eleven families survive the pressures of being rooted in an English-speaking society. In addition, it exerted a significant impact upon the surrounding neighbourhoods, contributing to a wider shift towards bilingualism. Furthermore, the Shaw's Road Community inspired other community enterprises throughout the North, particularly in the area of Irish-medium education.

Linguists have written prolifically about the various types and degrees of bilingualism which exist throughout the world. Definitions of bilingualism have ranged from a 'nativelike' command of two languages (Bloomfield, 1933), or an 'equal proficiency in two languages' (Rayfield, 1970: 11) to a much more relaxed, minimal acquaintance with the less dominant language (Haugen, 1956; Macnamara, 1967: 59–77). In the present book, the focus is directed at the emergence of bilingualism in West Belfast. However, an evaluation of the nature and degree of language dominance has not been a primary objective in this work. Rather, a broader approach was considered more meaningful and, indeed, necessary in this particular study.

Over the past few decades, it has become widely recognised that a study of language involves more than an evaluation of linguistic data. This is evident from the development of a multi-disciplinary approach to language, particularly within the areas of education, sociology and psychology. In a bilingual situation, where a minority language is being reinvigorated in certain districts within the community, the study must encompass a variety of other pertinent issues. In such a situation, a linguistic examination cannot be fully understood unless the author provides some insights into other issues, such as the self-respect of individuals as part of a community and nation. Such insights help to bridge the gap between analysis and full understanding. Without wishing to overstate the point, a scientific analysis of linguistic phenomena will have a limited relevance if the researcher doesn't reach the spirit of the speech community. One example of a work which strikes the balance to considerable effect is Dorian's investigation of East Sutherland Gaelic in decline, in *Language Death* (1981).

The aim of this present book is to examine a unique bilingual situation in Belfast from a sociolinguistic perspective. However, it also records a story of remarkable achievement which will hopefully inspire any group of people interested in reintroducing or strengthening a minority language in a satisfying and functional way. It is hoped that a fairly comprehensive picture is given, portraying this Community's role in the diffusion of Irish as an effective means of communication in urban life. The linguistic profile of the Irish itself commanded primary attention during the years of research. A fuller and more detailed account is given in the thesis than could be presented here. However, the overall trends described here should be of as much interest to readers who are unfamiliar with Irish as to fluent speakers.

When the research for this work was initiated, the Irish-speaking Community at Shaw's Road was thriving quietly. Visitors came and went — mainly people interested in minority languages. However, local media had not yet paid any serious attention to the Community. The Irish-medium primary school (Bunscoil), founded and managed by Community parents, had expanded and begun to attract growing numbers of children from outside the Shaw's Road vicinity. As pressure on the Government persisted and increased, aimed at securing official recognition and support for the school, the national media became alerted to the emergence of a new sociolinguistic phenomenon in their midst. Incongruities in the treatment of Welsh, Scottish Gaelic and Irish attracted more overt criticism as the public eye focused on the growth of this Community's school in West Belfast.

The thesis and subsequent book were prepared during an exciting period, both for the Shaw's Road Community and for Irish generally. The campaign for official support was drawing to a climax when research was just under way. During the first two years, the primary school was being funded largely by the organised activities of parents. Other parents had spent periods teaching in the school or providing educational materials for the children. A dramatic change followed the announcement by the Minister of Education that the Bunscoil was to be recognised as a Voluntary Maintained School, entitled to official financial backing. Pupil numbers continued to swell. More Irish-medium nursery schools sprang up in various community centres throughout the city, while similar developments were occurring elsewhere in the North. Indeed, the latest problem to be tackled by Belfast's Irish speakers has been how to overcome the need to restrict pupil intake into the Shaw's Road school and still respond to the mounting demand by parents for Irish-medium education. A second Irish-medium primary school was opened in the area in 1987, with the process of campaigning for official support initiated once more. Progress in the area of Irish-medium education was not paralleled in other schools where Irish is taught as a subject. Curriculum changes designed for secondary schools threatened to reduce the status of Irish at that level (DENI, 1988). The response from Irish-language teachers and other Irish speakers was vehemently opposed to official proposals. Later, certain concessions and modifications were made by the Minister.

Outside the realm of education further advances were made which suggest a more enlightened attitude towards the Irish language. For example, the total absence of official data on the position of Irish in the North has been, to some extent, corrected. The contribution of the Shaw's Road Community upon these developments is significant. In some ways, this influence has a direct bearing. Fundamentally, the fact of the Community's existence and survival have sufficed as a source of encouragement and motivation for other cultural and language-related projects.

In telling the story of the Shaw's Road Community in Belfast, it is vital to look beyond that core of eleven families to the families from surrounding neighbourhoods whose children attend the Bunscoil. These parents were given the opportunity to introduce their families to some degree of bilingualism by sending their children to the Bunscoil. All of the parents make some effort to acquire Irish in order to support their children. Accordingly, not only do children from predominantly English-speaking homes become competent, active bilinguals but, to varying degrees, the Irish language penetrates the home. This extended network of families is referred to, throughout the book, as the 'Bunscoil families'.

Content

The Shaw's Road Community was planned throughout the 1960s and the first couples took up residence towards the end of that decade. The emergence of this Irish-speaking community in Belfast was a pioneering initiative in many respects. However, it represents an important development in the history of the

Irish language — a development which grew out of a long series of preceding events. This development was an almost inevitable reaction to a peculiar interaction of social, political and educational circumstances within Northern Ireland's historic make-up. Yet, also within this contextual account of the Community's emergence, it becomes clear that the strengths and commitment of certain individuals have great significance and relevance. This background is discussed in chapters 1–5. Therein, some insights are provided into the historical context which resulted in some young Belfast couples taking the initiative to cater for their own linguistic needs. This is followed by an outline of the current position of Irish in Belfast and the account of how the Shaw's Road Community came into existence.

Chapters 6–10 deal with the process of language diffusion which is inspired by the Bunscoil. The nature of the Shaw's Road Community's impact on neighbouring districts becomes evident. As access to the language via the Bunscoil is availed of, the wider shift towards bilingualism gains momentum and the patterns of language behaviour which evolve are moulded by a complex of social and psychological factors. Language shift is defined by Fasold (1984: 213) in the following terms:

> Language shift simply means that a community gives up a language completely in favor of another one. The members of the community, when the shift has taken place, have collectively chosen a new language where an old one used to be.

Within the context of this book, however, language shift may represent a more intermediate stage in the changing patterns of language behaviour in a community. In some domains the shift is, indeed, complete. However, the overall shift referred to among the wider community of learners is just as significant even though it is at an incipient stage.

At the outset of this work, the children of Bunscoil families were still very young and were predominantly in the junior classes. Accordingly, their command of Irish was still much more receptive than active. For this reason, the Irish spoken by these children was not included in the linguistic analysis of this particular study. Rather, it was more appropriate to base the linguistic description on the children who resided in the Shaw's Road Community itself. Chapters 11 and 12 present these findings.

Methodology

The methodology for these two aspects of the research was, naturally, very different. It was not possible to give more than an outline of some of the ways

in which the Shaw's Road Community galvanised a wider active interest in
Irish. Individual members of the Community have initiated or assisted many
other language-related projects. However, it is undoubtedly the Community's
primary school which most effectively opened the door to the acquisition of
Irish in surrounding neighbourhoods. In order to examine the nature of the bilingualism evolving as pupil intake at the Bunscoil increases, a sociolinguistic survey was designed and administered to the full population of Bunscoil parents.
This involved interviewing 98 families in the spring of 1985.

A postal survey was not considered satisfactory for this work. In order to
note any additional relevant information about the families' experiences which
did not fall into the categories of questionnaire responses, it was necessary to
personally interview each of the families from outside the Shaw's Road
Community who had a child at the school. As it transpired, many of the parents
made further comments about their children's language behaviour after the questionnaire was completed. These were noted and added to the overall picture of
the bilingualisation process. The pilot study indicated the usefulness of having
two versions of the questionnaire so that the parents' answers would not be prej-
udiced by lists of possible responses. The parents were given one copy so that
they could read the questions independently. This allowed parents to consider
their responses and to elaborate upon them if they desired. Responses were
recorded by myself on the second copy of the questionnaire. A relaxed atmosphere prevailed during the survey administration once the initial introductions
were made. Most of the answers and comments given were quite detailed.
Various categories of questions were built into the survey, investigating the patterns of bilingualism emerging among Bunscoil families and the role of the
Bunscoil in this development.

The linguistic analysis of the Irish spoken in the Shaw's Road
Community also necessitated numerous interviews with the children, as one
dimension to the work carried out with them. It was important to spend as
much time as possible in the company of the children and to build up a sound
rapport with them, so that their Irish could be studied in a natural
environment. A formal linguistic analysis of parents' Irish was not carried out.
Shaw's Road parents had learned Irish as a second language; their children, on
the other hand, were being raised with Irish as their first language. Obviously,
parents influence the Irish spoken by their children. However, interest in the
parents' Irish was motivated only by that relationship, rather than for its own
sake. The Shaw's Road children belong to a particularly significant phase in
the Language Revival in Northern Ireland. Within this context, they are the
first generation to be raised and educated through Irish. A record of their
language behaviour in this particular urban bilingual setting, as well as their
attitudes towards the role of Irish in their lives, merits attention in any future

framework of language planning. Subsequent revival endeavours could learn much from these children.

Although Irish is the children's first language, they are subject to heavy pressures from the English-speaking world around them. It is not surprising, therefore, that the linguistic trends which characterise the children's Irish are fairly typical of those occurring in the Irish of Bunscoil children who come from English-speaking backgrounds and, indeed, in the Irish of the wider population of second language learners. The advantages enjoyed by the Shaw's Road children are more clearly manifested in their fluency and confidence as Irish speakers.

Linguistic data were accumulated over a period of four years, while the thesis was being prepared. Recording sessions ceased in 1986, although contact with the children has been maintained on a regular basis since and linguistic developments have been observed. Twenty-two of the Community children participated in the main corpus of recording sessions. These participants were aged between eight and eighteen at the outset. During the period of fieldwork, and since then, I spent a considerable amount of time in the children's company, through participation in a variety of activities. Material noted on these occasions supplemented recorded data.

It is important to state, at this point, that this analysis was based on the casual, everyday linguistic output produced by the children. Some samples of written material were gathered and examined and a few recordings of the children reading pieces of text were made. In addition, my interaction with the children meant that I was in their presence on formal as well as on informal occasions. Accordingly, some references are made in the book to stylistic variations in their linguistic output. However, it should be borne in mind that the account given in chapter 12 is based predominantly upon the relaxed and natural conversational style of speech rather than a more careful, consciously monitored style.

In view of this emphasis upon casual speech, it was imperative to arrange recording sessions in a suitably relaxed environment. Several settings were used. An available room in some of the children's homes was used on a few occasions. However, this was not the most appropriate setting. Rather, in the parents' absence, the young 'hosts' took the opportunity to create a party-type atmosphere which made recordings a little difficult. The most successful setting for recordings was the Irish nursery school, situated behind the children's homes. At that time, the Bunscoil and affiliated nursery were still quite small and used for a multitude of activities. The setting was not very formal. However, some light refreshments and the friendly chatter of the children themselves reduced the formalities even further. Some recording sessions were made in other settings, for example in Donegal where the eleven-year-olds spent a fortnight, once the Transfer Examination (11+) had been done in their final Bunscoil year.

Individual differences in the Irish spoken by the children were, of course, observed and noted. However, they were not so distinctive as to merit a presentation of data in relation to particular individuals. For example, recording sessions tended to be carried out with particular peer groups and, indeed, different groups showed some distinguishing characteristics. However, these were much less numerous and significant than might have been expected. Obviously, the language skills of older groups were more highly developed. Overall trends, however, were relatively uniform.

One factor which did exert some influence upon the children's language behaviour and repertoire of Irish was the transfer to English-medium secondary schools. Although this move coincided with reaching a particular age, it was the sudden exposure to a more concentrated English-speaking environment which triggered certain changes.

Overall Aim

It is hoped that the contents of this book will be meaningful to anyone interested in language revival. The overall aim runs parallel to the objectives of the Shaw's Road Community itself. The founder members of the Community set out to prove that their language was accessible and of practical relevance in the modern urban setting. Having closely examined multiple aspects of this sociolinguistic phenomenon it becomes clear that this story can inspire not only the population of West Belfast but also other language groups throughout the world.

When the core members of the Community decided upon this project they did not consider failure. Those who did stepped back in those early days. The resolution to realise the ambition of creating a cohesive Irish-speaking neighbourhood was in itself remarkable. So many factors militated against it. Yet, this turned out to be but a first stage in a broader development which embraced the wider population of Northern Ireland. The Shaw's Road Community made other people take Irish seriously. It continues to fulfil that function. This book examines that function and its implications for the Irish language in Northern Ireland.

1 A Language Initiative in West Belfast

Shaw's Road lies on the periphery of one of the large working class housing estates in West Belfast. Until recent years, the unique character of the community residing on Shaw's Road attracted little attention. Only local residents and a few Irish language enthusiasts were alerted to the emergence of an interesting and exciting development in the Language Revival Movement.

Today, the name 'Shaw's Road' represents more than just another street name in Belfast. It has become a living symbol of the improving fortunes of the Irish language and an encouraging landmark along the route to its revival. For anyone who loves that language this symbol evokes an emotive response. It is laden with a strong conviction of the feasibility of reclaiming and reinvigorating a neglected cultural patrimony. It also evokes the living experience of using the Irish language as a functional tool within a modern urban context. Just as Lower Abbey Street, in Dublin, is forever linked with the establishment of the Abbey Theatre and the Anglo-Irish literary revival, so is Shaw's Road indissolubly linked with the re-establishment of Irish as a normal means of communication in a place where it has not had this role for centuries.

To the casual onlooker, the appearance of this site in West Belfast yields no clue as to its significance. A group of eleven houses is situated directly opposite a public authority housing estate. The houses stand in an L-shaped formation around a primary school. Further housing development is in progress immediately behind the school. However, the expanding population is not the significant factor. The true importance of the place is apparent to the ear, rather than to the eye. As small children enter the school gates, or as one of the community residents calls out to the family pet, a stranger would be startled to recognise Irish as the language being used. In fact, this core of eleven houses is referred to locally as the 'Irish-speaking houses'. Behind them stands the 'Irish-speaking school', or Bunscoil Phobal Feirste.

Families rearing their children through Irish are not unknown in Belfast. However, a whole community whose creation and existence successfully share

the common purpose of raising and educating children through Irish is
unprecedented in twentieth-century urban Ireland. Indeed history shows the
process of urbanisation to be among those forces which have weakened the
general usage of the language, at least since post-Norman times. Belfast,
therefore, might appear at first glance to represent an unlikely and
unpromising ground for the cultivation of the Irish language. Even within the
city itself many people cannot fathom the question: how could Belfast have
been made to accommodate the emergence and obstinate survival of a
community of Irish-speaking families? After all, for centuries the odds have
been weighted heavily against the continued use of Irish, not only throughout
Ireland but particularly within the six north-eastern counties and most
especially in Belfast.

The Odds Against a Revival

Official attitudes

Belfast's pre-eminence as a city of community divisions was crystallised by
the division of the country following the Government Of Ireland Act, 1920.
Partition, and the establishment of the Stormont Government in Belfast, tended
to undermine the cultural heritage of the minority population living within these
new boundaries. Belfast became the official guardian of colonial interests and,
by this stage, the English language had taken up a position of total dominance
leaving the indigenous language in a position of low status. However, a sense of
sociopolitical stability and security, which could foster confidence in the solidity
of political integration with Britain, had never been achieved. Therefore, the
Irish language and culture were regarded with suspicion as a threat to the established political framework and as running counter to majority interests. The
problem of facilitating the cultural needs of the minority Catholic population
was resolved with expedience by proclaiming the non-existence of any such
needs.

In this way, both the refusal to recognise and the neglect to make provisions
for the cultural values of the minority sector were construed as a judicious and
rational relegation of obsolete relics, such as the Irish language, into the confines
of history books. The possibility that Irish deserved attention as a living modern
language was consistently denied. In the 1930s, Viscount Craigavon, who was to
become Prime Minister of Northern Ireland, expounded this official view of the
language in response to a parliamentary question raised regarding the removal of
a grant for Irish.

What use is it to us here in this busy part of the Empire to teach our children the Irish language? What use would it be to them? Is it not leading them along a road which has no practical value? We have not stopped such teaching; we have stopped the grants, which I think amounted to £1,500 a year. We have stopped the grants simply because we do not see that these boys being taught Irish would be any better citizens ... I hope the honorable member is satisfied that, on the whole, the Government is carrying out its duties fairly and justly among all sections of the population. (N.I. Parliamentary Debates, Commons, vol. XVIII c. 646, 24th March 1936.)

Such a pattern of neglect can often be more effective, in extinguishing a minority language, than an explicitly hostile policy. The absence of favourable provisions for the development of indigenous cultural manifestations is less likely to provoke a hostile response than is the presence of overt antagonism.

A further example of the official rejection of the language's value or validity was demonstrated in October 1949, by another future Prime Minister, Mr Brian Faulkner:

Apparently certain local authorities in County Down are at the moment naming streets in a language which is not our language and I do not think that should be allowed (N.I. Parliamentary Debates, Commons, vol. XXXIII, c.1546–1547).

The MP went on to request that the prohibition of Irish street names be enshrined in the Public Health And Local Government Act. The motion was opposed by a Nationalist MP, Mr Healy, who outlined some of the educational and cultural advantages of preserving local forms of placenames. His statement ended with an allusion to the crucial question of identity: 'You want British names which have no connection with Ulster. Ulster is part of Ireland.' The concluding response (from Dame Dehra Parker, minister of Health and Local Government) declared that Ulster was part of the United Kingdom. The complex interrelationship between the Irish language and the Nationalist identity which attracted Unionist suspicion was left unresolved and the requested amendment to the Act was passed, rendering the erection of street names in Irish illegal.

Northern Ireland's broadcasting authorities further endorsed the Government's treatment of Irish as a language without relevance. Planners in the areas of television, radio and newspapers swelled the numbers of powerful public and private sector administrators who were antipathetic to or, at best, indifferent to the Irish language.

Even within the domain of the Roman Catholic Church, facilities for Irish speakers or for members sympathetic to the language were not forthcoming.

Following Vatican II, the Latin liturgy was replaced by English. Irish belonged to the past.

Urbanisation

Over the centuries, the development of this unsympathetic official attitude took place not only within the context of political change but also against the background of continuing urbanisation. This process brought increasing numbers of people within social and economic spheres of influence controlled by an English-speaking elite.

Traditionally, it has been the rural areas which have provided a haven for Irish-speaking refugees from the confiscated eastern regions. It is not surprising, therefore, that it was in the rugged terrain of the west coast that the native language survived as the mother tongue. These areas wherein the English language never displaced Irish as the mother tongue are known as Gaeltacht areas. (The term 'Galltacht' refers to the rest of the country where the English language gained supremacy. 'Gall' means foreigner in Irish.) As a consequence, the term

MAP 1 *Ireland: traditional Gaeltacht areas.*

'Gaeltacht' is traditionally associated with rural, rather than urban, Irish-speaking areas. The establishment of an urban Gaeltacht anywhere in Ireland, and most particularly in Belfast, is an initiative which moves against the long established flow of a very powerful tide.

Against the background of history, it is now evident that there were many trends and tendencies which damaged the fortunes of the Irish language. Among these, the process of urbanisation has proved to be a powerful anglicising agent. It has reinforced the position of English as an outward sign of social advancement and undermined the value of Irish in that context. Those who left their rural homes for employment in the fast growing industrial cities of the nineteenth century usually found it necessary to acquire and use English. As economic circumstances uprooted large numbers of people from their rural environment so also did cultural and political necessity dictate that these people should change their language. The association of urbanisation with anglicisation hinges upon the relative economic prosperity of urban centres wherein the English language was totally dominant. In the nineteenth century English became most firmly established as the language of political and economic power and the process of linguistic assimilation became as inevitable in Ireland as it was in the countless other instances of language extinction. In this regard it is worth noting that Nancy Dorian delineated certain parallels with Scottish Gaelic (1981: 40).

> The great numerical superiority of Irish speakers through the first half of the eighteenth century could not preserve Irish in the mouths of the people when it was clear to every man, woman, and child that English, the language of the ruling elite, was the prerequisite for social mobility (Macnamara, 1971: 65). Similarly in eastern Sutherland, in the early nineteenth century, Gaelic quickly passed from the status of majority language to that of minority language once an English-speaking elite established itself in significant numbers — despite the fact that those numbers were tiny in comparison to the body of Gaelic speakers present in the area.
>
> Political resistance to linguistic assimilation was disastrously slow to develop both in Ireland and in Highland Scotland, presumably because of the low level of economic and sociopolitical development in those areas during the centuries when an elite of alien tongue was becoming most visible.

It is recognised that, within most developing economies of the nineteenth century, urban centres were inevitably associated with elite social groups. After all, such centres were already the seat of administration and law. Now they were also to become centres of industry on a technological scale foreign to their rural hinterlands. Little wonder that such a situation — within which progress, power and influence all spoke with an English tongue — should prove to be a powerful anglicising agent.

Against the Tide

At first sight, it might appear paradoxical that the urban environment, previously so hostile to the language, should prove to be the springboard for its resurgence. However, experience has shown that the success of language movements usually requires the creation of formal educational and cultural structures. The formation of such structures demands the commitment of a critical mass of language enthusiasts. If such a group of committed people is assembled, and if its corporate consciousness is alerted to the possibilities offered by the urban environment, cities can provide a convenient matrix for the implementation of language initiatives.

Historically, cities have provided an environment in which coteries of like-minded people could develop common cultural interests. To appreciate this, one has only to think of the literary and artistic groups which have flourished in London, Paris and many other cities. Upon reflection, it is not surprising that the unique social circumstances of Belfast with its ghettoisation and its high level of political and cultural consciousness should produce the impetus for a new and radical approach to language revival.

So it was within the unfavourable sociopolitical context of this urban setting, rather than within any of the traditional rural Gaeltacht regions where the language had found some sanctuary, that a unique language initiative was taken some twenty years ago. A conscious course of action was decided upon and implemented by a small group of Irish language learners. These young couples set about building a community — in both a physical and a social sense — wherein life in the home, neighbourhood, school and church could be experienced naturally through Irish. Neither the legal implications of their project nor the absence of official support were considered too daunting. In fact, the degree to which they were considered at all was minimal.

Once the original idea of establishing a Belfast neo-Gaeltacht had been conceived, the magnitude of the challenge and the historic importance of the initiative seized the imagination of those involved. This very positive attitude to the work in hand helped the embryonic community to tackle apparently insuperable obstacles. Indeed, both the immensity and the significance of such an undertaking were anticipated in an essay by one of Ireland's foremost literary figures, Mairtin Ó Cadhain.

If the people wanted the language or were made to want it — which need be only compulsive rather than compulsory — the language could take roots in fifteen or thirty years. You could have in the Galltacht, if not study book, if not Lebor Gabala, at least real Gaelic communities, juvenile delinquency, Beatles, shebeens and all. There must be one big community in Dublin. It is a challenge. Are we worthy to take it up? If we had flourishing communities such as I say throughout Ireland, and specially in the big urban areas, the Gaeltacht itself — the historical Gaeltacht — would no longer be anything except one other Irish-speaking community. (Ó Cadhain, 1964: 5)

This writer would probably not have been surprised that the challenge was taken up in Belfast. The decision to create an urban Gaeltacht neighbourhood aimed at supporting the conscious choice of the Irish language — not just as a functional medium of communication but as a way of life and as a necessary means of being true to an important component in a community's system of values — is unique to Belfast. This fact will be more clearly understood by considering the social and physical character of Belfast. One deeply ingrained feature of Belfast's social fabric has been alluded to already, namely ghettoisation (Poole & Boal, 1973). As a phenomenon characteristic of Northern Ireland, and more specifically of Belfast, the spatial segregation of the city, though carrying many social disadvantages to its residents, has provided a wealth of hard-earned experience in the business of seeking protection within cohesive social units. It is therefore necessary to cast some light upon the politico-religious divisions with which Belfast is riven.

Enforced ghettoisation is one of the consequences of the sad politico-sectarian history of Belfast. This pattern of residential segregation is particularly characteristic of the working class population. Many areas of the city have come to resemble separate urban villages, densely populated by either Roman Catholics or Protestants. Popular references to the two ethnic communities as Protestant and Catholic are only fully comprehended within Northern Ireland. Outside its boundaries the terms may be misleading, for in effect religious denomination is not the crucial divisive issue between the two groups. Rather, this is availed of by the media to provide convenient labels. It is true that religion features as a component in the different self-images of the two groups in question, as do other cultural values. However, it does not represent the central source of conflict (Fennell, 1983: 104–17).

The larger community is composed of people who value political affiliation with Britain and who wish to be represented as part of the British nation along with England, Scotland and Wales. Pickvance (1975) applied the term 'Ulster British' to this community (as opposed to the term 'Ulster Irish' which he

applied to the Catholic community in Northern Ireland). The vast majority of
this sector descends from the Protestant planter stock of the seventeenth century
and is today Protestant.

The smaller community considers itself to be part of the indigenous Irish
population and perceives itself as a component of the Irish nation as a whole.
This community does not regard itself as British. Nor does it place much faith in
the prospects for cultural equity within the political context of Northern Ireland.
This community is made up of Roman Catholics. Although some Catholics partially share an Ulster British code of values, and some Protestants identify
strongly with the Irish nation, the preponderance of Protestants or Catholics
within the respectively described communities gives rise to the use of these religious terms as conventional labels.

The disparity between both the political ambitions and the economic status
of these two communities in Belfast — indeed, throughout each of the six counties — generated and sustained an atmosphere of tension which was reflected in
the periodic eruption of sectarian violence. The latest phase in this bleak series
began in 1969 and remains ongoing. The other most notable periods of violent
strife occurred in 1835, 1843, 1857, 1864, 1872, 1880, 1884, 1886, 1898, 1920,
1935, 1964 and 1966 (Boyd, 1969).

This pattern of sporadic outbreaks of inter-community confrontation was
characterised by parallel waves of large-scale population movement when working class areas became more solidly segregated. The term 'population movement', however, casts no light upon the reality to which it refers. Vicious
sectarian attacks forced people to abandon their homes and seek refuge within
safer territories, more densely populated by their own community. At peak periods of inter-community violence the majority of families displaced from their
homes have been Catholics (Farrell, 1976: 263). In such circumstances, flight
was not constrained by adherence to standard legal requirements or administrative processes. Refugees took up residence in unoccupied or vacated premises.
The practice of squatting became widespread. In his book, *Housing A Divided
Community*, the chairman of the Northern Ireland Housing Executive, Charles
Brett (1986: 69), highlighted the particular form which squatting took in Belfast.
Unlike other major cities, where this phenomenon exists as a reaction to accommodation shortages, squatting resulted from a 'well justified fear' in Belfast.
Families were compelled to act upon their own initiative in order to find safe
accommodation. Support at community level became more organised as schools,
halls, churches etc. were used as temporary refuges.

Ironically, social bonds developed within each community as the gulf
between the two grew. In the case of the Catholic community, it is relevant to
note that the common misfortunes associated with forced relocation stimulated a

propensity to independent community action. The relevance of this fact not only applies to the creation of an urban Gaeltacht neighbourhood and community, but also applies to a range of other co-operative activities carried out by founder members of this community. An example of this is the rescue work carried out during the early days of this latest spate of civic disturbances.

At that time, community founders were engaged in the preparation of their site and the construction of their houses on Shaw's Road. The group had possessed no financial resources to invest in the enterprise. Therefore, a company was created which could secure the necessary loans. Local legal and architectural consultants provided their services gratis. A considerable range of skills and expertise was accumulated at this vital initial stage. However, members decided to suspend work on this undertaking so as to make their experience and skills available to victims of the sectarian onslaught. The decision was taken specifically in response to the plight of Bombay Street families. This entire street, situated on the Catholic Falls Road, was burnt out on 15th August 1969. Work ceased on the Shaw's Road site and efforts were channelled into the rebuilding of Bombay Street. The Irish speakers' company, de Brun & Mac Seain Ltd, used its healthy relationship with creditors in order to support the financial exigencies of reconstruction. Plans were drawn up even as the foundations were being laid. No one postponed the operation to satisfy conventional requirements such as applying for planning permission. Rather, a decision was made and action followed. This model for action proved to be the basis of a philosophy crucial to the development of the Gaeltacht Community itself. The spontaneity and generosity with which these human resources were shared illustrates the sharpened degree of cohesion within the increasingly ghetto-like community in West Belfast. The growth of independence and self-sufficiency within the Catholic community, along with an expanding store of experience and abilities, is of particular relevance to the emergence of an urban Gaeltacht in this setting.

So, the spatial distribution pattern in Belfast, which reflects the community divisions, also reflects the close-knitted character of each of the two conflicting sectors. Residential segregation has been a feature of Belfast working class life since the early nineteenth century. Though long standing, it has not remained at a constant level. Upsurges in sectarian violence resulted in population retreat into ghetto-like neighbourhoods. Relaxed periods in social and political tension have been accompanied by tentative movement into mixed areas. This alternating process of ghettoisation — followed by a degree of integration — followed by further ghettoisation, in dreary succession, has long marked the pattern of population distribution in Belfast. However, even during periods of relative peace, the degree of residential integration has been limited by an awareness of past tensions (Boal *et al.*, 1978: 37).

Among the Catholic neighbourhoods, West Belfast is the largest, most enduring and cohesive area. As thousands of families flooded into this area from previously mixed districts new housing estates have been erected to relieve the pressure. It was originally on the periphery of this territory that the Gaeltacht Community was situated. However, the rapid expansion of West Belfast has now given the Shaw's Road Community a more central position in the area. Of all the ghetto-type areas in the City, West Belfast provided the most fertile ground in which a community initiative such as the creation of an urban Gaeltacht could be accommodated. Therein, community cohesiveness was already intense. This provided the support necessary for the successful implementation of a project such as the one envisaged. So the very ghettoisation which had been the hallmark of an oppressed cultural group proved ultimately to be culturally advantageous.

The growth of a tradition of self-help within the ghetto produced a community which was accustomed to taking defensive action. The plan to build a neighbourhood for Irish-speaking families within the confines of West Belfast, therefore, was perceived in those same terms as the only possible means to defend a particular way of life. One or two families moved from Belfast to the Donegal Gaeltacht — where the language had traditionally found a retreat — in order to lead a freer fuller life as Irish speakers. However, this could not provide a satisfactory overall solution since a substantial range of practical obstacles impeded any serious consideration of movement from the city to rural Gaeltachts. The overriding factor which pointed to an urban Gaeltacht as the only effective answer could be paralleled to the rescue operation in Bombay Street. It was a contribution by a small but cohesive group to the overall welfare of the larger community of which it formed a part. In West Belfast the project would receive support. It would also, in turn, build cultural resources and awaken an awareness of the viability of Irish as a useful and accessible medium in today's world.

It is unlikely that a stable harmonious society would have engendered the drive to implement the Shaw's Road project. However, West Belfast, more than any other area in the city, has emerged and expanded against a background of sociopolitical unrest and economic constraints. This atmosphere of tension cultivated the mood for radical, innovative action. It also reduced the very natural fear of taking an unprecedented step without certainties or guarantees in view. Contrary to prevailing orthodoxy, therefore, certain key components within this particular urban matrix created a climate which was uniquely receptive to the creation of a Gaeltacht community in its midst.

The founding of the Shaw's Road Community represents the most promising and important phase in the city's language revival activities. It is significant both in terms of the language's overall struggle for survival and in terms of Belfast's more localised endeavours over the last century. However, the fortunes of the Irish language in Belfast cannot be understood in isolation from the great historical movements which determined the fate of the language in Ireland as a whole. Accordingly, the next chapter will summarise the historical developments which brought about the demise of Irish as a normal means of communication throughout most of the country. It will describe the resistance against these developments and will focus specifically upon the growth of the Language Movement in Belfast.

2   The Historical Backdrop

The emergence of a Gaeltacht Community in Belfast in the 1970s and the sub-sequent creation and development of Irish-medium educational facilities may be considered as a remarkable phoenix-like phenomenon. However, the early history of Ireland leaves no doubt about the resilience of the language brought here by the Goidels several hundred years before Christ. The incorporation of Latin, Norse and Anglo-Norman loan words into the Irish system and the influence of these languages upon the native indigenous linguistic system are indicators of the ability of the native vernacular to adapt to social change and, so, to survive. Until relatively recently Irish was powerful and flexible enough to resist dis-placement by the languages of foreign cultures. Indeed, a pattern of adjustment and mutual assimilation was operated.

Before the arrival of Christianity to Ireland in the fifth century AD the native Gaels had many centuries in which to establish their social, cultural and legal systems. These had been developed into a sophisticated and well-organised social fabric by the time of the Christian missionaries' arrival. It is probable that the early missionaries were antipathetic towards the native tongue in which the Pagan philosophy was so firmly entrenched. However, Christianity superimposed itself upon native Pagan traditions and feasts without undermining the status of Irish as the vernacular. Indeed, both the monastic schools and the native Druidic schools represented prestigious centres for learning and much of the rich ancient oral tradition of the latter was preserved by the innovativeness of native monks who applied the Latin alphabet and orthography to the vernacular. Corkery (1968: 13–26) refers to the relationship between the two cultures in their respective schools as a companionship which 'was possibly the greatest thing that has ever happened in Irish history'.

Norse influences are not generally hailed in the same manner although they too did not undermine the position of Irish as the vernacular. The beginning of the Norse invasions in 795 heralded a violent period of some two hundred years of incursions and raids. Monasteries were the most lucrative targets. Subsequently, the scholarly activities of the monastic settlements were seriously disrupted. These major social upheavals were reflected in the collapse of the standard language (the Old Irish period) — which had been rigorously upheld in both church and secular schools from 600 to 900 AD — and in the transition to the Middle Irish period (900 to 1200).

Further upheaval followed the Norman Invasion of the twelfth century. This may be viewed as the starting point in an historical era which resulted in the change from an Irish-speaking nation to an English-speaking one. Such a statement, however, should not cloak the early centuries of mutual cultural enrichment which also emerged from this relationship. Within this context De Freine (1978: 20–23) addressed the question, 'What constitutes the breaking point of national endurance and resilience?' This certainly did not occur during the early Norman presence and De Freine proceeds to give an account of the contribution which this gifted people made to life in Ireland as they had elsewhere in Europe. As the Normans advanced the extent of their political dominance their own languages were losing ground. Flemish soon disappeared and French later gave way to English or, in places, Irish. Many of the Norman nobles themselves were assimilated to, and became patrons of, the culture which they found to be thriving in Ireland. The most famous of these was Gearoid, Earl of Desmond, whose title as Lord Chief Justice of Ireland in 1367 was no more reputable than that which he earned as an Irish language poet.

By the fourteenth century the native cause was recovering itself. Conquered territory was reclaimed with the Norman and English settlers driven back and the native language restored where it had been lost. Measures deemed necessary to counter the Gaelicisation of Norman houses illustrate the bouyancy of the native vernacular. The weakened position of English was reflected in the writ issued in 1360 to the sheriff of the Cross of Kilkenny, forbidding people of English descent to speak Irish and, indeed, ordering them to learn English! The ineffectiveness of this document is evident from a subsequent attempt to curb the Gaelicisation of Anglo-Norman lords and nobles by means of the Statutes of Kilkenny. This famous set of laws, issued in 1366, lamented the colonists' adoption of the Irish language, laws and customs and prohibited any continuation of such practices. The supreme Council in Dublin was unable to implement the Statutes successfully and the Norman houses continued as before. This flourishing of the Irish language and way of life continued for over two hundred years. As an indicator of this healthy state we are often reminded that, as late as 1541, all but one of the Anglo-Irish Lords attending the English Parliament in Dublin were non-English speakers. Consequently, the Bill to declare Henry VIII King of Ireland had to be read in Irish (Corkery, 1968: 57; Ó Cuiv, 1971: 13).

At the close of that decade a further statute was enacted to restrict the activities of Irish poets and minstrels (Ó Cuiv, 1971: 13). This shows that the role of the Irish poet was still influential enough to be perceived as a threat to English rule. Nevertheless, that shattering of the poets' world, referred to below by Corkery, was by this stage looming closer:

> If it was not with our student (i.e. the student poet) somehow as we have indicated, those schools could not have maintained the status they actually did maintain for five or six centuries until, and utterly for political reasons, the English State scattered them. Nor could those who had gone through them write of them in such moving words as they did. For an Irish student then to think of his language as not enduring would be to imagine the world he knew as falling to pieces. (Corkery, 1968: 48).

Within a very few years, not only the poets' world, but that of Gaelic Ireland would be pushed perilously close to that breaking point of national resilience.

It was during the Tudor reign that Ireland would seriously experience political subjection and the destruction of her native political and social structures which had long upheld the Irish language. A policy of de-Gaelicisation went hand in hand with the Tudor conquest (Ó Fiaich, 1969: 101–11). The assault was directed at the principal supports of the Irish way of life — Irish chieftains; the native system of law and social institutions; the native language and culture; the Roman Catholic religion. Ironically, a changed attitude towards the language was adopted within the religious domain. Elizabeth I saw the Irish language as a means to promote the established Church and to convert natives. Elizabeth herself sponsored the translation of the New Testament into Irish and the provision of the first font of Gaelic type for this end. Ministers in Ireland were therefore encouraged to learn Irish and to use it in sermons (Ó Snodaigh, 1973: 6).

This missionary objective did not lessen the drive to undermine the Irish way of life. The great Irish-minded houses of Kildare and Desmond had been wiped out. Many of the sons of the nobility were 'taken to court', i.e. brought to England to be educated as loyal subjects. A most significant consequence to these events was that each time a great house or chieftain fell or fled another important patron of Irish culture disappeared. The aristocratic stratum which had always safeguarded the old Gaelic order was crumbling. The turning point in the fortunes of the Irish language is often identified as the defeat of the Irish at Kinsale in 1601 and the subsequent 'Flight of the Earls'.

After Kinsale the story of the Irish language must deal with its decline. The destruction of the native social structure in which the language was inherent did not, even then, occur in one fell swoop. The following famous verse believed to be by the blind poet, Raifteiri, was written over two hundred years later. The verse evokes an image of the poet's waning grasp on the old tradition.

> Mise Raifteirí, an file, lán dóchais is grá,
> le súile gan solas, ciúnas gan crá,

ag dul síos ar m'aistear le solas mo chroí,
fann agus tuirseach go deireadh mo shlí;
tá mé anois le m'aghaidh ar Bhalla
ag seinm cheoil do phócaí falamh'.

I am Raifteirí, the poet, full of courage and love,
my eyes without light, in calmness serene,
taking my way by the light of my heart,
feeble and tired to the end of my road:
look at me now, my face toward Balla,
performing music to empty pockets!

Despite the major historical events which directed severe blows at the fate of the language, it still showed remarkable tenacity (De Freine, 1978: 20–32).

Ó Cuiv (1971: 22) concludes that in the first quarter of the nineteenth century well over two million people still spoke Irish. Undoubtedly this figure rose considerably within the following two decades in accordance with the dramatic population increase of that pre-Famine era. At this stage, however, the status of the language was gravely diminished. Nevertheless, as a living idiom it had survived a disastrous period. The brutalities of conquest and political subjection had not obliterated it. The Penal Laws were implemented during the eighteenth century, denying Roman Catholics basic civil rights such as religious freedom and education. By the time their severity was modified, land ownership in Catholic hands had been reduced to 5% (Corkery, 1968: 70). Nevertheless, despite this loss of land and civil rights, the two cornerstones of Irish culture remained even yet: language and religion. Indeed, the Irish language contributed signficantly to Ireland's resistance to the Reformation. To some extent the language insulated the native faith from this dramatic religious development. Even when the vernacular was used as a vehicle by the established Church providing Irish-speaking ministers and Parish Schools, the novelty impact was nullified because the natives were already so accustomed to practising their own faith through Irish.

Throughout the eighteenth century examples of cultural resilience continued despite the weakening position of Irish. Courts of Poetry took over from the bardic schools. The traditions and skills passed down from family to family in other native institutions such as schools of medicine were also preserved for some time yet. The deprivation of educational facilities for Catholics was countered by the emergence of hedge schools (i.e. small informal schools, which offered the only real chance for elementary education to the poorer native classes whose civil rights were denied by the Penal Laws). However the endurance of the language was being quickly eroded as it became more and more associated with the socially disadvantaged.

This change prompted a new attitude towards the language. When social opportunities came within the reach of Catholics they were only attainable through the English language. Hence the co-operation between non-English speaking parents and hedge school teachers to equip children with English. Parents must have believed they were exercising cruelty for the child's sake when they used the infamous tally stick. Other signs of dramatic language shift appear. Early in the nineteenth century the role of Parish Schools (i.e. based upon parishes of the Established Church) was becoming obsolete, according to the Commissioners of the Board of Education,

> For the original objects of their Institution, namely, the introduction and diffusion of the English language in Ireland, the Parish Schools can no longer be deemed necessary (Ó Cuiv, 1971: 19).

The National System of Education, introduced in 1831, continued this anglicising policy. English was now established as the language of government and of education. The Catholic Church too went with the tide after the laws prohibiting or restricting its administration were relaxed. English gained ground, not just as the language of the upper social stratum, but also as an essential tool to survival in a changing world. The mass emigration which followed the Great Famine must have been a less terrifying prospect to those who could speak and read English. The value of acquiring English also increased as the Irish masses took a more active interest in politics from the eighteenth century on (Wall, 1969: 88–9).

Census returns in the nineteenth century indicate a steady decline in the numbers of Irish speakers. Monoglot Irish speakers, in particular, were fast approaching extinction with the numbers of speakers falling from 319,602 in 1851 to 38,192 in 1891 (Ó Droighneain, 1936). The fact that these records are undoubtedly underestimations, showing a widespread reluctance to admit a knowledge of Irish, reflects sadly on changing attitudes towards the language. At this point, as Irish seems about to disappear as a living idiom, its story takes a new turn. Once more its resilience surprises. The underestimation of Irish speakers, referred to above, was no longer the problem at the start of the twentieth century. Ironically, overestimation became the phenomenon to be aware of when considering later statistics. Despite this fact, the number of Irish speakers in Gaeltacht areas continued to decrease. However, this pattern was paralleled by an increasing number of speakers in the eastern urban centres. It was no coincidence that this growing interest in the language followed an important date in terms of the Revival: 1893 and the founding of the Gaelic League.

The climate of revival had been stirring for some decades. Precursors to the Gaelic League had, in their own way, prepared the way for a language movement. The character of this first phase was mainly academic. From the first half of the nineteenth century societies had been emerging which paid tribute to the value of Irish studies from an historical perspective. Such societies included the Gaelic Society of Dublin, Iberno Celtic Society, Celtic Society, Irish Archaeological and Celtic Society, and the Ossianic Society. This image of Irish studies as a revered worthwhile pursuit was reinforced by the work of reputable scholars abroad.

Belfast's contribution to the efforts of this language movement was considerable. As early as 1795 the academic attention which the Irish language and literature received abroad was hailed as an example to Irish people in *Bolg an tSolair*, a Gaelic magazine published in the city in that year:

> The Irish language is acknowledged by very learned foreigners to be the best preserved dialect of the Gauls and Celtiberians ... an acquaintance with Gaelic as being the mother tongue of all the languages in the West, is necessary to every antiquary who would study the affinity of languages, or trace the migrations of ancient races of mankind; of late it has attracted the attention of the learned in different parts of Europe ... Shall Irishmen alone remain insensible?

Pioneers of the Irish Revival in Belfast worked zealously throughout the nineteenth century. This scholarly industry was carried out principally by middle-class Presbyterians. Emphasis was placed on learned activities such as the compilation of manuscripts, the collection of folkloric material and the publication of texts. Societies such as the Belfast Harpers' Society provided Irish-language classes as one branch of their work. By the time this society ceased to function a more language-orientated group, the Ulster Gaelic Society, was in operation (Ó Snodaigh, 1973: 17). An account of the various groups and individuals involved in Belfast's Language Movement up until about 1860 was recorded by Ó Buachalla (1968) in *I mBeal Feirste Cois Cuain*.

A survey of those organised groups — the areas into which they channelled their efforts; their founders and members etc. — reveals an interesting pattern which has a relevance even today. The same personal names appear as we consider the efforts of groups and individuals involved in the Language Movement in the city. Usually a society was inspired by a predecessor, perhaps as a splinter group branching off into one of the areas more lightly covered by the earlier organisation, or it might show a more clearly defined change in direction. The Gaelic League, for example, grew out of 'The Society For The Preservation Of The Irish Language' (Ó hAilin, 1969: 94–5). However, members of the former group often set up or contributed in some other way to the development of successive initiatives. Each development in the build up to a Revival Movement, and each subsequent initiative taken as part of that more concentrated drive to restore Irish as a viable medium of communication in the twentieth century, may seem insignificant as an independent, often fleeting project. However the experience garnered by each member involved in drawing up and implementing the aims of a group was injected into the subsequent activities of some of those participants. The cumulative effect of this process was far from insignificant. In this way even the more fantastic schemes (and the twentieth century has witnessed a few!) made a contribution to the overall body of experience which, after all, had to comprise mistakes as well as achievements. In this way, therefore, a movement of limited numbers benefited from the maximisation of resources.

The shift in emphasis from scholarly or antiquarian pursuits to the promotion and propagation of Irish as a living language was most dramatically and effectively realised by that leading organisation, already referred to, the Gaelic League. The League aimed to halt the decline of Irish and to promote it as the vernacular. Its activities were both educational and social. The language classes which it provided increased in numbers fom 58 in 1898 to 593 in 1904. In order to equip these classes with trained teachers the League established training colleges. It also inaugurated a publishing scheme and devoted itself to filling the vacuum of modern Irish literature in original and translated form, and also supplying textbooks to facilitate learners. Other cultural activities such as evenings of Irish music and dance provided light relief from classes. The movement championed the language cause in education, working tirelessly to improve the status of Irish in schools. In 1904 it succeeded in introducing its own bilingual policy for primary schools whereby in districts where Irish was the vernacular, or in bilingual districts, both languages could be taught or used as a functional medium. It also later won the right to have Irish recognised as a compulsory matriculation subject in the National University.

Yet, the Gaelic League represented much more than an educational institution, and was more than an advocate of educational reform at all levels. Padraig Pearse, refers to the Gaelic League as a spiritual movement, in his essay 'The Spiritual Nation' (1976: 64). A recognition of two basic facts shaped the League's work. Firstly, that a language enshrines the mind and soul of a country. Secondly, a language acts as an energising force only while it functions as a living idiom — 'I mbéal na ndaoine a mhaireas an teanga' ('A language survives on the lips of its people').

The League viewed the restoration of Irish as the means to counter the anglicisation of Ireland. This fundamental philosophy had significant implications for the struggle for Irish independence. Although the Gaelic League itself was not a political organisation, many of its members fought in the 1916 Rising and subsequent War Of Independence. Padraig Pearse, himself, was to the fore in the Rising just as he had been in the realm of Irish literature, and in the League's efforts to develop 'the intellectual independence of Ireland'.

As yet the aspirations of the Gaelic League have not yet been fulfilled despite its vast achievements. Indeed, many people assumed that the role of this revolutionary organisation became obsolete with the founding of the Free State in 1922 and the recognition of Irish as the official language in Ireland. The Irish Government accepted that it was its responsibility to safeguard the native language. However the belief that this acknowledgement guaranteed the preservation and diffusion of Irish proved false.

Within the Six Counties such an assumption could never have been made in the first instance. The Northern Ireland Government chose to ignore the existence of Irish and the cultural rights of an ethnic minority. The continued need for Gaelic League branches was, therefore, never questioned by Northern Gaels. It was in Belfast that the second branch of the movement had been founded. This step was of major importance in Belfast because of the public apathy towards Irish which had taken root in the city during the second half of the nineteenth century. This occurred in stark contrast to the preceding decades of industry and application by lovers of the language in Belfast. During the later decades Irish had come to be regarded with some suspicion. The painstaking business of copying Irish manuscripts stopped (Ó Buachalla, 1968: 270). Classes in Irish in Queen's College Belfast (later to be awarded the status of University) ceased. The chair of Celtic Studies lay vacant from 1861 until the middle of the twentieth century.

Ó Buachalla (1968: 265–274) described the accumulation of factors and events which precipitated the close of that first era in the Language Revival activities in Belfast. The city's industrial boom in the early nineteenth century together with the hardship inflicted on rural areas by poverty and famine led to a dramatic population increase in Belfast over a relatively short period. It was chiefly Catholics who flooded into the city at this time. Their proportion increased from 8% in 1800 to 34% in 1861. This shift in the population profile caused unrest and a certain anxiety amongst the Protestant community which was reflected in the intensification of religious divisions and residential segregation. Divisions between the two communities in Belfast were strengthened by the economic expansion in the nineteenth century. This split was deepened by the campaign for Home Rule in Ireland which was bitterly opposed by Protestants. The relationship with Britain became more and more advantageous to the Protestant community as Ulster's industrial development continued. Catholics, on the other hand, were disadvantaged within this political context as is evidenced by the analysis of social variables definable in terms of religion, e.g. representation in professional and skilled employment; illiteracy; housing conditions etc. (Bell, 1976: 15–33). The growing rift between Protestants and Catholics was widened in the nineteenth century by the unifying control which the Orange Order asserted upon upper, middle and lower classes of Protestants.

Thus the economic dominance of upper class industrialists was secured by dividing the overall working class population of Ulster.

One of the consequences to this polarisation of the two communities was the alienation of each community from the more distinctive values of the other. We have seen that a recognition and appreciation of the language's worth had been manifest in the labours of many liberal Ulster Presbyterians. Its historic roots, however, were so deeply embedded in the Roman Catholic heritage that the language too suffered from the sectarian hostilities engendered by a fear, on the part of Protestants, of losing their economic and political dominance.

A growing suspicion of the Irish language led to this 'twilight period' in the Language Movement activities after about 1860. The advent of the Gaelic League in the city was therefore of major significance. It not only created a Revival Movement at ground level rather than on a more exclusively academic sphere but it also injected momentum and drive into a situation which had become stagnant. This public lethargy towards Irish in Belfast in the decades preceding the founding of the Gaelic League was described succinctly by a young scholar at The Queen's University Belfast, Deirdre Morton (1956):

> Is cosúil gur deireadh ré cultúrtha a bhí ann anois, nó comh fada is tá eolas agam ní chuirtí mórán speis arís sa teanga dhúchais sa chathair go dtí gur bunaíodh Conradh na Gaeilge ... Idir an dá linn tharla an réabhlóid tion-scála a chuir crot úr ar an chathair agus ar mheon na ndaoine a tháinig ina sluaite chun cónaí inti.

> The end of a cultural era occurred then (i.e. following the death of John O Donovan, Professor of Celtic Studies at Q.U.B., in 1861. The professor's academic position was not filled again until 1945.) As far as I know, little interest was invested in the native tongue in the city, until the founding of the Gaelic League ... In the meantime the Industrial Revolution changed the shape of the city and also the attitudes of those who crowded into it.

Ó Buachalla (1968: 273) pointed out that it was mainly Protestants who sat on the committee of the Belfast branch of the Gaelic League when it was first established. However, before long it was predominantly Catholics who were left. The League too was tainted by suspicion and always felt the need to defend and reiterate its non-political stance.

> With the advent of the Gaelic League the language in Belfast came, at least partly, into its own. But the League was never considered quite 'respectable' — that awful Belfast word — by the planters. To be a Gaelic Leaguer was to be suspect always. The League might shout at its loudest and longest that it was non-political and non-sectarian. The slogan did not impress Belfast. With the League's membership ninety-nine per cent

Catholic, what could one expect? 'Scratch a Gaelic Leaguer and you'll find a Fenian' was the formula in the old days ... (Ó Byrne, 1946)

Nevertheless, it may be justly attributed to the Gaelic League that it stimulated an interest in the Irish language and culture in Belfast when that had waned. The Belfast committee participated fully in the business of the central branch. It campaigned to have the position of Irish secured in the schools. It established adult language classes and cultural activities. In 1906 the Belfast committee founded a college to train language teachers. A second college, An Ard Scoil Ultach (The Ulster College), was established shortly afterwards in order to assert the place of the Ulster dialect of Irish in teacher training programmes and language classes. The Ard Scoil acquired central importance in the Revival Movement in Belfast.

The idea to create An Ard Scoil Ultach emerged because of a controversy about dialects. Many members were concerned about the position of the Ulster Irish dialect. Munster or Connacht Irish was being taught at all the Christian Brothers' schools. Also, some of the League classes were being taught by speakers of Munster Irish who were working in Belfast. The concern that Ulster Irish was not being adequately catered for was also one of the various factors which prompted another development in the Revival Movement — the establishment of Comhaltas Uladh. This organisation, affiliated to the Gaelic League, was created specifically to represent the interests of Ulster, with special emphasis on the needs of the Six Counties. At this time of political turmoil in the 1920s the Language Movement was at a low ebb. The Gaelic League had lost some of its momentum. It was also encountering financial difficulties. Members in the Six Counties had very particular problems which they felt were ill understood elsewhere in the country. Following Partition in 1922, for example, some Catholic teachers refused to recognise the new political boundaries. They received their salaries from the Dublin Government. This arrangement was stopped, however, and the teachers in question were left to negotiate with the Northern Ireland Ministry of Education. This example indicates the level of confusion and dismay experienced by League members in the Six Counties at that time. Comhaltas Uladh aimed at countering the state of disillusionment then prevalent. One important aspect of its work was the establishment of Irish Summer Colleges, situated mainly in the Donegal Gaeltacht. Attendance by Ulster learners was encouraged by introducing scholarship schemes. Comhaltas Uladh also negotiated with the Ministry of Education and secured modest amendments to regulations for teaching Irish in schools.

The founding of Comhaltas Uladh follows the chain-like pattern already referred to. It grew out of an already established organisation in response to the specific requirements of one area of the latter's responsibilities. This pattern was particularly strong in Belfast because the Irish-speaking circle was not only a minority but a minority within a minority. It also operated on a cross-sectional plane, in the sense that membership of many of the societies in operation at any one time showed a considerable overlap. Premises were also shared, for example between League branches, the Gaelic Athletic Association and perhaps a literary or drama society.

Revival activities in Belfast throughout this century have provided variety. Some of Belfast's older language enthusiasts recall how the learning of Irish was in some ways simpler than it is today. The powerful anglicising influence exerted by the technological media was less overwhelming and less manipulative of the public's social life. The Irish speaker or learner would attend the Ard Scoil, situated near the city centre, several nights a week — for a language class, a ceili or lecture, or perhaps for the storytelling evening held at weekends. On another night he or she might visit a local branch of the League. Contact with traditional Gaeltacht was quite tenacious, even though the mode of transport was commonly the bicycle (without ten gears!). During the 1930s and 1940s the Irish-speaking circle in Belfast included young men and women from the Donegal Gaeltacht who were working in the city. The men found various types of employment. About twenty of the girls worked as maids in the more affluent houses. Traditionally these girls had Thursday afternoons free when they regularly congregated in one of the local branches of the League.

The Feis was another feature of Belfast's cultural life when Irish speakers gathered for competitions in various categories such as language, music, dance, history, sport, recitals etc. Belfast's Feis was first held in 1900 and later became an annual event usually lasting three weeks. Schools and League members participated and prizes included scholarships to the Gaeltacht.

Any visitor to Belfast who is interested in Irish will inevitably spend an evening in Cumann Chluain Ard. This branch of the Gaelic League was established in 1936 in order to encourage a less centralised network with independent premises in local areas. Cumann Chluain Ard will be referred to again as it was here that the founder members of the Shaw's Road Gaeltacht Community first met, socialised, learnt Irish, and eventually planned the building of an Irish-speaking neighbourhood as a natural and necessary extension to their lives as Irish speakers.

The 1940s and 1950s saw other societies, campaigns and enterprises come and go — but each, somehow, left its mark on the revival story. 'Glún na Buaidhe' which had a branch in Belfast between 1943 and 1945 introduced a rigid 'English prohibited' rule. Before this the Language Movement had shown a leniency towards the speaking of English during the various events.

'Fal', a group operating in the mid-1950s, drew attention to the dependence of Irish speakers on English-medium institutions. Members of Fal believed that this situation greatly impeded the progress of revival efforts. In the August 1954 edition of their monthly paper, *Dearcadh*, the group deplored the lack of a national press. Current Irish periodicals and magazines could not fill the vacuum. Major daily newspapers of the time were criticed for their lip service to the language in the form of the one or two articles in Irish which they printed. Other editions of *Dearcadh* give an insight into the close affinity which Belfast Irish speakers felt with traditional Gaeltacht and their concern about the decline of Irish in those areas. The October 1954 editorial opened with the words,

Bás na Gaedhealtachta — Bás an Náisiúin.
(Death of the Gaeltacht — the death of the Nation.)

Support for the Gaeltacht cause was urged in this article which closed with the following warning,

Slánú na Gaedhealtachta an obair is práinnighe atá le déanamh againn. Sinne an ghlún dheireannach a bhfuil ar ár gcumas an Náisiún a shábháil ón bhás.

(Saving the Gaeltacht is the most urgent aspect of national work to be realised. We are the last generation with the possibility of saving the Nation from death.)

The preservation of Gaeltacht areas wherein the position of the Irish language was fast diminishing was perceived as vital to the nation's welfare. Fal created a pressure group to support the campaign which called upon the Dublin Government to allow Gaeltacht areas more autonomy.

A series of fleeting operations speckle the continuation into the 1960s in Belfast. An Irish-medium credit union lasted a short period. A small shop was opened wherein negotiations were through Irish. A variety of Irish-language papers appeared and disappeared. Many schemes were suggested, discussed, planned, but never saw daylight. Others were implemented and failed drastically. One member of Fal, for example, endeavoured to make his contribution to the Gaeltacht's cause by selling his Belfast business and setting up a small craft industry in the Donegal Gaeltacht. However, the project failed. No financial rescue was forthcoming and it ended in disillusionment and bitterness.

Each achievement, whether long-term or fleeting, each plan which remained on some committee table, each unsuccessful attempt, represented, at the least, a contribution to a community's self-assertion of its Irishness. They prevented the ideal of an Irish-speaking nation from slipping into oblivion. Sometimes it was propelled forward. Sometimes it was just kept ticking over. It never quite died. What Irish speakers were determined to prove to themselves and to others was that the Irish language was a viable and satisfying medium of communication in today's society.

The recollections of many of today's older Irish speakers point to the 1950s as the high point of revival activities in Belfast. At this time the founder members of the Shaw's Road project were just learning Irish. The social dimension to learning activities would have been particularly attractive to these young people. The Gaelic Cycling Club organised trips of historic interest every Sunday and provided accounts of these outings in its periodical, *Roth* (Wheel). A swimming club was in operation also. Church services were not provided in Irish during these years, although two religious groups 'Cuallacht Mhuire' and 'Réalt' held prayer meetings in Irish. The latter group extended its programme with social evenings during the winter months. This included poetry readings, lectures, debates, music, dance and games. An Irish choir, active at this time, was very successful at the Welsh Eistedfodd. Various literary societies were part of the language scene also. 'Cleití', a club for writers, endeavoured to inspire its members to produce written material and to publish it in Irish journals and magazines. A reading circle also lasted a few years. Irish language drama societies in the city became quite well organised in the early 1950s. A co-ordinating council was established to oversee each season's programme, grant aided by Comhaltas Uladh.

The Irish Language Movement in Belfast was developing within a closely knit community. This explains the significance of each episode or enterprise along its course, for most members of the circle would be acquainted with each other. The atmosphere created and sustained by this movement ultimately produced a network of couples and young families who were not satisfied with participation in various educational or social events. These people wished for a permanent setting within which they could be more fully true to themselves as Irish speakers and as Irish people. This could only be realised within the context of an Irish-speaking community and neighbourhood. As children appeared, the second fundamental requisite would be the provision of Irish-medium education.

As yet the question of the position of Irish in the educational system has not been considered. We have seen how, in the nineteenth century, the school was used as an anglicising instrument. Sadness pervaded the words of Robert Mac Adam, Belfast's leading patron of the language in the nineteenth century, as he described the arrival of that twilight era which education and the industrial expansion of Belfast precipitated:

That which conquest and colonisation failed to effect in centuries, steam and education are now accomplishing peacefully and rapidly; so that ere

long, the traces of the olden time will have faded from our view. (Ó
Buachalla, 1968: 231)

It is also evident, however, that the language has proved more resilient than
could have been anticipated. With the arrival of the Gaelic League air was blown
into the embers. The language had found champions in the realm of education.
But what was the status of this language which the League was endeavouring to
improve? What was the position of the language in schools when young adults
were attending the Ard Scoil or evening classes at a local League branch? Was
there any possibility of Irish-speaking families in the 1970s being adequately
catered for within the existing educational system? In order to answer these
questions and provide a more complete background picture of the Irish language
in Belfast the following chapter looks solely at its position within the context of
formal education.

3 Irish and the Education System

... because they find a great inconvenience in moving their suits by an interpreter they do for the most part send their children to schools, especially to learn the English language; so as we may conceive an hope that the next generation will in tongue and heart and every way else become English. (Ó Cuiv, 1971: 16–17)

These words came from the pen of Sir John Davies, an English Attorney General in Ireland during the early seventeenth century. The principal duty of that post was to establish the English legal system in Ireland. The native code of law, known as the Brehon code, had survived the prohibitions introduced much earlier in the Statutes of Kilkenny and, indeed, had continued to operate for a further three hundred years. We have already considered the remarkable resilience of the native tongue in the face of various legal and military steps which aimed to impose the English language and English social structures. When, however, during the Tudor conquest, the English language successfully gained dominance in the legal and other domains, the native vernacular suffered further loss of esteem and value. The ancient language of the Irish nobility and aristocracy and the native learned professions was being eliminated or demoted as military defeats caused the collapse of the upper social strata of the country. Before long, the education system would be used to reinforce and hasten this language shift.

The aspirations, expressed above, for the demise of that unique ingredient of Irish identity were somewhat overly ambitious. Nevertheless, the Attorney General's observations serve to highlight a key factor in the decline of the native tongue. The English language was establishing its dominance in areas of social and economic prestige. Accordingly, Irish was slipping into a fatal association with impoverished, low status areas of life.

This process was based on a double-edged approach involving the destruction of existing native social order and administration, together with a deliberate use of the new administration as a consciously anti-Irish language instrument. The Irish language was to suffer demoralisation as a result of the assault on the native learned and aristocratic classes. Surprisingly, it survived many of the tactics employed to achieve this end and even the proscription of the native bardic order in the sixteenth century did not halt the quill of some of Ireland's best-loved poets. However, the old traditions which had long upheld the Irish tongue could not continue that function once the native social order had waned and disappeared, following the military defeat at Kinsale. On that occasion, the last real chance for national independence had been seized by the Irish chieftains. When their valiant attempt failed, the military defeat itself was of less significance for the language than the death blow which was dealt to native morale as the old Gaelic order crumbled. English administrative authorities established their own social and economic order. The native language lost its long standing guardians following the Tudor attack on legal, religious and economic institutions. Ancient educational structures, which had supported the native vernacular, were destroyed. The highly prestigious professional schools of learning came to an end; the system of poetic patronage vanished as the aristocratic families fled or were evicted. Those families who did not flee to Europe reeled under the intensified impact of colonisation during the seventeenth century and the vast majority of the land was granted to the English settlers. A new landlord class was introduced from England as native aristocratic families were ousted from their estates and 'resettled' in the impoverished western regions of the country.

Therefore, that double-edged approach of colonisation brought about the systematic elimination of the native classes and their culture from domains of economic and social significance on the one hand, and, on the other, effected the firm introduction of English language dominance in situations associated with social and economic prestige. Consequently, the ancient privileges afforded to scholars of native learning were not only removed but reversed. The social acclaim and status, traditionally enshrined within those native social institutions which had upheld the old Gaelic order, were stripped from them. That loss of functional value in higher domains and the subsequent loss of dignity would come to be reflected in the public perception of the Irish language.

This situation may be illustrated by briefly comparing the following two poems, both written in the seventeenth century. The opening verses of the first poem, written by an anonymous poet in the early part of the century, illustrate how the learned profession of the bard was still revered and cherished in certain parts, and how privileges were still enjoyed by him.

Beatha an Scolaire	*The Scholar's Life*
Aoibhinn beatha and scolaire	Sweet is the scholar's life,
bhíos ag déanamh a leighinn;	busy about his studies,

is follas dibh, a dhaoine,	the sweetest lot in Ireland
gurab dó is aoibhne in Éirinn.	as all of you know well.
Gan smacht riogh ná rofhlatha	No king or prince rule him
ná tighearna dá threise	nor lord however mighty,
gan chuid cíosa ag caibidil,	no rent to the chapterhouse
gan moicheirghe, gan meirse.	no dredging, no dawn-rising

However, the second extract, from a poem by Daibhi Ó Bruadair, was written in the second half of the century. Like many of the poems of that period, these verses describe the poet's sense of loss and injustice as the old value systems disappear. The tide of Gaelic civilisation, in which the noble craft of poet-scholar was immersed, was being swept away in the name of colonisation. The poet expresses his wrath at the fact that the 'stuttering' of broken English commands more respect than the eloquence of Gaelic verse, and English customs take precedence over native ways:

Mairg Nach Fuil Ina Dhubhthuata	*O Its's Best Be A Total Boor*
Mairg nach fuil 'na thrudaire	It's best to be, good people
eadraibhse, a dhaoine maithe,	a stutterer among you
ós iad is fearr chugaibhse,	since that is what you want,
a dhream gan iúl gan aithne.	you blind ignorant crew.
Dá bhfaghainn fear mo mhalarta,	If I found me a man to swap
ris do reacfainn an suairceas;	I'd give him my lovely skill
do-bhearainn luach fallainge	He'd find it as good as a cloak
idir é 'gus an duairceas.	around him against the gloom
Ós mó cion fear deaghchulaith	Since a man is respected more
ná a chion de chionn bheith	for his suit than for his
tréitheach;	talents
truagh ar chaitheas le healadhain	I regret what I've spent on my art,
gan é aniogh ina éadach.	That I haven't it now in clothes.

This poignant change in the fortunes of the native learned classes was paralleled by the declining fortunes of the language which had been the cradle of their intellectual formation. Economic advantages were exclusively associated with the English-speaking population. The introduction of an English system of land tenure, implemented and maintained principally by the population of English settlers, undermined the native socio-economic infrastructures. English was, of course, the language of this new class of landlords, as well as the professional and commercial classes which accompanied it. The indigenous language of the country represented only one aspect of an entire culture reeling in degradation under the impact of military suppression, plantation, evictions, religious persecution, famine and mass emigration.

The incessant assaults upon the old Gaelic civilisation did not effect the obliteration of the Irish language. Indeed, even throughout the years of famine, culminating in the Great Famine of 1847, Irish was the vernacular throughout most of Ireland. Nonetheless, the linguistic profile of the country was subject to a fatal process of change. Whereas Irish was used by all classes of society in the sixteenth century, that situation changed considerably in the wake of the defeat at Kinsale. English superseded Irish in areas of socio-economic significance. English language dominance extended from public affairs and administration through other high status areas such as law, commerce and the professions.

It is deeply significant that Daniel O'Connell, born in 1745, a native speaker of Irish and one of the first Catholic Irishmen to be admitted to the bar (he was also the man who achieved the repeal of the last of the anti-Catholic penal laws), should have turned his back on the language. O'Connell believed that a utilitarian approach necessitated the abandonment of the Irish language in order to embrace the English tongue as the more universal and useful medium.

Even the Catholic Church, the most influential institution standing outside the formal framework of British government in Ireland, increasingly saw itself within an English language context. The survival of Irish among the common people of the country after the political collapse of Gaelic Ireland had been largely due to the courageous efforts of priests as well as poets in defence of the native vernacular. However, the relaxation of the harsh and restrictive Penal Code allowed Catholics a limited degree of freedom and social mobility. When Catholic colleges became legal, the language of higher education was that language associated with the upper social strata — English. Therefore, the Royal College of Saint Patrick, established in Maynooth in 1795 for the training of Catholic priests, adopted English as its institutional language. This, despite the fact that the overwhelming majority of Irish Catholics spoke Irish.

Education reinforced this bilingual diglossic situation whereby the English language gained dominance in areas of high social status and Irish retained its position as a viable medium of communication only in the less formal situations such as in the homes of the poorer classes. In the seventeenth and eighteenth centuries the native Catholic population were deprived of educational facilities. Brief, sporadic periods of a more relaxed religious tolerance allowed the occasional appearances of Catholic schools. However, these periods were few and short lived. Generally, the small gentry and professional classes suffered most. The more affluent parents could afford to send their sons to be educated in Europe. The lower, peasant classes — whether Catholic or Protestant — considered education as a luxury beyond their reach, and therefore did not expect it. The desire for education was nevertheless reflected in the establishment of 'hedge schools', in the eighteenth century, where small groups of children gathered to be taught secretly and clandestinely. The fact that children were taught to read and write English, as well as Irish, in these illegal schools reflected the increasing need for the lower classes to familiarise themselves with the language of landlords, the courts, local government, public meetings and the commercial world. (Wall, 1969: 85–6)

Valuable insights into this historic period may be gleaned from the diary of one of these hedge school masters, Amhlaoibh Ó Suilleabhain (or Humphrey Ó Sullivan) which was written between 1827 and 1835. O Suilleabhain possessed unusual gifts for a man of his times. In the introduction to his translation of 'Cin Lae Amhlaoibh', Tomas de Bhaldraithe commented upon the significance of the author's decision to employ the Irish medium rather than English in this literary work (de Bhaldraithe, 1979: 12). Not only did Ó Suilleabhain adopt a literary form which had, with a few exceptions, ceased to exist in the Irish tradition, but he elected to do so through the medium of Irish. He was not deterred by the tendency of contemporary scholars to abandon that language in favour of the emerging dominant vehicle of expression — English. Rather, Ó Suilleabhain displayed his appreciation of Irish as a versatile and effective medium with a rich literary and oral tradition behind it.

An entry in Amhlaoibh's diary, dated 14th May 1827, describes the primitive cabins where the author, and his father, had taught school. Those makeshift shelters had, by then, disappeared, and Amhlaoibh wonders if the native language confronts a similar destiny:

> Will it be long until this Irish language in which I am writing will disappear? Fine big schools are being built daily to teach this new language, the English of England. But alas! Nobody is taking any interest in the fine subtle Irish language, apart from mean swaddlers who try to lure the Irish to join their new cursed religion. (De Bhaldraithe, 1979: 23)

Illiteracy in Irish would also have reinforced the association of that language with the poor and uneducated. This situation was consolidated by the attitudes of many scholars, together with the lack of publishing facilities for Irish material. On 5th January 1828, Amhlaoibh laments that strengthening of English as the language associated with social and educational privileges:

> ... Some of the townspeople are organizing a circulating library for a limited number of members. It has been established for the last year. Every member of the society pays five shillings a year. Alas! Who will establish an Irish language library? No such person is available. The English language of the Saxons is every day getting the upper hand of our native language. Add to that a thousand million other blemishes and deficiencies under which we are suffering since the day the English once got hold of our native land.

A similar love of the Gaelic language stirred the consciousness of another pioneering figure in Irish prose — Canon Peadar Ó Laoire. Indeed, this leading figure in Irish literature was motivated in that direction by his realisation that the efforts of the Revival Movement were hindered by the sparsity of suitable published material (Ó Ceirín, 1970: 150). His autobiography was written against the background of historical events spanning the second half of the nineteenth century.

Peadar was educated at home until the age of thirteen when a schoolhouse was built in the vicinity of his home. He referred to his early schooling at home as a blessing which prevented him from being exposed to 'bad English'. Peadar's mother had come from a wealthy family which was able to equip her with a sound education. The difficulties experienced by other school children who lacked that advantage from which Peadar benefited is well attested in the book: 'They would never hear a word at home but of Gaelic or broken English. The English which they had in the books was the same to them as Greek' (Ó Ceirín, 1970: 54). Peadar also reflected upon the serious decline in the use of Irish which he witnessed over a short period. Indeed, the author's concern for the future of the language was stirred most dramatically on first encountering many of his colleagues at Maynooth College who were unfamiliar with Irish. He envisaged the transition from national bilingualism to the loss of Irish.

Peadar Ó Laoire was born shortly after the introduction of the National Schools. This system of education, introduced in 1831, opened the door to free primary education at public expense. The term 'National', however, is rather misleading, as the objective of these schools was to create that loyal, English-speaking British citizen which Sir John Davies had visualised some two hundred years previously. Pupils were taught to speak, read and write English and were also taught Arithmetic.

In terms of its language goals, the National School System was successful. Its contribution to the dissemination of English and the decline of Irish was therefore significant. Parents co-operated in this process of language shift. The difficulties and restraints encountered by persons with no understanding of English were instrumental in cultivating that parental enthusiasm for children to acquire English. O Laoire also provided insights into this attitude:

In Ireland at that time, the people who had nothing but Gaelic had their minds pinioned where everyday business was concerned. For example, in any kind of legal affair, the man with English was able to turn black into white on them and they had no means of defending themselves. If they gave their own account in Gaelic, none would understand them — except, perhaps, the man who was planning to do them an injustice. They used to have interpreters, but, if the interpreter had accepted a bribe, how would things be with them? From whatever way it was looked at, it could be seen that the man without English was in disastrous straits. (Ó Ceirín, 1970: 148)

The new degree of social freedom and potential social mobility, afforded to Catholics, also acted as an inducement to encourage the learning of English. The education system would provide the means of securing that goal. Accordingly, not only did education now fully endorse the position of English as the language of higher domains but it also rendered it accessible to the native masses.

Padraig Pearse, that renowned patriot, writer and educationalist, referred to the National School System as 'the murder machine', in his series of essays under that title. Pearse attributed the undermining of 'a national consciousness enshrined mainly in a national language' to the efficiency of Ireland's National and Intermediate systems (Pearse, 1976: 22–3).

Entry into the National Schools meant stepping into an English-speaking world. Irish was only accepted onto the curriculum at the turn of the century, under pressure from the Language Revival campaign, then gathering momentum. One of the stated objectives of the Gaelic League was to secure Irish as the medium of instruction in National Schools in areas where it was also the home language. Furthermore, the League was committed to establishing a strong position for the Irish language in National and Intermediate Schools throughout the country. This commitment met with some success. The Commissioners of National Education had already been successfully petitioned to allow the teaching of Irish as an optional subject. Subsequently, since 1879, it was legal to teach Irish in school premises outside school hours. Language enthusiasts had also secured its entry into the Intermediate School curriculum with teachers being remunerated on the basis of exam results. Few schools availed of this provision.

The Gaelic League eventually succeeded in stabilising this position of Irish within the school system so that it could be taught within school hours. The League also prevented the exclusion of Irish from secondary schools and won the acceptance of its bilingual programme. Then, in 1918, Irish gained recognition as an essential subject for matriculation in the new National University of Ireland. Meanwhile, the organisation was also engaged in the task of setting up Irish Colleges, offering short-term teacher training courses. Certificates of merit were recognised by the National Board of Education and, therefore, entitled the teacher to fees for teaching Irish in the National schools.

Within a couple of years, the story of Irish in the educational system would diverge along two separate paths. The political division of the country, consequent upon the Government of Ireland Act, 1920, resulted in a division of the educational system along two separate courses. While Irish, in the Republic of

Ireland, progressed towards the status of the first national language, the story was very different in the Six Counties.

The new independent Government in the South adopted an ambitious package of policies which were designed to realise the objectives of the Language Movement. These goals aimed to preserve the language where it was still the vernacular of the community, and to revive it throughout the rest of the country where it had been lost. The latter commitment would involve a range of policies which secured the constitutional and legal rights of the language. These measures included provisions to have Irish displayed on road signs; introduced into the media; used alongside English in Government publications and required of applicants for the Civil Service. Other proceedings catered for the standardization of the language's orthography and spelling, and the publication of Irish language material. (Ó Riagáin, 1988: 29–53). However, the educational system was perceived as the principal hope for propagating the language outside the Gaeltacht. Therefore, Irish continued as a compulsory requirement for entry into the National University. It also became a compulsory subject in all primary and secondary schools. (Until 1973 it remained a mandatory subject in state examinations.) These educational policies were not directed only at Irish as a school subject. In addition, efforts were channelled into the development of immersion programmes whereby children would be taught entirely or partly through the medium of Irish. These types of schools were increasing in numbers at a steady pace until the 1950s.

The educational system in the Twenty-Six Counties would therefore bear much of the responsibility for reversing the anglicising influences of the National Schools. Within the context of a newly independent state this role placed a considerable strain on the available resources. Despite the achievements of the Revival Movement, most of the country's primary school children, and many of the older children, were still not being taught Irish in 1921. Subsequently, teachers were ill equipped to respond confidently to the demands placed upon them. New teacher training facilities had to be introduced immediately and the overall package included summer crash courses in Irish. In addition to these provisions, competence in the language was made mandatory for entry into Teacher Training Colleges.

This package of positive language-related initiatives in the South was not paralleled in the post-partition Six County state. The position of Irish within the educational framework of Northern Ireland remained relatively unchanged after 1920, and no favourable language policy was formulated. In fact, a formal language policy of any type, concerning Irish, was never presented. The Irish language, as perceived by the Northern Ireland authorities, was a ghost of the past. Officially, it did not exist. As a logical consequence to this attitude, special provisions for its preservation or promotion could never arrive on the agenda.

This lack of improvement in the status of Irish, following partition, was expressed concisely by Tomas Ó Fiaich:

> Across the border the State's attitude towards Irish in the education system remained much as it was in the rest of the country in 1920. While the days when a government spokesman would refer to it as an archaic tribal tongue were probably over, it is tolerated rather than encouraged by the State. (Ó Fiaich, 1972: 74)

If this absence of positive support was true of the general attitude to Gaelic culture it was also evident within the more specific area of education. The teaching of Irish in schools was permitted. However, the set of regulations governing its position in schools was restrictive rather than encouraging of the language's scope and potential as a valuable cultural commodity.

The first regulations for the teaching of Irish in the primary schools were issued in a circular by Lord Londonderry, Minister for Education, in April 1923. This document was entitled, 'Instruction in Irish in Public Elementary Schools in Northern Ireland' (Circular P21: File Ed. 13/1/878. Public Records Office, Northern Ireland). Therein, the Minister informed teachers and school managers that the maximum time allowed for teaching Irish as an ordinary subject was to be one and one half hours per week. In schools where Irish was taught within school hours, history could be omitted from the timetable and replaced by Irish. As an ordinary subject, it could not be taught to children below the third grade. Irish could also be taught as an extra subject, outside school hours, to children of the third grade and higher. Fees would be paid to qualified teachers who gave at least forty hours' instruction of Irish as an extra subject per annum.

Both the teaching of history and of Irish were viewed with similar suspicion by the Education Authorities. The following memo to Lord Londonderry, in September 1922, referred to the forthcoming regulations:

> History may be dropped where Irish is taught within school hours. N.B. I agree with this recommendation in as much as the kind of history that would be taught in schools where it is desired to foster the study of Irish would be likely to have a bias of a very undesirable character. (File Ed. 13/1/156. Northern Ireland Public Records Office)

If the values of the Gaelic League were incorporated into the policy making and planning procedures of the Twenty-Six Counties, the Ulster branches of that organisation faced a Government machine which operated in an entirely different mode. Negotiations and appeals for improved conditions were protracted and unproductive. The Language Movement needed a solid base in the North from which to immerse itself in the very particular problems which it encountered within the context of the new political framework of Northern Ireland. This objective was one of the factors which resulted in the founding of the Ulster-based language organisation, Comhaltas Uladh.

One of the earliest undertakings of this organisation was to send a deputation to the Ministry of Education to lobby for a more flexible attitude to Irish in schools. In February 1927, ten representatives of Comhaltas Uladh formally requested the Minister to permit the introduction of Irish to classes below the third grade. Other changes to the system were also requested, some of which had been in effect during earlier years. In 1926 the teaching of Irish as an extra subject was further restricted to classes in grades V, VI, and VII. The Comhaltas deputation appealed to have these limits extended (Ó Muimhneacháin, 1974: 155). Efforts to secure greater opportunities for learning Irish at school met with stalwart opposition. In the instance referred to, the Minister suggested the irrelevance of Irish within the new political boundaries.

> The Minister pointed out that the Commissioners of National Education controlled Elementary Education over all Ireland, whereas the purview of his Ministry extended only over six counties, where the Irish was admittedly dead or dying.
> The Minister also suggested that a knowledge of French would prove more useful to a boy than knowledge of Irish. (File Ed 13/1/516. Northern Ireland Public Records Office.)

The limited success of the deputation resulted in the one concession that Irish could once more be taught in place of history from the third grade. (In an earlier programme this lower age limit for introduction to Irish had been set at fifth grade.) Otherwise, however, the Minister was adamant about maintaining the current position, even though he acknowledged that certain changes had caused a reduction in the number of schools teaching Irish as an extra subject.

From 1926 the grants for teaching Irish as an extra subject at third and fourth grades were withdrawn. Some seven years later, all special grants for teaching Irish were terminated. At that time about ten and a half thousand children were learning Irish at primary school (i.e. 14.11% of children at Roman Catholic schools, and 5% of the total primary school population). The principal reason given for this removal of these grants was the heavy financial commitments of Government. The Parliamentary Secretary, Mr Robb, also stated that the elementary school was not an appropriate place for the instruction of Irish. He supported this claim by stating that a large number of schools under Roman Catholic management had not availed of the grant (Northern Ireland Parliamentary Debates, Commons, vol. XV, col. 1077, 25th April 1933).

The Ministry's impartiality in this matter was not universally trusted. This is evident from the parliamentary debates of the day. Mr Mc Neill, MP for the university area, expressed fears about the Ministry's 'spirit of antagonism to the Irish language'. He informed the Northern Ireland House of Commons that, 'I have a very shrewd suspicion in my mind that it is being discontinued, not in the interests of economy, but in the interests of party politics in Northern Ireland. (Northern Ireland Parliamentary Debates, Commons, vol. XV, col. 1084–1085, 25th April 1933). The Member for Central Belfast, Mr Campbell, expressed these same doubts, more explicitly, when he accused the Ministry of provincialism, obscurantism and pettiness (Northern Ireland Parliamentary Debates, Commons, vol. XVIII, col. 640–642, 24th March 1936).

The response of the contemporary Prime Minister to these objections from nationalist Members of Parliament, validated their declared suspicions:

What use is it, in this busy part of the Empire, to teach our children the Irish Language? What use would it be to them? Is it not leading them along a road which has not practical value? We have not stopped the teaching; we have stopped the grants, which I think amounted to £1500 a year. We have stopped the grants simply because we do not see that these boys being taught Irish would be any better citizens.

These comments provide an insight into the political make-up of Northern Ireland at that time. The Irish language was perceived in political terms by the Government. Its propagation was considered a threat to the balance of power which was firmly controlled by the Unionist majority within the Six Counties. Schools were expected to play their part in propagating the cultural and political value systems of the ruling party — a party which was to rule the Northern Ireland state continuously for fifty years. The Irish language could not be accommodated within that tight framework. It could not be accepted as the cultural heritage and right of all Northern Ireland citizens — and especially of those who desired to cultivate and cherish that aspect of their identity.

Indeed, if culture can be likened to the personality of a community (Brennan, 1964), then the nationalist community in Northern Ireland was expected to undergo a personality change. The children of that community were destined to miss that valuable opportunity to share in the self-knowledge and self image which the Irish language could provide to the population as a whole. One writer, Padraig Ó Snodaigh, referred to the Irish language as the 'Hidden heritage' which had been obscured from the Ulster Protestant by short-sighted educational policies (Ó Snodaigh, 1973: 25).

Northern participants in the Language Revival Movement endeavoured to reduce the detrimental influence of the abolition of special grants by accepting the responsibility of paying those fees which had been withdrawn. This challenge was met for one year by Comhaltas Uladh. However, this organisation was unable to sustain the burden in the long term. Once this fact was faced, Comhaltas Uladh channelled further efforts into the provision of Gaeltacht scholarships for school children. Thereby, the Comhaltas hoped to compensate for the loss of fees for Irish as an extra subject by encouraging its effective teaching as an optional subject (Ó Muimhneacháin, 1974: 156). This work of Comhaltas Uladh made a significant contribution to the promotion of Irish in schools. The prospect of a month or two on a summer Gaeltacht course, organised by Comhaltas Uladh, or one of the other language organisations, continues to add an enjoyable dimension to language learning for the thousands of school children who annually attend these courses.

Language campaigners continued to oppose the restrictions placed upon the teaching of Irish, during the years which followed Partition. In some ways, the situation deteriorated from the already limited scope for Irish teaching which had existed within the framework of the National School System. For example, the Irish Colleges, which had been set up by the Gaelic League in order to train Irish language teachers, suffered along those lines. Most of the colleges which had been recognised by the Commissioners of National Education were refused recognition by the Northern Ireland Ministry of Education. Applications made on behalf of the colleges, requesting the Ministry to accept their teaching certificates as qualifications for teaching Irish in Northern Ireland's schools, were rejected. (Memo. File Ed. 13/1/878, Northern Ireland Public Records Office.)

An application was also made to introduce Irish as a compulsory requirement for Catholic students entering Teacher Training College, in accordance with resolutions adopted by the Armagh Provincial Council of Catholic Clerical Managers in May 1929 (File Ed. 13/1/878). The application was refused. Indeed, a Celtic Department was not created in the two Roman Catholic Training Colleges in Belfast until the mid-1960s.

The position of Irish in the educational system of Northern Ireland continued to suffer from the Government's attitude which vacillated between hostility and disregard. On various occasions it was pointed out that this view diverged from the more favourable attitudes emerging towards Welsh and Scottish Gaelic in schools. Indeed, Irish has also been treated as a less valuable and relevant subject than any of the European languages. In 1947, one MP objected to the contrasting official attitudes towards Irish and French. Whereas the grant for teaching Irish as an extra subject was removed, a decision was taken to introduce grants for conversational French classes. The Minister for Education defended the differential treatment. 'French is much more practical and useful than Irish, and I make no apology for trying to cultivate it.' (Northern Ireland Parliamentary Debates, Commons, vol. XXX, col. 4641, 5th March 1947.)

This narrow attitude towards the value of Irish to the entire Northern Ireland community was consistently reflected in the lack of status afforded the language within the educational system. No comprehensive policy for its promotion, within that context, has been developed. For example, no facilities for the publication of Irish language materials for Northern Ireland schools, comparable to the Welsh and Scottish Gaelic Book Councils, have, as yet, been developed. However, if these negative policies impeded the language's progress within the schools under Roman Catholic management, they were even more detrimental to the language's prospects in the State schools. The latter sector caters mainly for children of the Protestant denomination, although there are a few schools which are attended by both Protestant and Catholic children. This dual system in Northern Ireland partially reflects the prevalent sociopolitical situation which has resulted in residential segregation. It is also true that the Catholic Church accepts and cherishes the responsibility for educating Catholic children within an environment where a Catholic ethos pervades. Unfortunately, the failure of policy makers to consider Irish as 'a purely educational and cultural issue', (Northern Ireland Parliamentary Debates, Commons, vol. XXV, col. 2711, 8th October 1942) has resulted in its relatively limited development within Catholic schools, and its almost complete exclusion from the curriculum in the State Schools attended by Protestant children. Despite this situation, the Irish language remained the second most popular language, other than English, taken in public examinations in secondary schools. (French still represents the most popular subject.) This fact is illustrated in Table 1.

Certain glimmers of hope for a more enlightened attitude towards Irish in the educational system have emerged sporadically within recent decades. In 1974, the Department of Education published a report which suggested a more

TABLE 1 *Combined O Level and A Level Entries*

	Irish	French	German	Spanish
1960	1163	4350	599	97
1965	1624	7402	1114	357
1970	2348	8859	1287	903
1975	2124	8904	1330	1133
1980	2065	9799	1341	1215
1985	1991	9226	1118	1248

favourable and tolerant view of the language. Second language teaching in the primary school was advocated generally. However, the particular attributes of Irish were also acknowledged.

> In dealing with the teaching of Irish in the primary school, consideration can be given to certain environmental factors which bear on the subject in Ireland. Unlike other languages, Irish does have immediate historical relevance for school pupils here. Surnames, Christian names, names of towns, counties, rivers, fields and numerous other geographical features are in most cases derived directly from Irish. Indeed, the majority have still preserved the distinct phonetic form to this day ... In every conversation in town and country children here make use of words and idioms which are obviously peculiar to our language environment and cannot be overlooked in a consideration of the teaching of Irish. Since children here are in relatively close proximity to Irish-speaking areas, they can familiarise themselves with Irish sounds and speech without serious difficulty. These factors are of considerable help in the teaching of Irish and confer certain advantages which no other second language can claim to the same extent in Ireland. (DENI 1974: 106)

This statement was welcomed by Irish language teachers and lecturers at the Teacher Training Colleges. It conveyed a promising willingness to modify the neglectful official attitude towards Irish which had, until then, prevailed. The encouraging comments of the report, however, were not reinforced, in any practical sense, by follow-up language planning or policy initiatives. At a more localised level, the focus upon Irish in the primary school bore certain positive results. The Gaelic League appointed a part-time organiser who visited various primary schools in Northern Ireland, with the aim of investigating and stimulating interest in the teaching of Irish. The Catholic Training Colleges directed their attention at the provision of in-service courses to equip those teachers who were enthusiastic about Irish, but lacked proficiency or self-confidence. Also, about this time, a teaching package of books and tapes for young school children was designed and produced by a primary school teacher, Seamas Ceitinn. Subsequently, a first step was taken to filling the void of suitable teaching materials for schools.

This peak of activity, unsupported by an overall co-ordinating policy for improving the position of Irish in schools, could not sustain momentum. The level of progress might justifiably be measured as one step ahead of animosity and passive neglect, towards recognition and accord. The next logical step towards active, practical support within a policy framework was not realised. Consequently, the onus remained on Irish language enthusiasts and upon the dedication and motivation of individual language teachers, to ensure that pupils had an opportunity to gain real insights into their own heritage via the language. Its promotion as a viable, functional medium was also left up to language organisations and individual Irish speakers. A concrete, well planned programme to introduce the language into all schools, to provide well tested, attractive materials and to develop strategies outside the educational system which would provide real motivation for a broader range of young people to learn and use Irish remain as future challenges.

The latest curriculum proposals by Dr Mawhinney, Minister for Education, add another episode to this tale of the Irish language in Northern Ireland's schools. An outline of this latest development is presented in the following chapter, bringing the story of Irish in the educational system up to date. This account is dealt with within the context of the current position of Irish in the Six Counties.

4 Irish in the Present Day Context

Many of Belfast's older generation of Irish speakers look back on the 1950s as a climax in the Language Movement. Colourful anecdotes abound about that period when people enjoyed considerable variety in their social activities as Irish speakers and learners. After subsequent years of a declining pace, the Language Movement began, once more, to gain momentum. Today, a vibrancy reigns among the various groups working for the language — a feeling that something stirs. In Northern Ireland, Irish is very much the learners' language. The urban revival is under way. It is not a phenomenon to be observed and monitored from a safe academic distance. Here is a real social issue which breathes and sweats and bleeds and smiles. It demands to be taken seriously. So, yes. Something stirs.

Yet, the old paradoxes still exist in the official attitude taken towards the language. Government legislation reveals signs of the old ambiguity and doubt about the nature of the language's potential. On the one hand, for example, enlightened views permitted the recognition of the Bunscoil. Since 1984, the Irish-medium primary school has enjoyed all the advantages of other grant aided schools. A modest increase in radio time for Irish language programmes has also been facilitated. Furthermore, in August 1988, the Government published a preliminary report of a survey on the Irish language in Northern Ireland (Sweeney, 1988). That publication represented a significant step forward for the language. It proved that the Irish language was now recognised as a relevant aspect of life in the Six Counties — an aspect which merited the attention of policy makers. Until then, even the data acquisition form for census returns ignored the existence of Irish as a viable, quantifiable phenomenon.

However, although these improvements in the position of Irish engender hope for the future of the language, other measures systematically detract from that hope. Indeed, an erratic trail of sensible positive gestures runs alongside another set of initiatives and measures which demote the status of Irish in the North.

Education

The latest proposals for educational reforms concerning Irish in Northern Ireland's schools provide an important example of this type of attitudinal dichotomy. At the time of the Government's survey publication, the Irish language could be chosen as an optional subject in secondary schools, alongside other subjects of the schools' or pupils' choice. As we have seen, the language maintained its popularity as an exam subject. During the formulation of proposals for changes on the curriculum, educationalists favouring Irish hoped for legislative changes which would strengthen the position of Irish in primary and secondary schools. The published report, *Education Reform in Northern Ireland: The Way Forward* (1988), showed a confused attitude towards the role of Irish in Northern Ireland's schools. On a positive note, the Minister for Education acknowledged that the cultural value of Irish was relevant to all Northern Ireland school children.

> Several respondents suggested that there should be opportunities for pupils to gain awareness of aspects of history, culture and traditions which contribute to the cultural heritage of Northern Ireland. The Government welcomes and accepts this suggestion as a positive measure aimed at lessening the ignorance which many feel contributes to the divisions in our society. The Government also believes it to be both appropriate and necessary that the curriculum of every child should include elements of Education for Mutual Understanding, which has already helped to foster valuable cross-community contacts among many of our schools. (DENI, 1988: 3)

However, while recognising its potential, in this broad sense, the more specific curriculum changes originally recommended in the Report would, in effect, have diminished the status of Irish as a modern language with particular cultural advantages.

At secondary level, it was proposed that a study of French, German or Spanish be compulsory for all pupils. Irish was excluded from this category of modern languages and placed in a separate category as an optional, additional modern language. As such, a child could no longer choose to study Irish in conjunction with scientific or environmental subjects only. French, Spanish and German were afforded this privilege. Irish could only be studied as well as one of these languages, plus English. The option for that percentage of pupils who would like to take Irish as their only modern language, was subsequently eliminated. Within the framework of these proposals, European languages were awarded greater status than the Irish language, in Northern Ireland schools.

Irish in the primary schools has been subjected to the same class of inconsistencies. The Primary Teachers' Guide (DENI, 1974: 106) acknowledged its potential contribution to the curriculum. Other official documents reported similar observations about the advantages of second language learning at primary level. (DES, 1988, 012). It is not surprising, therefore, that educationalists expected to find concrete, constructive proposals for the development of Irish in primary schools within the framework of the Minister's reforms. In fact, none were given.

Consequently, a sense of frustration was expressed by Irish speakers in Northern Ireland, particularly within the realm of education. Fears about the effect of the Minister's proposals on Irish inspired an angry response by language enthusiasts from an early stage in their formulation (Mc Kendry, 1988; Comhar Mhúinteoirí an Tuaiscirt; Ó hUiginn & Ó Mairtín, 1988). Despite this protest, the dual approach continued. While one page of the Report inspired optimism by recognising the cultural value of Irish yet another page recommended changes which would, effectively, have damaged its previous position in secondary schools.

Some months later, the Minister for Education announced certain amendments to his proposals, in response to the range of objections made by Irish speakers and educationalists. The significant aspect of this announcement was the reassessment of the position of Irish in secondary schools. Accordingly, rather than placing Irish in a 'special' category which was, in effect, inferior to that of other modern languages, it was to stand on a par with those languages. This news was welcomed by various spokespersons within the Language Movement.

It is hoped that some fruit may be borne from the Minister's recommendation that Northern Ireland pupils should be given the opportunity for insights into various aspects of cultural heritage. It seems that a door has been left open whereby improvements to the language's position may be introduced. However, this is perceived by Irish speakers as a side entrance, at best. The challenge of introducing new, direct, forthright initiatives which would ensure opportunities for all Northern Ireland children to learn Irish has not been met. A policy for teaching Irish in primary schools throughout Northern Ireland and for encouraging schools to avail of opportunities remains a future aspiration.

The present day position of Irish in Northern Ireland primary schools can only be estimated from local, unofficial information (Mac Éinrí, 1981). Official statistics for individual subjects are unavailable. Educationalists describe a general rise in the numbers of primary school children learning the language over the decades, based upon teachers' attendance at in-service courses and visits made to schools. The Government Survey addressed questions to parents about their children's knowledge of second languages (Sweeney, 1988: 20–1). It was reported that 11% of all children aged between three and fifteen had a

TABLE 2 *Knowledge of languages by children aged 3–15 years by religion of parent*

Age group	Total		Catholic		Protestant	
	3–10 (%)	11–15 (%)	3–10 (%)	11–15 (%)	3–10 (%)	11–15 (%)
At least one language	6	71	10	76	7	72
Irish	3	24	10	51	—	—
French	3	66	2	67	5	72
German	1	7	—	4	2	10
Spanish	0	4	—	7	1	3
Base = 100%	1,291	816	198	256	277	300

knowledge of Irish. This figure represented one third of the Catholic population, including 10% of children of primary school age. The Survey found that only among Catholic children under eleven did substantially more know Irish than any other second language. Table 2 shows these results within their full context.

Discussions about the position of Irish in primary schools refer mainly to the teaching of Irish as part of the curriculum in English-medium schools. The full cross-curricular potential of the Irish language in primary schools has not been developed. Some of its unique advantages were recognised in the Primary Teachers' Guide, 1974. The recent Reform proposals by the Minister of Education express an interest in a cross-curricular approach towards Cultural Heritage as an instrument to promote inter-community harmony. This reference to diversity and mutual understanding is not generally interpreted as heralding solid, well-structured programmes for developing familiarity with and the use of the Irish language.

Beyond this context, an important trend regarding the position of Irish in primary schools has been emerging at the community level: education through the medium of Irish. This trend grew out of the Shaw's Road initiative. The support which it has engendered is very evident at pre-primary level. Irish language nursery classes exist in three of the Six Counties. Nine classes operate in Belfast. This network of nursery classes necessitated the founding of Belfast's second Bunscoil in 1987. Like the nursery schools, it was set up by enthusiastic parents and is financed by contributions from voluntary organisations in addition to the arduous fund-raising efforts of parents. Twelve children attended the school during its second year (1988–89) and, due to increasing numbers, a second teacher was appointed in September 1989. These small classes facilitate an accumulation of experience without the added pressures of large classes with which most schools today are forced to cope. The physical classroom layout of Bunscoil na bhFal (this second school) has begun in a makeshift fashion. A permanent site, which is more convenient, will have to be found in the future. So far, no obstacle has proved insurmountable for the parents who founded this school. The achievement of these people may be better understood by considering that they could have chosen to enrol their children at the Shaw's Road Bunscoil which was already well established. Rather, they faced up to the need for a school in their own locality as well as the limitations on numbers which the Shaw's Road School would soon have to implement. Their decision involves the tedious process of struggling to win Government support. Efforts to secure official backing for the second Bunscoil become forever more crucial as the expanding network of nursery classes cannot be accommodated at the Shaw's Road school. An awareness now mounts about the urgent need to bring the development of Irish-medium education under a central co-ordinating umbrella. This move is becoming more widely recognised as imperative.

Parents living in Newry have shown the same initiative by employing a primary teacher to provide classes through Irish for those children who have passed through their nursery system. The same struggle for support and official backing is under way there.

Another interesting project, which is officially supported, has proved successful in Derry. There, an Irish-medium stream operates within an English-medium primary school. Accordingly, some of the school's pupils learn through Irish within an Irish unit, while the rest of the school are taught through English. The process of immersing the children in the Irish language suffers certain disadvantages within this environment. Nevertheless, the system benefits from obvious advantages, also, which the second Bunscoil does not yet enjoy.

The position of Irish in secondary schools is more easily evaluated because of existing records. Approximately 25,000 children are learning Irish, as a subject, at secondary schools. Examination statistics have already been outlined in order to illustrate the persisting popularity of Irish as a modern language. In the past, this fact could not have been used as an indicator of oral proficiency. Exam syllabuses and contemporary teaching methods tended to dictate against communicative skills, more in favour of the translation of texts and grammatical drills. Modern curriculum and exam changes shift considerable emphasis onto the creation of an awareness of the functional value of modern languages. Practical skills are incorporated into the teaching programme. Children are expected to be able to understand road signs, to elicit essential information in particular situations, and to become more familiar with the language spoken by native speakers.

However, even before the widespread adoption of teaching techniques based upon practical communicative skills, one aspect of Irish teaching served to encourage the use of the language: attendance at summer Gaeltacht courses. These three to four week courses, run by Irish language organisations such as Comhaltas Uladh or Gael Linn, have long formed an integral part of learning Irish at secondary school. Pupils lodge with native Irish-speaking families and attend daily classes and cultural activities. Use of the Irish language is encouraged with varying degrees of firmness. A weakness in this system results from the lack of follow-up activities related to Gaeltacht visits.

Facilities for Irish-medium secondary education do not yet exist. The temporary provision of all-Irish secondary education at Shaw's Road, 1978–80, was valuable, in itself, as a pilot project. Since then, however, Bunscoil children have been passing through to local English-medium secondary schools. Later, the effect of this step on the children's use of Irish will be discussed. Certainly, the long standing annual increase in the number of children learning through Irish at pre-secondary levels is creating a growing pressure for the provision of continuity through subsequent levels. A Secondary School Committee, comprising mainly parents, was set up in 1988 in order to co-ordinate the work of establishing Irish-medium facilities at secondary level. An early response to its efforts resulted in the introduction of some limited facilities into a local Boys Grammar School. Bunscoil children transferring to this school are taught three subjects, on the curriculum, through the medium of Irish. However, the Committee is currently involved in finding the most suitable site for a permanent Meánscoil (Irish-medium secondary school) where both boys and girls can experience secondary education through Irish. The target date for opening the school is September 1991, commemorating the twentieth anniversary of the founding of the Shaw's Road Bunscoil. This objective is being approached with the same determination and resolve which secured that earlier achievement.

Irish-medium education has not filtered through to the tertiary level. Irish may be studied as a degree subject at the Queen's University of Belfast, the New University of Ulster, and at the Catholic Teacher Training College in Belfast. A chair for Irish exists at both universities. The degree courses offered at each of these third level institutions vary somewhat from each other, although the emphasis is universally placed upon the modern language. Queen's University offers a degree in Celtic Studies. A Celtic department is also based in St Mary's Training College. The New University of Ulster offers Irish in its Department of Irish Studies. Both Universities provide courses for students without prior familiarity with the language. This facility is particularly relevant in light of the general absence of opportunities to learn Irish in non-Catholic schools.

Outside the confines of formal education, another important dimension to the learning of Irish pumps vitality into the Revival Movement. Hundreds of voluntary evening classes, throughout the Six Counties, cater for adults who wish to learn Irish. In West Belfast, over 60 such classes are run by voluntary organisations. Learners of all ages attend classes, although the majority are within the 17–35 age bracket. These learners want to be able to speak and use the language. The demand for adult classes is also reflected in the development of the range of Irish classes being offered within Further Education.

Most Bunscoil parents attend one of these classes in their attempt to support their children. People attending these classes are inspired by the desire and need to express their own sense of national identity. The existence of an Irish-medium school in the city generated confidence in that identity and their right to active participation. In one study, 74% of this learning population identified the Bunscoil as a contributor to the overall revival of Irish (Ó hAdhmaill, 1985).

The network of voluntary classes intensifies the demand for resources, such as Irish-medium education, within formal structures. Amazingly, this process of mutual advantage survives despite the absence of a central co-ordinating organisation to oversee present fragmented branches of the Language Movement. Indeed, it survives despite the absence of an organised structural framework for voluntary classes. These classes are generally taught by dedicated individuals who have themselves learnt the language in adulthood. In these cases, a lack of professional training does not curb motivation and enthusiasm. Undoubtedly, however, the teachers' efforts would be enhanced by the establishment of a support service from within the formal framework. Again, at community level, several weekend courses have been provided in Belfast for voluntary teachers. More solid gains could be derived from exposure to the resources and expertise available in the Teacher Training College and within Further Education. Courses on the language itself and on teaching methodology would equip voluntary teachers with added confidence and skills. It would also demonstrate a recognition of the valuable service which these people provide.

Evidently, the many contributors to the Language Movement in Northern Ireland often participate in a rather fragmented sense: without the guidance of a centralised co-ordinating body. There is a general feeling of a common goal and a willingness to pull together. Nevertheless, the pooling of resources is limited. For example, as yet contact between the well established Bunscoil at Shaw's Road and the recently founded second all-Irish primary school, situated a couple of miles away, has not been fully developed. However, this would seem to be an obvious area where co-operation would be particularly fruitful. Other areas, penetrated by the language, experience the same restrictions because of the lack of official policies and centralised resources to co-ordinate efforts. Meanwhile, the diligence and dedication of individuals and various cultural and pressure groups remain the cornerstone of the Language Movement's progress.

The emergence of an all-Irish nursery network and two primary schools in Belfast has resulted directly from the initiative taken by the city's most esteemed promoters of the language — the founder members of the Shaw's Road community. This educational facility introduced hundreds of families, from outside the community, to the Irish language. However, for the Shaw's Road children, it represented only one aspect of life as Irish speakers. To satisfy the individual and community needs of their families, Shaw's Road members sought to achieve access to the language in many other areas. We have already seen how they strove to assert the right of their children to lead full lives in their mother tongue. In many of these areas, the Shaw's Road parents secured a foothold for the language. Establishment of Irish in further domains was often tenuous at first, but it did lay a basis for later developments. Today, the position of Irish remains strongest within the framework of learning activities. However, its expansion is evident in other areas also.

Church

Another response to the quickening momentum of the Revival Movement has been the provision of religious services for Irish speakers. One central parish in Belfast celebrates an Irish mass every Sunday and Holy Day. Irish-speaking priests operate a rota system in order to provide the service in addition to the obligations to be fulfilled in their own parishes. The spiritual needs of children being educated through Irish are also met. The Shaw's Road Gaeltacht Community provided the necessary impetus to the build-up of this current position, given the support and co-operation of individual Irish-speaking priests in the city. Indeed, it would have run counter to the most basic aims of the Community to have, simply, availed of existing religious provisions in English. Practising religion through Irish was essential for self-fulfilment on an individual and community basis.

A further development in the growing awareness of the Irish language as a very real, living fact of life, is the extension of Irish language services throughout other parishes in Northern Ireland. One diocese operates a system whereby parishes take turns in celebrating Sunday mass in Irish. Other parishes throughout the North provide regular services through Irish. Still, it cannot be said that the Church works to encourage the use of Irish. Indeed, many Catholics could attend Sunday mass over a lifetime without ever hearing a prayer recited in Irish. That fact reveals the distance which the Revival (and the Church) has yet to travel. Nevertheless, the Language Movement owes much to the dedication and diligence of particular priests who took a lead in the promotion of Irish, and indeed, to those who continue this work. The death of Cardinal Tomas O Fiaich, in May 1990, was most sorely lamented by lovers of the Irish language. During his lifetime, the Cardinal contributed to efforts to promote the Irish language and, since his demise, other cultural events have been held in his honour. Other local priests are well known and appreciated by the city's Irish speakers for their constant support.

The developments made within the religious sphere are generally restricted to the context of the Roman Catholic Church. Although the pioneering Revival Movement of the last century was built upon the work of a group of esteemed Presbyterians, that participation in the fortunes of the language ceased under the strain of divisive forces. The association of the Irish language with the Catholic population meant that it too would be labelled 'suspicious' among other factors marked as threats to the interests and values of the majority. This misconception has never been clarified.

Media

Over the years, Irish language campaigners objected to the inconsistencies and uneven policies towards lesser used languages in the UK, which catered for media output in Scottish Gaelic and Welsh. Until 1981, Irish was not acknowledged on television or radio. It remains excluded from Northern Ireland television, although viewers in some areas can receive Irish language programmes from the Dublin-based station, RTE. Very occasionally, over the years, an Irish language item may have featured on a radio programme. Indeed, one experience, related by a local priest from Downpatrick, tells of a particular BBC radio broadcast during the 1950s. Sunday Mass (celebrated in Latin) was being broadcast from the parish of Tyconnaught. According to custom, then, a closing prayer was recited by priest and congregation in Irish. Two members of the broadcasting team were listening through earphones in the vestry. Upon hearing the 'Hail Mary' being recited in Irish, one of these gentlemen was overheard asking, 'I say, what language is that?' His colleague informed him, 'Why, Latin of course!' This incident might lead some people to ponder the ignorance of Irish which was demonstrated by someone in a position of public responsibility. A more likely response might be to smile at the ignorance of Latin! At any rate, regarding Irish and the BBC, the relationship has progressed some way since then.

Actually, it has only been during the 1980s that the position of Irish on the radio has improved. The local BBC radio station has employed two Irish language producers and output has expanded to include daily and weekly adult programmes as well as a schools' series. Northern Ireland listeners also avail of programmes broadcast from the Twenty-Six Counties and can now receive the Gaeltacht-based station. Irish language material on radio is also provided by a small pirate station. Irish speakers applied for franchise on a new community-based radio station but learned, in June 1989, that they were unsuccessful. However, a one hour slot for a bilingual programme is included in the new station's daily output. The other major radio station, based in Belfast, does not broadcast any Irish language material. It has expressed no response to the call for coverage in Irish, nor to the growth of a bilingual community with particular cultural interests in Irish.

Interestingly, however, the Independent Television Company, UTV, did commission an investigative survey into the potential demand for Irish on television. This question was explored within the context of the public's interest in language programmes generally. (Omnibus Survey, May, 1985.) The Report concluded that the potential audience for educational programmes in the Six Counties was 70,000. These potential viewers were found to be predominantly Roman Catholic from within the 15–34 age bracket. No evidence was found of any class or regional concentration among this population. It may seem surprising, in view of these results, that no plans for producing Irish language programmes of any type on UTV have materialised or are presently being prepared.

Concerning the area of publications, a significant development during the 1980s has been the introduction of a daily Irish newspaper, produced in West Belfast. This paper, *Lá*, has survived various setbacks, and continues to circulate throughout many parts of the country. A literary supplement to the paper was introduced in June 1990. The contribution of *Lá* to the Language Movement is not only due to its informational function. Equally important is the degree of pride and self-esteem which is instilled in Northern Irish speakers by the fact that Ireland's only Irish language daily paper is published in Belfast. Several other newspapers available to the Northern Ireland reading population carry regular feature articles in Irish. Various Irish language periodicals and magazines are also based in the Six Counties. In a broader literary sense, the Six Counties is not without its contributors to the corpus of modern Irish literature, although they are far from abundant.

Despite the progress of Irish within the area of publications (and, indeed, within the overall context of the media), one only has to reflect upon the vast body of English language material, dominating the market, in order to perceive the degree of that progress in its true perspective. The promotion of Irish publications is seriously impeded by the absence of Government support, such as in the establishment of a Books Council. This type of organisation could direct and hasten the expansion of Irish publications by developing and co-ordinating schemes aimed at encouraging young writers and financing publications. One positive step was taken by the Queens' University, Belfast, in 1988, by appointing a writer in residence at the Celtic Department. The possibilities for promoting and facilitating a wider range of publications in Irish are limitless. Of course, these will remain unexplored until the introduction of favourable policies and a genuine willingness to respond to cultural needs.

Easy accessibility of Irish language literature has been introduced to Belfast by the opening of an Irish book shop, 'An Ceathru Poili', in 1984. This book shop represents the only base in the North which specialises in Irish language material. It caters for readers in Belfast and also delivers stock to centres throughout the Six Counties. Like other projects, such as the daily newspaper, the Irish book shop evolved due to the initiative and drive of a few particular individuals who were motivated by a commitment to the language. It has been precisely this type of individual who has taken a lead in other initiatives which originally seemed inaccessible. The founding of an urban Gaeltacht Comunity, an Irish-medium school in Belfast, and an Irish language daily newspaper are examples of these ideals. Indeed, given the traditional official stagnancy with regards any promotion of Irish, the revival of Irish in Northern Ireland has fed and thrived upon the work of individual Irish speakers of this calibre. Whatever disadvantages the Language Movement knows, it has been fortunate in this sense. At critical times, there have been competent individuals, willing to take a chance on a radical project which they believed to be feasible. That fact has played an essential part in the story of the revival of Irish in Northern Ireland.

Government

Generally, it is from the community platform that the Irish language finds its way into more formal domains. This process has been evident regarding education, the media, and religion. At Government level, the 1980s have witnessed some signs of enlightened attitudes running alongside parallel signs of old hostilities. Unfortunately, within the Northern Irish context of divisions, conflicts and prejudices, the Irish language is just one more victim.

This fact is illustrated by the attitudes of local councils towards cultural issues. Where a Nationalist majority exists on the council, legislation may be passed which promotes the Irish language. For example, Fermanagh, Omagh, Newry & Mourne and Derry councils have recognised the basic cultural rights of their rate payers by establishing Cultural Committees and appointing Cultural Officers. Regrettably, however, it is the political make-up of each council which determines whether or not these fundamental rights may be enjoyed. Therefore, Belfast's population of Irish speakers, learners, and supporters are not acknowledged or supported by the Belfast City Council, which is predominantly Unionist. This situation persists despite Belfast's leading role in the diffusion of Irish. In Belfast, one finds a landmark in the emergence of urban Irish. In quantitative terms, Belfast's community of Irish speakers is much stronger than in any other city in the Six Counties. Yet, the majority of representatives on its City Council cannot be persuaded to introduce any amenities which would enrich the cultural experience of the city's population of Irish speakers.

Attempts made to secure practical support from Government include applications made by Glór na nGael — an Irish language organisation with locally based branches throughout Ireland — for the consideration of the Commission for the Belfast Urban Area Plan Review, in 1987. Therein, Irish speakers outlined their proposals to be taken into consideration by planners and policy makers, during the preparation of plans for the city's physical development over the next decade. These proposals were not incorporated into the definitive version of the Plan. Indeed, a vigorous campaign is currently underway in a response to the withdrawal of Government funding from Glór na nGael in the autumn of 1990. Much of the work done by this organisation is related to the Irish-medium nursery provision.

Neglect of the Irish language over the years has been identified as one of the factors constituting cultural deprivation and causing feelings of resentment and alienation in the Catholic community. A sharpened awareness of the full implications of this fact has encouraged a greater Government tendency to release funding for Irish language initiatives. In order to provide a channel for Government funds, an independent charitable organisation called the 'Ulster Trust' was set up in the autumn of 1989. The Trust is responsible for distributing grants for language projects totalling £50,000 per annum.

Language Organisations and Activities

Glór na nGael has also provided motivation for community projects aimed at promoting the language. Indeed, various communities in Northern Ireland have featured among the winners of its top awards. These awards pay tribute to the efforts made by particular communities on behalf of the Irish language.

Traditionally, competitions form an exciting part of Irish culture, dating back to pre-historic times in Ireland. That tradition has always been especially strong in the field of sport. Today, national sports continue to thrive as a fundamental component of the country's cultural fibre. Football, handball and the two stick games — hurling and camogie are among the major games. National sports draw support from the entire country and are not perceived within a Six County context. The Gaelic Athletic Association, which promotes national sports among Ireland's youth, is the largest sporting organisation in the country. This organisation is formally committed to the propagation of the Irish language and Irish culture generally. Many local branches appoint Language Officers. The Derry County Board also runs a cultural centre where Irish language courses and festivals are held.

Competitions among schools are also used to generate interest in the language by other organisations such as Comhaltas Uladh and Gael Linn. The major annual schools' competition in the North is aimed at encouraging oral proficiency. Apart from awards presented to winning schools, some children from each participating school also receive scholarships to summer Gaeltacht courses.

The Belfast Feis shares similar aims. These do not emphasise the cultivation of competitive skills, but rather, seek to create an environment wherein children derive enjoyment and satisfaction from their participation in learning activities. This event is currently being built up after some lapsed years. As yet, the programme is still quite limited, focusing on poetry recitals and some language and history work. However, it is hoped that competition classes will be extended to reintroduce further aspects of language skills and a broader general spectrum of events. The Belfast Feis is particularly valuable as a stimulant to the teaching and learning of Irish in local primary schools.

Events such as the Belfast Feis have a further significance in view of one major void in the cultural amenities available to Irish speakers. That area of neglect concerns the lack of facilities for young people outside school hours. Leisure activities for teenagers are largely restricted to the English-speaking environment. These may be found at local sports centres, youth clubs, discos, cinemas etc. The stability of Irish as a spoken medium is seriously threatened by the intense exposure of young people to English language dominated activities without any approximation towards a balanced range of social possibilities.

Young children, educated through Irish, enjoy activities, friendships, etc. associated with the school, and therefore with the Irish language. Adults can usually participate in social activities associated with the language class which they are attending. Many classes are situated in clubs where entertainment may form an added dimension to the class, such as quizzes through Irish or social evenings. Parents of children being educated through Irish are encouraged to attend fundraising social events on behalf of the nursery or primary school. A social dimension to Irish could also be enjoyed by participating in some other adult clubs or societies, for example, amateur drama work. However, teenaged Irish speakers are restricted socially. Some participate in the city's Irish language youth choir. Some may use the language at certain traditional music or dance classes. Naturally, however, young people require a more extensive, varied programme of activities. At present this must be sought outside the Irish-speaking circle. In general, these young people find that an English-speaking environment rapidly intensifies its dominance over aspects of their lives both within and outside the education domain. A real need exists for the provision of cultural centres which would offer young Irish speakers and learners social opportunities, resources and amenities comparable to those available to the general public.

Urban Irish is very much the language of the learner. Learning activities are focused around classes. Ways of providing Irish-medium education at secondary level and of establishing leisure-type amenities for teenagers have not yet been perceived as priority issues. As more children pass through the primary system, pressure may mount for these questions to receive serious, concentrated attention. In the meantime, the greatest progress continues to be made in the area of pre-school and primary Irish-medium education and in the area of adult learning activities.

Another phenomenon which reflects that awareness of national distinctiveness is the increased popularity of native Irish names for children. This trend is also very clearly evident at the Irish-medium nursery schools, at the Shaw's Road Bunscoil and, indeed, at the more recently opened second Bunscoil. The vast majority of children enrolled have been christened with native Irish names. This growth in popularity has soared over the past ten years, or so. Before this, Catholic parents were influenced by saints' names, or by fashionable names encountered in the media. Today, native names are in popular currency.

Children at the Bunscoil are taught to use the original Irish version of their surnames. More generally, however, the Gaelic versions of surnames have not received the same widespread support as the use of Christian names. Some Irish speakers have officially changed their names. It is more common, however, for Irish speakers to retain the English language version and to use the Irish version in particular situations or settings. Founder members of the Shaw's Road Gaeltacht community and school described their decision, as young learners of Irish, to take the legal steps necessary to change their names into Irish. Some of these people were then employed in work-places which were predominantly non-Catholic. Subsequently, they felt nervous and vulnerable about this change. Such a confirmation of identity could have attracted antagonism in a mixed working environment. Yet, the decision was adhered to as a necessary step towards self-fulfilment and, for these people, it marked a significant point in their efforts to assert their sense of national identity.

Personal names are important expressions of that personal and national identity. The original Irish version of surnames usually gives insights into family origin or physical characteristics or the traditional family profession, e.g. Mac an Bhaird (= son of the poet), Ó Branduibh (= descendant of the black raven, i.e. dark person). The Gaelic version of surnames appears strange to persons totally unfamiliar with the Irish language. Usually, the English version is simply an anglicisation of the spoken form and therefore approximates the Gaelic version.

However, the two written forms differ considerably. Many people are unprepared to take the chance of using the Irish form on official documents, not trusting that it will be treated seriously and with respect. The same difficulty arises all over the world where people from one culture are subsumed into a more powerful and economically dominant culture. This is particularly evident in the case of immigrants. Consider the emergence of names such as 'Flarity' in the United States. The original Irish version of 'Ó Flaithbheartaigh' would have posed extra problems for any newcomer trying to enter into and adjust to another culture which, for Irish speakers, included a different linguistic system.

The same phenomenon arose in Ireland when it became apparent that the language of social mobility and economic survival was English. The resulting conflict of interests was a painful experience for many children. We have already referred to the infamous tally stick used by parents and school masters to curb the use of Irish. Writers at the beginning of the twentieth century relate poignant accounts of similar experiences, aimed at establishing a sense of identity with those values associated with Irish. *Caislean Oir*, by the Donegal writer, Seamas Ó Grianna, opens with such an episode. The young protagonist's first day at school begins with confusion and tears when the master punishes him for not responding to roll call. Later his mother explains to him that he had not recognised the name used because 'James Gallagher' was, in fact, the English version of his own name and one to which he must now become accustomed.

> 'Agus, a mháthair', arsa an gasúr, 'nár shíl mise riamh gur Seimí Phádraig Duibh a bhí orm. Nach é sin an t-ainm a tugadh i gcónaí orm?'
> 'Is é, a thaisce', arsa an mhathair, 'ach seo d'ainm i mBéarla. Agus Béarla a bhíos i gcónaí i dteach na scoile … Agus, a leanbh, an bhfuil tú 'gheall ar a bheith gan bhéal gan teanga agus gan ábalta do leitir féin a léamh nó a scríobh nuair a rachas tú i measc na gcoimhthíoch?' (Ó Grianna, 1976: 9)

> 'And mother', said the boy, 'didn't I always believe that my name was Seimi Phadraig Duibh. Isn't that the name I was always called?'
> 'Yes, love', replied his mother, 'but this is your name in English (i.e. the form used by the master). And English is the language used at school … and son, would you leave yourself unable to communicate and to read and write your own letters when you move out among strangers?'

One of the factors inhibiting a rise in the use of Gaelic surnames, which parallels the increased popularity of Gaelic Christian names in recent years, is the absence of the Irish language from official documentation. The personal name is used so often on official literature that, indeed, it does not occur to many people that they could legally use the Gaelic version of their own name.

Others fear confusion or discrimination of some sort. Some Students' Unions at third level institutions have recently addressed this problem by introducing bilingual documentation.

One area where striking progress has been made, at community level, concerns the erection of Irish language street name signs. This work of translating and displaying Gaelic street names has been supported by various language organisations, such as Glór na nGael. In Belfast, the west of the city has taken a lead in the project by erecting bilingual street signs throughout most of its neighbourhoods. Elsewhere in the Six Counties, other local communities have also financed this work and erected the Gaelic version of street names. It has long been felt by Irish speakers that the use of Irish language street names has always been discouraged by the General Post Office. Indeed, reference has already been made to that clause, added to a Government Bill, in 1949, which prohibited the use of street names, 'in a language which is not our own'.

The campaign for bilingual signs offers real educational advantages. Street signs erected by the city councils may exhibit a name such as 'Owenvarragh Park', which is devoid of any semantic value in the English language. However, the Gaelic name, from which it derives and which is pronounced almost identically, is 'Páirc Abhainn Bhearrach'. This signifies the park where a pointed river flows. Indeed that river has since been enclosed in a tunnel and is no longer visible. So, the Gaelic version of the name often allows an understanding of the environment which cannot be derived from the anglicised form. Other names contain anglicised forms of 'dún' (fort), 'cluain' (meadow), 'Tulach' (mound) 'cill' (church) etc.

The cultural and educational value of becoming familiar with the Gaelic forms of place names has been clearly attested in the 1974 *Teachers' Guide*, referred to in the previous chapter. Furthermore, in 1988, the Northern Ireland Department of the Environment commissioned a five-year project aimed at producing a comprehensive ordnance survey map of the Six Counties, in Irish. Yet, despite this example of progress, the appearance of Gaelic street names in certain areas has only been realised because of the cultural awareness of the communities concerned who were prepared to accept the responsibility for organising and financing the project.

The value of the project sponsored by the Department of the Environment, could extend beyond the obvious informational service which it provides to the Northern Irish public. It may also make some contribution towards the education of the entire population about the all-round relevance of the Irish language. The relevance of Gaelic place names and street names is not restricted to one part of any area. The Irish language pre-dates the divisions and conflicts which exist today. Therefore, citizens in both Nationalist and Loyalist areas could benefit from a knowledge of the Gaelic origin from which their street or townland derives its name. Ironically, it is because the Irish language is often identified with the Nationalist section of the population that its use and propagation has been officially discouraged. In one queer sense, it is the people who have inherited that distorted vision of cultural values who lose most.

Sometimes the conflict reaches ludicrous levels. Yet, the underlying issue of community and national identity remains a serious and sensitive one. One glaring example of this absurdity resulted from the decision of one city council to formally change its name from 'Londonderry' Council to 'Derry' Council. (The Gaelic name for this city is 'Doire Cholm Cille', or 'Doire' as an abbreviation.) A political row erupted. The decision also aggravated the dilemma of the media. Should the county and city be referred to as 'Derry' or 'Londonderry'? Public speakers' political affiliations could certainly be recognised from their choice. Amongst ordinary people on the street the distinction is less clear cut. 'Derry' might represent the speaker's preference for severance from London, or it could simply represent a common abbreviation. However, usage in formal situations usually depends much upon political views. Representatives on the media sometimes endeavour to project an objective outlook by alternating the two forms during a report. This style can attract the derision of listeners because of the heightened awareness of the Northern Ireland population to the issue. One local radio DJ amusedly adopted the term 'Stroke City', derived from his earlier tongue-in-cheek version of Derry/Londonderry city.

On a more serious note, the fear of discrimination experienced by some people, regarding the use of Gaelic names in official domains, is sometimes unjustified. However, the fact that it is possible is often all that is required to discourage the use of the language. In many situations discrimination could also be alleviated by the cultivation of a more educated and enlightened view of the language. Partly because of the limited support given to the Irish language and culture on the school curriculum, ignorance of the all-embracing values of this heritage is not restricted to the uneducated sections of society. Indeed, this unfortunate fact was highlighted at a recent meeting of academics and business consultants which discussed proposals for the economic development of West Belfast. One leading consultant questioned the credibility of proposals made by a community group entitled 'Obair'. The comment made implied that this organisation, which endeavours to promote employment opportunities in West Belfast, must be considered sectarian because of its Gaelic name. Other educated representatives agreed with this deduction. 'Obair' is the Irish word for 'Work'. This type of bias is founded on an uninformed and misconstrued vision of reality, all the more tragic when it operates among the educated classes, trusted with public responsibilities.

Government has a duty to promote a code of values which transcends such a narrow and distorted view of Irish culture. This could be achieved by developing a policy for the protection and propagation of the Irish language. In the package of educational reforms referred to at the beginning of this chapter, the Minister for Education acknowledges the potential role of Irish within the context of community integration. The existing problem of ignorance and intolerance requires a much more committed and dynamic approach to developing the position of Irish in the curriculum. Educationalists, concerned with Irish, remain unconvinced that any genuine, earnest intention exists to cultivate respect for Irish as a living, spoken language which has a deep reservoir of cultural relevance for every Irish person.

The progress yet to be made is, clearly, vast. Irish speakers were both disillusioned and roused by the latest educational reforms, before these were amended. Nevertheless, the overall feeling is one of optimism. The language is solidly established in the area of Irish-medium education. A platform exists from which to work towards extensions into further educational levels and increased Government support at existing levels. The language is used by one community in Belfast across a spectrum of domains. Other communities have erected Gaelic street names, introduced language classes, arranged cultural activities, etc. Furthermore, thousands of people throughout the Six Counties have expressed a desire for further access to the language in the media and in schools. This substantial public desire for exposure to Irish has, for the first time, been officially recorded.

The main thrust of activity is still occurring at community level. Pressure generated by the momentum of this activity has led to some positive responses by the authorities. The ultimate aim is to reach a situation whereby those in official domains not only react to public pressure, but accept a responsibility for nurturing favourable, informed attitudes towards the Irish language. The present day position of the language is en route towards that difficult goal. A consciousness is currently emerging that the advent of this objective cannot be patiently awaited. Rather, disparate initiatives should be co-ordinated in order to assert a more integrated and effective impact upon the diffusion of Irish. At present, any account of the Irish language's position in the North reveals a scattered range of developments. The industry and dedication of various groups and individuals have propelled the language forth into the public eye and ear. The current situation is now ripe for the establishment of a major centralised body with responsibility for drawing together the many strands in the movement which work towards individual aims. Such merging of resources within the framework of an overall strategy for development is now vital.

5 An Urban Gaeltacht: Formation and Development

In 1969 the first family of Belfast's own Gaeltacht Community took up residence on Shaw's Road, in one of the small cluster of houses which they and their fellow members had just built. There was no celebration of popping champagne bottles and snipping coloured ribbons, no speeches nor official photographs. That sort of ceremony would come in later years when subsequent projects — inspired by this community's achievements — would be launched. In those early days the efforts of Irish speakers received little public attention. Therefore, with a low public profile, founder members channelled their energy and drive into immediate concrete challenges such as procuring a site for the project, finding financial backing and building houses. Each obstacle was met head on. Anyone stepping back to view the overall implications of this undertaking would have been overawed, if not petrified. It is not surprising that most of the nineteen families originally interested in the scheme withdrew from it at an early stage. Five families were left to fulfil the dream.

It is ironic that, as well as being seemingly impossible, the founding of a Gaeltacht Community in Belfast was also inevitable. For years the city had known isolated individuals or couples who raised their children through Irish. However, an Irish-speaking family living in an English-speaking area could enjoy a very limited degree of social interaction with other Irish-speaking families. Young adults learning the language could participate in the fairly varied social life which was associated with the Irish language, attending ceilithe (dances), classes, competitions, or one of the language clubs. However a bilingual child whose neighbours, playmates, school friends and relations are non-Irish speakers is in a difficult situation. There was only one solution to this problem — the creation of a supportive and cohesive Irish-speaking environment. A newspaper article, as early as 1965, reported the intention of this group of Irish speakers to establish their own neighbourhood and school, and estimated that approximately 36 Irish-speaking families were then living in Belfast. These families were scattered throughout the city. Some of the couples — and those of previous generations — had connections with the Donegal Gaeltacht. Most, however, had learnt Irish in adulthood and chose to give the language to their own children. If this was possible for isolated families who lacked the advantages of belonging to a corporate social unit, would it not be so much easier to achieve within the context of an Irish-speaking community?

Previous Generation of Irish-Speaking Families

The earlier generations of isolated Irish-speaking families contributed to the language movement by showing that Irish was viable as the language of the home in an urban setting. Naturally, that isolation within English-speaking neighbourhoods restricted the language behaviour of the families. Experiences recalled by some of these families provide insights into the pressures exerted by the dominant language in a society which was as yet unaccustomed to bilingualism. Additionally, in many of the families only one of the parents was an Irish speaker. It is not surprising, therefore, that in some cases it was only the eldest child who was reared bilingually. By the time subsequent children arrived, the efforts to make Irish the principal language of the home had been abandoned. In other families, some of the children later rejected Irish while others kept it as the language of their own homes or even became actively involved in its promotion. In such families, it was usually the eldest children who were numbered among the latter.

A look at one or two of these earlier families confirms the value of raising children bilingually (Saunders, 1982). However, what is most relevant is that the founder members of the Shaw's Road Community were well aware of the difficulties which these isolated Irish-speaking families had faced. They hoped to avoid these difficulties within a closely knit social framework of families with similar cultural commitments. In one of these earlier families, the eldest, whom we'll call Peadar, continues to make a significant contribution to the promulgation of the language in Belfast. He has inspired many with his own love of the language. One of his brothers also uses Irish through his work and likewise encourages its promotion. A third brother teaches Irish in a secondary school. The latter, however, made the decision not to rear his own family with Irish. He perceives that he thereby avoids the risk of forcing the language upon his children and possibly provoking their resentment towards it. He prefers to allow his children to make their own decision about acquiring Irish when they are older.

Peadar described a temporary phase of rejection of Irish which he himself experienced in his own childhood. This occurred when he was nine years old and was directly related to the clearly defined association of Irish with home life and English with school life. Peadar recalled the custom of describing the events of his day to his mother on returning home from school. Having encountered these experiences through the medium of English he developed a preference for relating his account in English also. However, this intrusion of English into the only domain where Irish was sacred was resisted strongly by his parents. A dispute resulted between parents and child which led to the child's refusal to speak any Irish at all. This situation was later aggravated by other school experiences. Peadar described the embarrassment to which he was subjected on entering secondary school. A well-meaning teacher endeavoured to inspire other pupils to further diligence by escorting the young wonder around all the senior classes in the school and showing off his mastery of the language. Needless to say, this episode does not feature among Peadar's fondest memories.

A similar experience was related by one of the children of another family raised with Irish in an English-speaking neighbourhood. This person, whom we'll call Seamus, had also been 'shown off' as a young Irish-speaking phenomenon at school. The eldest of this family is now raising children with Irish. Since commencement at a local English-medium primary school the children have been using English at home, even in their responses to their parent's Irish. This arrangement is working without disharmony. On the other hand, Irish has been rejected by Seamus and one of his brothers. The latter chose not to raise his children with Irish. He too associated his upbringing through Irish with being compelled to be different. He recalled a clear impression of being perceived as 'odd' by playmates and neighbours. In adulthood this person has come to terms with the negative attitudes which he had previously experienced. He has now developed a favourable attitude towards the preservation and progress of the language although he does not actively contribute to that aim. A degree of guilt results from this position. For him, therefore, the Irish language has connotations of conflicts and complexes.

Many factors influence the way a child perceives his own bilingualism. His own personality determines largely how he will handle the concept of being 'different'. For many children this could be enjoyable and indeed provide a rare opportunity for mischief! A more timid child may encounter difficulties. The status of the minority language will also play a significant part. Today, the Irish language has gained considerable strength in West Belfast and it is no longer very unusual to hear a child chatting in Irish. At best it would now evoke a quiet comment or a smile rather than the type of spectacle in which Peadar and Seamus were involved. Over recent decades the language has also increased in popularity and this influences how the Irish-speaking youth is perceived by peers. A further factor which merits consideration is the parents' manner of handling difficulties. If a child feels the language situation to be unnatural how do the parents strike a balance between flexibility and firmness?

The experiences of these isolated Irish-speaking families will strike a familiar note in any place where a minority language struggles for survival. Similar dilemmas and conflicts encountered by Norwegian-speaking families in the United States were recorded by Einar Haugen (1969).

> Wherever contact with English-speaking children was active, as in an urban community, the children brought with them home an active desire to speak English. Only by the establishment of iron-clad rules by which English was banned from the home could the parents resist this invasion. This counter pressure by the parents had to be stronger than the social pressure of the environment toward English. If the social pattern in the community was favourable to English, the parents were placed in a very difficult position. It now became a question of parental authority, with the children often sullen and rebellious, and the parents torn between a determination to impose their own linguistic pattern and a desire to see their children content ... Eventually the parents might also succumb to the pressure exerted by this uncomfortable situation and go over to English themselves.

The social pressures exerted by the dominant language could only be held at bay within a strong supportive and cohesive social framework. This crucial role of the community was also identified by Haugen:

> By living in a Norwegian-speaking community they multiplied their chance of being able to carry it out (i.e. protecting the position of Norwegian in the home), since their children were not under any strong social pressure to use English ... Most families cannot afford to carry on a bilingual tradition unless they are supported by the presence of other such families within the same neighbourhood. (Haugen, 1969: 234–6)

In the 1960s, Irish-speaking families in Belfast found themselves in precisely this position. The social pressures to use English were, and still are, intense. English is a necessary functional medium in Northern Ireland; Irish, on the other hand, lacked that functional status. This serious disadvantage could only be alleviated by creating a social situation wherein the Irish language assumed a genuine functional value. In the absence of an official body of language planners to make proposals and plans along these lines this obvious solution had long remained unexplored. When the proposal did finally evolve, it was not generated by a Government representative, an educationalist, an urban planner or architect. Rather, the idea for an urban Gaeltacht Community emerged from the midst of a group of young couples who were in the process of learning the language and extending its functional status in their lives. These young people were attending Gaelic League classes at Cumann Chluain Ard and participating in social events associated with other language clubs. Several of the couples were recently married or engaged. The build-up of personal relationships through Irish rendered the projection of the language into their future homes a most natural desire. They were aware of the gravity of such an undertaking within an English-speaking neighbourhood but they wanted to raise children who could enjoy a natural, happy childhood as Irish-speakers without having to resort to English every time they went out to play or to attend school.

This was not perceived as a lofty ideal or a grand goal in life. Nor was it discussed in simple terms of a demand which they would make to the Northern Ireland Government. Instead, it was accepted that this was a basic human right which would never be granted and must be realised by themselves. They could make it happen. Arguments about legality and the response of officialdom to the establishment of a Gaeltacht Community and school would inevitably arise. Founder members felt that action must take precedence over any debate with the Government in order to avoid lengthy delays and weakened resolve. This decision was quite crucial considering the fact that the Irish-medium primary school which the Community founded was not granted official maintained status for the first thirteen years of its existence.

The achievement of this small group of people should encourage others throughout the world who believe that their language could coalesce their common culture around a deeply felt and unique identity. The founder members of the Shaw's Road Community were mainly working class people with minimal financial resources. When they commenced their enterprise there was no example to follow nor were there any signposts to warn of the hazards ahead. A major advantage to this shaky starting position was the fact that, in the material sense, these people had little to lose. More affluent language enthusiasts would be reluctant to commit themselves to such a chancy venture. More academic Irish speakers would be similarly unexcited by the prospect of participating in such an unorthodox project. The qualities which these founder members possessed included their youth, energy, dedication and resilience. When other couples, originally interested in the scheme, had withdrawn, the core remained united in its resolve. This core included one or two key members who possessed personal qualities of an unusual calibre. The philosophy of 'action' which the group implemented would also play a significant part in the project's success. It was accepted that demands for social and educational facilities for Irish-speaking children would only receive serious attention once a group of families had united in a solid, closely knit community. Demands made by individual Irish speakers living in various parts of the city could never be productive. This premise was explained in a letter which the founder members addressed to other potential participants in the proposed project:

> Gan pobal den tsort seo ní féidir linn ár gceart mar shaoranaigh a
> dh'éileamh; nó ní thig le Bardas Conndae, nó Rialtas, riar do dhream atá

scaipthe fríd daoine eile nach mbíonn an t-éileamh céadna aca. Chreid muid má bhí an Ghaeltacht cheart le leathnú amach go gcaithfeadh Gaeilgeoirí na galltachta iad fein a neartú mar ionad go ndéanfaimis an réamh-obair leis an leathnú amach a chur i gcrích.

(Without a community of this kind we cannot assert our rights as citizens; nor can the County Council nor Government respond to the demands of an unco-ordinated group of people. We believe that the rural Gaeltacht can only expand if Irish speakers in Galltacht areas form concentrated units and thereby prepare for that expansion.)

By the mid-1960s the work of realising this goal was under way. The newspaper article referred to above outlined the aspirations of the families involved:

Irish-speaking families in Belfast have banded together to launch a unique building programme which will offer children an education exclusively in the Irish language. The scheme running into hundreds of thousands of pounds envisages a primary school and twenty private houses on a two and a half acre site at Shaw's Road. The building of the houses, each costing about £2500, will start next summer. Families who occupy them must speak Irish only.

The report carried an announcement by a representative of 'Teaghlaigh', the Irish-speaking families' organisation, which explained how the idea for the Community came about

... At the moment there are thirty six Irish-speaking families in Belfast but the school would be open to anyone who wants to send the children along. We estimate that something like two hundred children will be enrolled.

We understand nothing of this kind of education has been offered before, not even by Jewish or other communities living in Belfast.

The idea for the school and houses originated four years ago. At that time there were only seven Irish-speaking families in the city, and most of us had just got married. We came to the conclusion that one of the difficulties of bringing up a family through Irish was that we lived in different parts of the city. The idea of living together in one community emerged. (*Sunday Press* 14th November 1965.)

A striking feature of this statement is the note of determination which pervades it. This determination reveals the extent to which disadvantages and doubts were outweighed by commitment and perseverance. The question marks which hung over the project were very real and the potential pitfalls were also serious. Examples of the facts which demanded attention are as follows:

(a) As newly-weds or engaged couples these young people had few financial resources.
(b) The group had no experience of land purchase, urban planning or large scale fund-raising programmes. As their project was a pioneering one they could not seek advice from an experienced community.
(c) The couples involved in the project had built up sound social relationships with each other. Some were related to each other. However, this might not guarantee a harmonious and successful network of relationships as next-door neighbours.
(d) No educational facilities existed in Northern Ireland for children whose home language was Irish. Therefore there were no official resources of expertise to be tapped. Community members also lacked such specialised expertise.
(e) The pressures to speak English had traditionally been greatest in urban centres. Attempts to withstand these would be extremely taxing.
(f) These couples had only recently acquired Irish themselves. The task of raising children with Irish as their mother tongue would also place linguistic demands upon them.
(g) Participants in the project were engaged in regular employment. They attended language classes in the evenings. Some were now giving classes themselves. Time available for preparing a site and building houses was limited accordingly.

The cumulative presentation of possible obstacles is awesome. However, the five couples who remained as the nucleus of the project chose to handle each difficulty as it arose. 'Potential' problems were not dwelt upon. Despite long-term aspirations the scheme was tackled on a day to day basis. Having admitted that, logically speaking, a particular task was impossible, the group got on with the business of finding a means of carrying it out. Any other approach to this mammoth undertaking would have resulted in its early abandonment. Step by step, construction got under way.

The nucleus of the Community established a company which it named 'de Brún and Mac Seain Ltd'. This step was taken in order to meet legal requirements and to secure credit from Building Societies. The two and a half acre site at Shaw's Road was bought from the Christian Brothers. Comhaltas Uladh, the Ulster council of the Gaelic League, granted the Company a loan of £2,500 to facilitate this purchase.

The couples were given professional assistance gratis by a local architect and lawyer, who were also Irish speakers. The company applied to the City Council for grant aid to help with the building of new houses. It also sought credit for building materials. Basic utilities had to be provided for the

development as a whole — sewerage, drainage, electricity, water supply and
roadworks were all undertaken. Local tradesmen were employed for some of the
construction work. However, Community members themselves carried out as
much as possible of this manual work, dividing the labour between them. The
first house was completed in 1969. Before final commitment to the scheme, each
member made a promise to the Company that he would not sell his property to
a non-Irish-speaking family if a prospective Irish-speaking purchaser existed.

The experience gathered by the Community during the processes of
establishing a company, securing financial backing, purchasing land, preparing a
site and building houses, would thereafter be used to the benefit of West Belfast
generally. We have already seen how construction work at Shaw's Road was
brought to a halt while the company availed of its resources to assist with rescue
operations at Bombay Street. Later, the Company also contributed to other community enterprises throughout West Belfast. These community projects which
were set up included a credit union, an Irish bookshop, an industrial estate, a
knitting factory, an investment company and a petrol station. Some of the
schemes were Irish-language projects. Some were unconnected with the language, but simply aimed to generate employment in deprived areas. Some of the
community members were asked to take over and manage a community newspaper. This local paper, the *Andersonstown News* has now built up an extensive
circulation.

By 1970 three more houses were occupied in the Gaeltacht Community.
Another three families joined the Community between 1974 and 1976. Later, the
number of families rose to eleven. Although ground remained for further development, the Gaeltacht Community did not swell beyond these eleven families.
Many reasons explain this limit. Families who are already settled into a home
and neighbourhood must consider many factors before contemplating moving
house. First home buyers must also consider factors such as proximity to the
place of employment and the advantages and disadvantages of building a house
as opposed to renting or purchasing one, etc. Participation in a Community like
that at Shaw's Road requires a high degree of commitment which cannot be
expected from everyone. However, the lack of a continued growth of Shaw's
Road families nor any emergence of other urban Gaeltacht communities is not a
subject for concern. In many ways this Community has served its original purpose. It started the ball rolling. It had projected the language into domains which
had long been exclusively English-speaking in Belfast, even to Irish speakers.
The success of this Community had inspired the entire language movement in
Northern Ireland. Subsequent endeavours need not follow an identical route. The
generation of further urban Gaeltacht communities had never been the intention.
What was now certain was that the Irish language question must henceforth be
handled in terms of a relevant, modern living language.

The most significant single act by the Shaw's Road Community which influenced the direction of Irish revival today was its introduction of Irish-medium education. The Irish-medium primary school (An Bhunscoil), which the Community founded in 1971, would soon assume a prominent position as an issue in the language campaign in Northern Ireland. Until this time Irish had been taught only as a school subject in the Six Counties. In many schools it was treated in the same manner as Latin or Greek, rather than as a living means of communication. Some of the original members of the Shaw's Road Community recalled how they themselves abandoned the study of Irish at school because of this non-stimulating approach. An account of the future positions of minority languages, published in 1979, referred to this aspect of the language situation in Northern Ireland.

> Few children (except those in the Gaeltacht) hear the language spoken in everyday life, and the language has been taught almost as a dead language ... Similar problems have beset the teaching of Irish in Northern Ireland schools. Here the study of the subject has certainly been a claim to characteristic identity by the minority Roman Catholic group ... But again Irish has been taught — sometimes with inadequate textbooks and methods — as another subject on the timetable, studied for reasons of cultural heritage, possibly, but from the point of view of the learners, not useful for everyday communication ... So that although the language has served as a symbol of minority group membership, its use has not become characteristic of the group. (Alcock *et al.*, 1979: 58)

This attitude towards Irish partly explains why some of the children of Belfast's earlier Irish-speaking generation were paraded around their secondary schools as young wonders. As a spoken everyday medium outside rural Gaeltacht, Irish was not really taken seriously. The Shaw's Road Community was instrumental in changing that view.

An Irish-medium nursery playgroup had been operating in the city since the mid-1960s. Some families who chose not to participate in the Community project were involved in the introduction of this nursery class. Originally, the class was held once a week in one of the family homes. Although a qualified teacher took the class in her spare time, a lack of resources inhibited the success of this attempt. In 1966 another nursery level project was introduced — 'Naíscoil Phobal Feirste' opened in Cumann Chluain Ard. As funds did not exist for the appointment of full-time staff the group was taken by one teacher on Saturdays and during school holidays. One of the Shaw's Road mothers supervised activities on weekdays. At this time nursery education in Northern Ireland was not widespread. Advice was sought from other groups such as the 'Save The Children' organisation in Belfast and Irish-medium nursery bases in Dublin.

The main difficulties which the Naiscoil teachers encountered were language-related ones. People who had learnt Irish as young adults had little need for a vocabulary which incorporated words like 'sloshing', 'slurping', 'gurgling', etc. The solution found was to compile a suitable dictionary and decorate the classroom walls with colourful displays of words — less for the children's sake than on the teachers' behalf, at the outset.

Children at this nursery went on to attend local primary schools. However, parents of Shaw's Road children were determined to provide Irish-medium primary education for their own children. Two of the eldest children in the Community had already reached school-going age and were enrolled at a local English-medium school. Other parents had themselves accepted the responsibility of initiating their children's primary education. Decisive action was necessary to provide for the rest of the Community children. Decisive action had become a speciality!

The story of the Bunscoil has humble beginnings. Founder members relate — with a barely detectable note of mischief — how they bought a mobile hut for £100 on a Friday afternoon, assembled it at Shaw's Road over the weekend, and opened the city's first Irish-medium primary school on Monday morning! For some time before this, members had been searching for a suitable teacher for the school. It was felt that, because of the pioneering character of the school, an experienced teacher was required. Opinions differed about whether or not the teacher should be a native speaker from the Donegal Gaeltacht. Some members felt that this would give the children an advantage in acquiring the language. Others believed that a local Irish speaker should be given employment. Finally a native Irish speaker from Cill Charthaí in Donegal was appointed. (This person resigned two years later because of social unrest in Belfast and was replaced by a local teacher who had been raised with Irish.)

When the school opened, in September 1971, it had nine pupils. Seven of these children lived in the Gaeltacht Community; the other two children were from Irish-speaking families living in the outer community of West Belfast. Numbers swelled somewhat as the eleven households in the Community expanded. Clearly, the school would eventually close if it excluded pupils from English-speaking backgrounds. Therefore, in 1978, the affiliated nursery class opened its doors to children from non-Irish-speaking homes in order to give these children the grounding needed for progression into the primary sector. The nursery school became an important feeder for the Bunscoil. It enabled parents with little command of Irish themselves to ensure that their children acquired the language in a happy and natural environment. This step also provided Irish speakers living in other areas in the city with facilities which earlier generations of Irish-speaking families in Belfast had not known.

AN URBAN GAELTACHT   77

Following this expansion of the catchment population to incorporate
English-speaking families, enrolment at the Bunscoil began to accelerate rapidly.
In the 1984–85 school year 162 children were attending the school. Class years
were divided as follows:

Primary Seven (ten- to eleven-year-olds)	6 pupils
Primary Six	5 pupils
Primary Five	6 pupils
Primary Four	20 pupils
Primary Three	28 pupils
Primary Two	37 pupils
Primary One (four- to five-year-olds)	60 pupils

The swell of numbers in the lower years indicates the growing interest of people
outside the nucleus of the Gaeltacht Community in Irish-medium education.

For the past few years, between 70 and 80 children have been enrolling
annually at the Bunscoil. With nine nursery schools acting as feeders in
1988–89, the breakdown of class years was as follows:

Primary Seven	25 pupils
Primary Six	38 pupils
Primary Five	48 pupils
Primary Four	48 pupils
Primary Three	51 pupils
Primary Two	70 pupils
Primary One	57 pupils

Sixty-three children were enrolled to transfer into the Bunscoil from nursery
class in September, 1989. This increased school population has raised questions
about the upper limit in terms of controlling the standard and use of Irish.
Therefore, the establishment of a second Bunscoil in the city in 1987–88
responds to an ever-pressing need.

Naturally, the physical layout of the school has also changed quite dramatically. The first classroom, which the Community purchased, had been used
originally as a shelter for families burnt out of their homes. When new modern
classrooms were later added and educational resources acquired that first mobile
hut was dismantled and removed to a site in the Lower Falls area of West Belfast
in order to act as a starting point for the second Bunscoil.

This second Irish-medium primary school was also established as a community initiative. As yet it is not supported by the Department of Education. The
Shaw's Road school was financed by voluntary fund-raising programmes for
over a decade — the principal area of expenditure being the teachers' salaries.

Growing numbers of pupils resulted in increased costs; extra teachers had to be employed as well as extensions and annexes made to the school building. When the main thrust of expansion began in 1980 a Management Committee was formed to organise and co-ordinate fund-raising activities. Financial demands continued to soar and in 1983 the annual costs were estimated at £75,000. The chairman of the fund-raising committee was also responsible for maintaining correspondence with the Education Authorities about the school's application for official recognition and support.

The efforts to secure official recognition for the Bunscoil were initiated during the early stages of the project. As early as 1965 a delegation from the Irish-speaking families met with the Permanent Secretary of the Ministry of Education in order to discuss their intention to provide education through Irish for their children. This meeting marked the beginning of a not so wonderful relationship! Throughout many years of negotiations the families clung to their belief that the all-Irish Primary school deserved the same treatment as other local primary schools which educated children through English. The matter was not seen in this light by the Department of Education.

Initial queries about the status of the proposed Irish-medium primary school resulted in official warnings about its illegality:

> ... it is the Ministry's view that instruction given entirely through the medium of Gaelic would not constitute ... efficient and suitable instruction ... (paragraph (c) of section 66(1) of the Education Act) for the pupils of an Independent School. A complaint would therefore be served by the Ministry. (Letter from Mr Benn, Permanent Secretary of the Ministry of Education, to the secretary of 'Teaghlaigh', 29/11/1965)

The Irish-speaking families did not accept that instruction through their children's first language could be detrimental. The nine children, aged between four and six years, who entered the Bunscoil in 1971 were happily unaware of the acrimonious wrangle which would ensue concerning this projection of their mother tongue into the educational domain. Their parents realised that bringing about a more enlightened and positive official attitude was going to be an uphill struggle. This involved scrutinising and digesting the details of every relevant educational document and piece of legislation.

Early responses by the Department expressed two main reservations: firstly concerning the low intake of pupils during those first years, and secondly, concerning the future of the children when they were ready to transfer to secondary school. The long-term implications of these questions would naturally be of interest to the Department of Education. The viewpoint of the Community differed dramatically. Such questions did not assume the same stature of significance for a group of people who had successfully created an environment wherein the Irish language had a functional relevance for their children at home, at play, and at school. The existence of difficulties was taken for granted and certainly was not allowed to impede positive action.

The Community applied to have the Bunscoil registered as an Independent School. This recognition was granted, on a temporary basis, in April 1976. Attempts to have this recognition made permanent bore unsatisfactory results. Two and a half years later the School Committee appealed to Lord Melchett, Minister for Education, to give his support. The frustration and disillusionment experienced by the Committee during negotiations with the Education Authorities pervades the tone of that communique,

> Our main hope in writing to you is that you will use your influence on our transactions with the Department of Education and the Belfast Education and Library Board. There are two main problems here: the normal low-gear grind of any bureaucracy faced with a new problem, and the endemic hostility of the educational authorities here to Irish culture in general and the Irish language in particular. Their (particularly the Department's) facilities for stonewalling us are almost inexhaustible. (Letter from the Secretary of the Bunscoil Committee to Lord Melchett, Minister for Education, 7/12/78)

The Committee had also made an application for voluntary maintained status by this time. This status would entitle the school to financial help from the Educational Authorities. The application was accompanied by evidence of the projected increase in the school's intake. This security of numbers resulted from the decision to allow children from English-speaking backgrounds to enter the all-Irish nursery school and later transfer to the Bunscoil. It was also pointed out to the Education and Library Board that it was legally required to secure efficient education to meet the needs of its area, and also to provide for a variety of instruction as appropriate to the needs of all pupils (Articles 5 and 6(1) of the Education and Libraries (N.I.) Order of 1972). Some months later, in April 1979, the Bunscoil was allowed to register fully as an Independent School. The application for maintained status was, however, refused.

A further five years of negotiations passed before voluntary maintained status was granted. It was widely considered that the protracted and unproductive nature of those negotiations was caused by implicit Government policy and ill-concealed cultural hostilities on the part of the authorities. The Community believed that official objections to the application were invalid. The original refusal was made on the grounds that the potential enrolment figures were low and that adequate educational facilities were already provided in existing primary schools. However, the enrolment figures being quoted by the Department were already two years out of date. Also, the character of other schools did not cater for the special needs of parents who wished to have their children educated through Irish.

In 1982 the Department of Education carried out a general inspection in the school. The results were favourable and the follow-up report reflected positively on the standard of education being imparted to the children. It also noted the happy friendly atmosphere of the school environment and commented upon the advantages of parents' motivation and enthusiastic support for the school. The School Committee was encouraged by the constructive comments made in the Inspectors' report. It took note of references made to the physical constraints imposed by the school building and urged the Department to facilitate improvements by awarding grant aid. On this occasion, however, the Department refused the request, claiming that a fresh application would have to be made by the Committee. Accordingly, each stage of the associated bureaucratic process would have to be repeated. The basis for this demand was that the increased enrolment of pupils at the Bunscoil represented a change in the school's policy. The Community interpreted this posture as another obstacle intended to stall or prevent progress. It refused to accept the Department's claim as valid. The legal advice which the Committee sought indicated that the official legislation did not require a fresh proposal. The controversy over this point lasted a further two years. In the meantime political representatives from three parties added their voices in support of the Committee's application. Finally it was announced that the Bunscoil would be recognised as a grant-aided school from September 1984, subject to certain conditions. This decision meant that the teachers' salaries would henceforth be paid by the Belfast Education and Library Board. An 85% grant of capital expenditure was also part of the package.

This decision was widely welcomed as a gesture of goodwill on the part of the authorities. It did, however, attract a furious reaction from some Unionist politicians. A similar reaction was evoked from this quarter when it was announced, around the same time, that the Steelstown Primary School in Derry was to introduce and accommodate an Irish-medium unit within its school structure.

By the time the Bunscoil was awarded grant aid, many of the first children to enter the school had passed on to secondary schools. Two families sent their children to be educated in Dublin where a number of Irish-medium secondary schools existed. This was an expensive undertaking which involved considerable self-sacrifice. Other families sent their children to the local secondary school where they would be taught through English. Generally these students took Irish as one of their subjects. However, before these steps were taken the Community did operate an all-Irish secondary school (Meanscoil) for their children. This lasted from 1978 to 1980 and again showed remarkable initiative and commitment.

As the Bunscoil was then being financed by voluntary fund-raising activities the Community was unable to assume further financial responsibilities by
employing full-time teachers for the secondary school. Therefore, the
Community availed of the services of various individuals who were employed in
local English-medium secondary schools and who also spoke Irish. These teachers gave any free time which they had to the Meánscoil. In this way a timetable
was arranged for the students to be taught all the usual subjects on a secondary
school curriculum, through the medium of Irish. This project demanded a total
pooling of resources. The science teacher, for example, had a very limited command of Irish. One of the parents therefore took responsibility for compiling a
list of appropriate terminology and also acting as a language assistant or interpreter in the classroom. Needless to say, this parent has acquired an unusual
knowledge of science and the teacher's Irish has also improved considerably!

The goodwill of the teachers involved with the Meánscoil was remarkable.
Nevertheless, it was decided to shelve that particular project for a variety of reasons. The Bunscoil, at that time, absorbed most of the committee's energy and
attention. The secondary school was adding considerably to the demands placed
on Community parents. In retrospect, the parents involved express a satisfaction
that secondary school education was provided during those two years. Even
though the scheme was short lived it proved that secondary education through
Irish was viable in Belfast. Also, if it could be operated for two years with no
resources, other than professional expertise and co-operation of local teachers
who were already in full-time employment, its future success must be guaranteed should more concrete material support be secured.

The introduction and establishment of Irish in various sociolinguistic
domains was clearly being achieved by the Shaw's Road parents. From the
beginning, the home and later the school represented the strongholds in the work
of rearing Irish-speaking children. The neighbourhood was also supportive. The
cluster of eleven houses on Shaw's Road, with their nursery and primary school
situated just beyond their back gardens, comprised a closely knit community in
a physical as well as social sense. Indeed many of the families were related to
each other so that some of the children live next door to their cousins.

The diffusion of Irish into the surrounding areas was facilitated to some
extent by the entry of children from English-speaking backgrounds into the
Bunscoil. This too influenced the status of the language in the surrounding community of West Belfast in particular and contributed, in this way, to the build-up
of a favourable and natural atmosphere for Irish speakers.

Another area which would represent an important dimension to the children's lives as Irish speakers was that of religion. This also was an English language domain in Belfast before the Community was formed. Therefore, early in

the preparations for a Gaeltacht neighbourhood, members of Teaghlaigh urged the Bishop of Down and Connor to provide Irish language services for the city's Irish-speaking Catholics. This was followed by a series of petitions and further requests. In due course regular Sunday Masses in Irish were celebrated in a chapel in the city centre. Community members sought the co-operation of various local priests in arranging for the extension of these weekly services to include holy days and the administration of the sacraments. The first of the Community children travelled to Dublin to be confirmed. Today an Irish-speaking child can receive all the sacraments in that language without leaving his own city.

The use of Irish and range of learning activities in West Belfast has been influenced by that Community core of eleven families. By projecting the language into other domains, such as primary education and religion, the network of members has grown. The Gaeltacht Community remains based at Shaw's Road where the Irish-speaking families reside. However, members of the surrounding areas have been shown an alternative way of introducing Irish into their homes, namely by allowing their children the opportunity of acquiring the language at a young age in a natural environment. Irish-medium education has played a central role in the diffusion of the language as a useful and effective medium of communication.

Once the children transfer to local secondary schools, their opportunities for speaking Irish decline. The Bunscoil plays a substantial role in the Irish-speaking lives of the younger children and their families; as yet no substitute has been provided which fills that gap for older children. As teenagers, the children's education switches to English-medium. Their build-up of school friends also develops the non-Irish language situations in which they find themselves and their social life is enjoyed largely with these non-Irish-speaking school friends. A need exists for attention to this area. Irish language youth clubs and cultural events directed at teenagers, as well as facilities for Irish-medium education at secondary level, do not exist to help counter the increased exposure to English language domains which the children encounter as they grow older. This is particularly serious for English-speaking homes whose relationship with the Irish language depends principally upon their child's attendance at the Bunscoil.

The following chapter begins to look more closely at the families living beyond Shaw's Road who sent their children to the Irish-medium nursery and primary schools. It is suggested that the lack of facilities for teenagers represents a threat to their endeavours towards bilingualisation. That problem may be resolved in the future. Certainly its implications will be examined more closely in subsequent chapters. In the meantime, however, let us consider the nature of the language's diffusion from the Gaeltacht Community into the homes of

Bunscoil children living elsewhere in Belfast. What are the patterns of bilingualism which emerge among these families, and what part does the Bunscoil play in this process? The experiences of these families must have relevance for parents throughout the world who, in their own way, are trying to raise bilingual children. As the majority of parents are not themselves Irish speakers at the outset, this undertaking will be of special interest to anyone concerned with language revival. The following chapter, will describe the demographic background of those families from surrounding districts whose children attend the Bunscoil. This information will provide an outline of that population which evidently shares the cultural aims of the Shaw's Road Community and, so, becomes an indirect extension to that Gaeltacht nucleus.

6 The Bunscoil Families: Socio-economic Profile

The Bunscoil at Shaw's Road now attracts the majority of its pupils from outside the Gaeltacht Community. The catchment area from which these Bunscoil children come comprises a number of the wards of Belfast. As Map 2 shows, these wards are not contiguous and a few are three or four miles from the school. This is to be expected as the Bunscoil catchment reflects the social geography of Belfast — a city characterised by religious, ethnic and cultural segregation.

The city, as a whole, is confronted by a number of social and economic problems which have afflicted it for over half a century. Some of these problems have their roots in the political history of Northern Ireland while others are rooted in the economic history of the area. Following the partition of Ireland in 1920, Belfast became the capital of Northern Ireland, itself a peripheral area of the United Kingdom of Great Britain and Northern Ireland. At the time of partition, the industrial interests in Northern Ireland were firmly convinced that there was an important industrial role for the city within the United Kingdom. Unfortunately, there were a number of significant factors which militated against the realisation of this aspiration.

Firstly, the city was located in a peripheral situation with respect to the United Kingdom as a whole. The Irish Sea presented a transportation problem which has always increased the costs of both exports to and imports from Britain. Secondly, and perhaps of equal importance, there were major problems connected with Northern Ireland's industrial structure. As a result of its industrial history, the principal industries of Northern Ireland were agriculture, textiles and shipbuilding. While all of these industries were efficiently run, they shared the common characteristic of being declining employers of labour. The automation of industrial production has had a major effect on the number of people employed in textiles and shipbuilding. Similarly, the mechanisation of farming has replaced men by machinery on the land. Sadly, as these industries became more efficient, they employed fewer workers. The important position of these three industries within the local economic system has meant that their misfortunes have become the misfortunes of the whole community.

KEY

1	CLONARD	18	FORTWILLIAM	35	STRANMILLIS	
2	FALLS	19	CLIFTONVILLE	36	MALONE	
3	NORTH HOWARD	20	CAVEHILL	37	DONEGALL	
4	COURT	21	CASTLEVIEW	38	WINDSOR	
5	SHANKILL	22	BELLEVUE	39	UNIVERSITY	
6	WOODVALE	23	BALLYSILLAN	40	BALLYNAFEIGH	
7	ARDOYNE	24	LEGONIEL	41	ROSETTA	
8	CRUMLIN	25	BALLYGOMARTIN	42	ORMEAU	
9	NEW LODGE	26	HIGHFIELD	43	WILLOWFIELD	
10	DUNCAIRN	27	ST. JAMES'	44	ORANGEFIELD	
11	GROSVENOR	28	WHITEROCK	45	THE MOUNT	
12	ST. GEORGE'S	29	SUFFOLK	46	BLOOMFIELD	
13	CROMAC	30	ANDERSONSTOWN	47	SHANDON	
14	BALLYMACARRETT	31	MILLTOWN	48	BALLYHACKAMORE	
15	ISLAND	32	LADYBROOK	49	SYDENHAM	
16	CENTRAL	33	FINAGHY	50	BELMONT	
17	GROVE	34	UPPER MALONE	51	STORMONT	
				52	COLIN	

MAP 2 *Bunscoil catchment wards.*

Against this background, Belfast's long-term unemployment problems become more understandable. The social and political divisions within the city exacerbated the economic misfortunes by ensuring that the burdens of unemployment were not equitably shared. As a result, Belfast has the additional problem of significant variations in socio-economic circumstances from area to area of the city. To a large extent, these variations coincide with the cultural and political divisions between the city's two communities. Catholic areas tend to be worse off.

The city has 51 wards though, for our purposes, the Colin ward which is just outside the city boundary must also be considered. This ward forms a recently constructed part of the built-up area and forms an extension of the area often referred to as 'Catholic West Belfast'. It contains a significant number of Bunscoil families. The ward boundaries within the city were changed in 1984 but, since the most comprehensive and up to date statistics are still gathered on the basis of the pre-1984 boundaries, these have been used for the purposes of this work.

The wards from which the Bunscoil children are drawn are:

Andersonstown
Ardoyne
Ballymacarrett
Clonard
Falls
Finaghy
Ladybrook
Milltown
Saint James'
Suffolk
Whiterock
Colin

As a background to consideration of the socio-economic characteristics of the Bunscoil families, as a group, it is necessary to examine aspects of the catchment wards in comparison with the city as a whole. Fortunately, a good statistical base for such a comparison is available in the Northern Ireland Housing Executive's Belfast Household Survey (1985). This survey, taken in conjunction with employment data from the Northern Ireland Civil Service, provides the basis for a comparative examination of a range of socio-economic indicators. The population of the catchment wards comprises approximately 90,000 persons, some 28% of the city. Considering the size and extent of the catchment area it might be expected that it would represent a fairly typical sample of the socio-economic conditions in the city as a whole. In a number of important respects, this is far from the case.

In examining the general socio-economic situation in Belfast, it is possible to compare the incidence of a number of important factors as they occur from ward to ward of the city. These factors relate to such aspects of urban life as income, home ownership, household size, occupational skills and unemployment rates. An examination of the incidence of such factors highlights two important points. Firstly, Belfast is a city with high unemployment and poverty levels. Secondly, and this is recognised as a problem, there is considerable variation in the degree of economic misfortune experienced by different areas of the city.

The economic prosperity of any area is affected by a number of demographic characteristics, among which the dependency ratio is of foremost importance. In any community, the population will be composed of those who are capable of work and those who are not. Children, the aged and the infirm are dependent and must be supported by those who are capable of work. The ratio of dependants to the population as a whole tells us something about the financial burdens which a community bears.

In Belfast, the dependency ratio varies greatly from ward to ward with a percentage figure as low as 20.15 for Windsor and 22.35 for University wards, contrasting sharply with figures of 48.02 for Colin and 48.76 for Court. The overall dependency ratio for the city is 37.91%, while the corresponding figure for the Bunscoil catchment wards is 40.34%. The catchment area also has a higher average household size than the city as a whole — while the household size for the city is 2.8 persons per household, the corresponding figure for the catchment area is 3.4 persons per household. Household size varies significantly from ward to ward in the city with as much as 3.9 persons per household in Ladybrook ward and as little as 1.6 persons per household in Windsor ward. The Bunscoil catchment, with an average household size of 3.4 persons, exhibits a substantial variation from the average household size of 2.8 for the city as a whole. Indeed, the average household size of the population of Bunscoil parents interviewed was even larger than that of the catchment area, at 4.8.

Belfast has been a city of high unemployment since the Second World War. Since the beginning of the economic recession in the late 1970s, the situation has worsened. The prospects for improvement do not look good; indeed recent figures from Cambridge Econometrics and the Northern Ireland Economic Research Centre (December 1988) indicate that Northern Ireland's unemployment percentage of 17.4% for that year (the highest for any region in the United Kingdom) will increase to 20.4% by the year 2000.

The impact of unemployment increases when households have more than one member out of work. Looking at the situation in Belfast, and examining the distribution of households with two or more unemployed, the position is seen to be very serious. While the average percentage of such households for the city as a whole is 4.7, the variation from area to area is considerable. For example, in Castleview and Cavehill wards the percentage of households having two or more members unemployed is zero and 0.3 respectively. At the other end of the scale, Milltown ward has a corresponding figure of 16.7%. In contrast to the average figure of 4.7 for the city as a whole, the figure for the Bunscoil catchment wards is 9%.

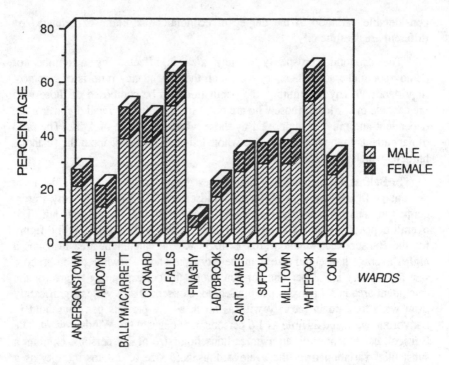

FIGURE 1 *Unemployment — male and female (as a percentage of economically active population).*

It is interesting to note that unemployment is higher among males than females. Of the economically active population, 23.2% are unemployed — taking the city as a whole. This unemployment is, however, composed of 6% female and 17.2% male. These figures match the comparative health of the service sector of the economy, as contrasted with the sad state of the manufacturing sector. Within the Bunscoil catchment the figures are worse, at 35.5% overall. In addition, the difference between male and female unemployment rates are even more pronounced with 27.4% of economically active males unemployed — in contrast to the corresponding figure of 8% for females.

Unemployment, and differences in its impact, have implications for income levels. It is not surprising, therefore, that all of those indices which point to prosperity show a mirror image of the unemployment statistics in their spread throughout the city. For example — although the average percentage of Belfast households owning their own homes is 51.8%, the variation ranges from zero, in Grosvenor ward, to 87.3%, in Fortwilliam ward. As compared with the figure of

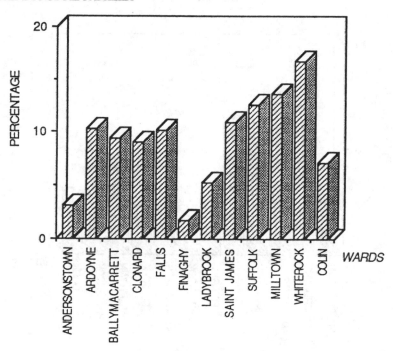

FIGURE 2 *Households having two or more unemployed (percentage in each ward).*

51.8% for the city, the Bunscoil catchment wards show a lower rate of home ownership at 40.1%.

Car ownership is another indicator of economic prosperity. Households without cars are at a disadvantage in terms of access to employment and are usually more common among the poorer sections of the community. The proportion of Belfast households in this category is 57.3% — quite high in United Kingdom terms. However, the variation between wards within the city is considerable — for example, Shandon ward has only 22.3% of households without a car while in Whiterock ward the corresponding figure is 91.9%. In comparison with the overall city figure, the percentage of no car households in the Bunscoil catchment is higher at 66.5%.

By the criteria of all of the indices examined, the Bunscoil catchment area shows a lower degree of economic prosperity than the average for the city of which it forms a part. However, this divergence is much less dramatic than the disparities between individual areas within the catchment itself. For example,

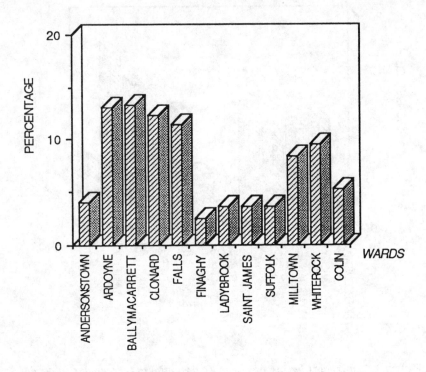

FIGURE 3 *Household heads who are unskilled (percentage of ward).*

the impact of unemployment within the various areas of the Bunscoil catchment differs significantly. While always very high, the differences between the wards are startling.

As Figure 1 shows, all of the wards suffer much greater male than female unemployment — however, the variation in total unemployment is astounding with Whiterock and Falls wards having 65.3% and 63.9% respectively while Finaghy ward has a 'mere' 10.3% unemployed. The differences are even more marked if we consider the male component of unemployment. While, in Finaghy ward, unemployed males constitute only 5.9% of the economically active population, the corresponding figure for Whiterock ward is 53.4%.

With regard to multiple unemployment in households, the differences are also very marked. For example, 16.7% of households in Whiterock ward have two or more members unemployed while the corresponding figure for Finaghy ward is only 1.8%. This exemplifies the considerable difference in economic circumstances to be found in different areas of the catchment. (See Figure 2.)

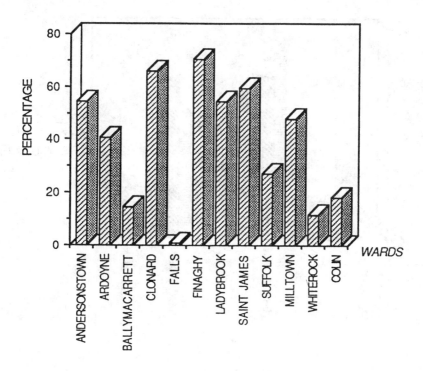

FIGURE 4 *Owner occupancy in Bunscoil catchment (percentage in each ward).*

In terms of the skill level of the workforce, the differences continue. Ardoyne and Ballymacarrett wards have 13.1 and 13.3% of their household heads within the 'unskilled manual' skills category while the corresponding figures for St. James', Suffolk and Finaghy are 3.6%, 3.6% and 2.5% respectively. This variation in skill levels is remarkable, especially within the context of a catchment area which has a great deal of homogeneity in terms of the educational provision within its boundaries. (See Figure 3.)

Although there is more public authority housing in some wards than in others, it should be remembered that Northern Ireland legislation gives tenants of such houses the right to purchase their dwellings. Therefore, it is interesting to note that the rates of home ownership within the wards of the Bunscoil catchment vary widely. For example, 70.6% of the households in Finaghy ward own their own homes — for Clonard ward the figure is 65.7% and for St James' 59.5%. These figures contrast sharply with Colin, Whiterock and Falls wards which have owner occupancy rates of 18%, 11.4% and 0.8% respectively.

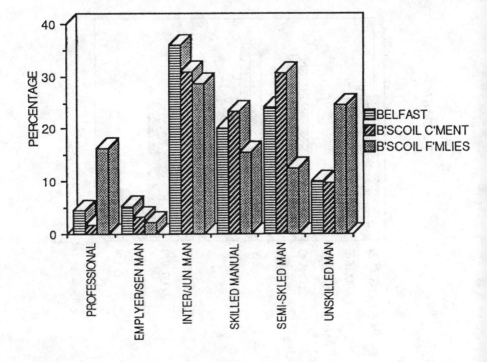

FIGURE 5 *Occupational skills — % breakdown (all over 16s, excluding house-wives and students).*

Again, we have another indicator of the great disparity in economic circumstances to be found in different areas of the Bunscoil catchment area. (See Figure 4.)

The message of the statistics is clear. While the wards forming the catchment area for the Bunscoil are generally less prosperous than the average for the city, the internal differences within the catchment itself are far more significant. Belfast is a city of profound economic, social and political differences. Within the catchment area of the Bunscoil, the economic and social differences are just as pronounced as in other parts of the city.

The profile of the Bunscoil families themselves, comfortably accords with the statistical evidence just considered. Indeed, as Figure 5 shows, the Bunscoil families as a group show unusual variety in the spread of their occupational skills.

At 16.3%, the proportion of professionally qualified people among the Bunscoil families is considerably higher than the corresponding figure for Belfast as a whole (4.5%). Again, the proportion of unskilled manual workers, at 24.6%, is more than twice the average figure for the city as a whole. It is appreciated that even a 100% sample of the Bunscoil Community is still, technically, a small sample. Nevertheless, the figures certainly show that the Bunscoil people are far from being a homogenous group in an economic sense. It is evident, therefore, that the cohesion and sense of community which the Bunscoil families exhibit so strongly cannot be explained by the socio-economic variables examined. Although the socio-economic background provides a context within which aspects of this language shift may be located, it by no means yields all the necessary clues to the sources of energy and commitment so abundantly displayed by the Bunscoil families. The sources of the motivation and commitment lie elsewhere within the deeper realms of culture and identity. This question is tackled directly in the following chapter.

7 Why Choose the Irish-Medium School?

Having examined the economic and social background of the Bunscoil parents it is interesting to look at the specific influences which motivated them to take the unusual step of sending their children to an Irish medium school.

When considered objectively, it is quite unusual for parents to forsake the benefits of a well tested non-fee-paying school system and to embark their children upon an unrecognised and untested educational course. It is all the more unusual when the unproven and novel course is conducted in a language which confers no economic advantages and which had previously been regarded as a badge of inferiority. In such circumstances, the motivation must be sought on the non-material plane. Ideals related to educational quality rather than economic utility may be expected to wield influence. This does not suggest that the economic and utilitarian aspects of the language should be ignored. On the contrary, those involved in the propagation of Irish are becoming more and more conscious of the utilitarian dimension of the language. However, it is true to say that Irish language educators have an enhanced awareness of the overall importance of cultural factors within the realm of education.

Since the question of motivation is central to any linguistic endeavour, examination of parental motives with regard to their children's education must command attention. Some of the Bunscoil parents' educational and cultural objectives may well be particular to the Belfast situation. Nevertheless, it is likely that most of the cultural and philosophical influences underlying these objectives will be of interest and relevance to parents and educators in a wider context.

The crucial role of educational programmes in strengthening the future of linguistic minorities is all the more apparent following the publication of a document summarising the positions of minority languages within the European Community (Commission of the European Communities, 1986). That report emphasises the importance of education generally in asserting the rights of linguistic minorities,

After what has been said in the present report, it is quite obvious that the educational dimension is absolutely central in securing a correct approach to the problem of minorities. It is through education that cultural values and attitudes are transmitted, that open-minded or intolerant approaches are instilled, and that the groundwork is laid for the behaviour of the adult citizen. The most vital of the European minorities have perceived this fact with absolute clarity, and have worked very hard to create, even in cases where their rights are not legally recognised, an effective educational network to secure the transmission of their cultural values to young people. It is thus quite clear that the *struggle for the protection of minorities is won or lost precisely in the field of education*, and that measures of an educational nature assume an absolutely predominant priority position in regard to all others. (Commission of the European Communities, 1986: 237)

Accepting the importance of educational factors within a minority language context, it is vital to attempt an understanding of the factors which lead parents to favour particular educational initiatives. The lessons learned from the Belfast experience should, hopefully, make a contribution to the development of a perspective on primary education in minority languages.

This chapter explores the factors which encouraged parents to participate in a linguistic and educational enterprise which was largely experimental and pioneering within this urban neighbourhood. Parents who enrol their children at the Bunscoil today are selecting a school which has proved to be successful from an academic viewpoint. It is supported financially by the Department of Education and therefore is well equipped with modern classroom facilities, teaching aids, sports facilities etc. The Bunscoil is also one of the few primary schools which is still expanding yearly despite the current economic climate of cutbacks and redundancies. However, when the Bunscoil parents involved in this study were interviewed the school was enjoying its first year of official grant aid. Therefore these parents had introduced their children to the school when it comprised a few makeshift classrooms, at a time when teachers' salaries, maintenance costs and teaching aids were financed largely by the fund-raising activities of the parents themselves. Choosing the Bunscoil demanded a strong commitment on the part of parents. Church collections, street collections, fund-raising functions and meetings are not always cheering prospects on winter nights. In addition to these extra obligations, which are not associated with other schools, parents were also confronted with the challenge of learning the Irish language so that they could understand their children's reading books and homework assignments.

It is important to realise that there were two distinct groups of families who sent their children to the Bunscoil. Children who lived in the Shaw's Road Gaeltacht Community were raised with Irish as their first language in the home. The demands placed on children and parents from surrounding areas with little or no Irish were very different. Many of the Shaw's Road parents had purposefully, and often with difficulty, acquired Irish as adults. The desire to give their children an Irish-medium education followed on naturally from their decision to raise bilingual families. The provision of Irish-medium education was, therefore, an obvious and necessary extension to their lives as Irish-speaking households. The difficulties experienced by adult learners of a second language had been tackled earlier during their own involvement in the various language learning activities. These parents had built up a sound basis for striving to meet the linguistic demands placed upon them as the functional role of Irish spread into the educational domain. They were, therefore, confident in their understanding of the language through which their children would be educated. In contrast, however, most of the parents from surrounding districts who decided to send their children to the Bunscoil had no such reserve of confidence. Their Irish was often minimal. Nevertheless, the doubts and anticipated difficulties associated with Irish-medium education were outweighed by the prospect of giving their children a full educational experience in the Irish language.

Parents from outside the Irish-speaking Community had also to confront a further reality. If they made the wrong decision, and their children's attendance at the Bunscoil did not work out, then changing to another school would mean changing to another language. This could present considerable difficulties for the children involved, above those commonly associated with a change of school. Standardised terminology for mathematics, science and other subjects would be unfamiliar to the child. Literacy skills in English would not be developed to the same level as peers until after the fourth year. These facts would complicate any decision to change schools.

In the light of these drawbacks it must be asked, what were the considerations that influenced parents' choice and led them to take a chance on an initiative unprecedented in Northern Ireland? From the survey, it is clearly evident that parents were not motivated by the success or otherwise of their own educational encounters with Irish at school. Indeed, the overall picture suggests that most parents' experience in this regard had been unsuccessful, and even unhappy. Of course, many parents had never formally studied Irish at school or college. However, even those who had done so were not generally enthusiastic about their experiences. Table 3 illustrates this point.

Even those parents residing in the Shaw's Road Community were far from enthusiastic about their experiences of learning Irish at school. Some of these Gaeltacht residents recalled negative experiences concerning their own Irish classes at the various schools which they had attended. Nevertheless, they

TABLE 3 *Percentage of the total respondents who studied and enjoyed Irish at school*

	Primary School	Secondary School
Fathers	16.3	23.5
Mothers	25.5	24.5

became motivated to learn the language at a later date and went on to create an environment wherein the language was given a real functional value.

It might be wondered whether the Bunscoil parents from the surrounding districts had also acquired Irish as young adults and perhaps sought to give this a real purpose in their lives by introducing their children to Irish-medium educa- tion. The survey results showed that this was not the case. These parents were not motivated by having attained a mastery of Irish and thus having enjoyed deep intellectual and cultural satisfactions through the medium of the language. In fact, most of them had a poor opinion of their own ability to handle the lan- guage prior to their children's attendance at the Bunscoil. As an illustration of this, the self-assessed competence levels of mothers' Irish prior to their chil- dren's attendance at the Bunscoil is laid out in Table 4.

As table 4 shows, oral fluency was rare and literacy was generally poor. If these facts are accepted, we must search elsewhere for the considerations which provided the parents' basic motivation. Undoubtedly, the decision to commit

TABLE 4 *Competence levels of mothers' Irish, before their children's attendance at the Bunscoil*

	No Irish (%)	Few words (%)	Simple pieces (%)	Most pieces (%)	Fluent (%)
Read	46.9	28.6	10.2	7	7
Write	44.9	28.6	9.2	7	6
Speak	34.7	43.9	12.2	2	7
Understand	35.7	37.8	12.2	6	8.2

(A fuller description of the competence levels of parents is given in the next chapter.)

their children's future to an all-Irish education was one which was not taken lightly. Only after long family discussions were the decisions made. Because of the unusual nature of the educational arrangements, and because of the fact that the Bunscoil had not, at that time, established itself fully and permanently, more consideration was given to the decision than would normally be the case.

During interviews with parents, it clearly emerged that they had devoted considerable thought to the advantages and disadvantages of sending their children to the Bunscoil. All parents were able to name at least three considerations which they discussed prior to finally deciding to send their children to the school.

The original suggestion that the child attend the Irish-medium school did not come from other Bunscoil parents or relatives or neighbours. Rather the idea was introduced by the parents themselves. Once the prospect was opened to discussion, the final decision was also influenced mostly by the views of one or other of the parents. This fact partly reflects the amount of media attention which the school and Community were receiving at that time. More parents were being reached directly by the publicity surrounding the school's history and struggle with the authorities. These reports usually examined the children's way of life at the school and gave positive accounts of the educational progress which they made. Hence, there was a growing interest in the school's welfare and in the type of education which it offered. Nevertheless, 20% of the parents interviewed stated that their decision was most influenced by another Bunscoil parent, some of whom also happened to be related to the respondent. Normal grapevine procedures were also in operation and other parents, who were happy about their children's attendance at the school, were encouraging friends and relatives to become a part of the school community.

Advantages

In the last analysis, however, couples evaluated the pros and cons for themselves and made what they considered to be the best decision. Some of the advantages or disadvantages which were deliberated over proved to be less significant than anticipated or feared. It is interesting, all the same, to look at those considerations and learn of the factors which create a favourable or unfavourable impression about the prospect of education through a lesser used language.

'Irish identity' and 'quality of education' were the two foremost advantages which parents anticipated would be associated with a Bunscoil education. 'Irish identity' was most frequently mentioned as the first single factor which had been discussed as a benefit of Bunscoil attendance. Parents usually enlarged upon this

TABLE 5 *Anticipated advantages of sending children to the Bunscoil (mentioned by respondents as being among the top three factors)*

Advantage	Percentage
Quality of education	73.5
Irish identity	71.0
Cultural awareness	48.0
Child acquires 2nd language	36.0
Language survival	26.0
Nationalist/Republican tradition	9.0
Parental involvement	9.0
Other	12.0

concept during the interview. The term 'Irish identity' represents for them a sense of belonging to the Irish nation as opposed to allowing themselves to be perceived as members of a British province. That consciousness of the opposition between nation and state can be one of the principal characteristics of a minority (Commission of the European Communities, 1986: 14). Clearly, parents felt that the Irish language would strengthen their grasp on that identity which provides a solid link with a rich cultural heritage as well as distinguishing them from the model of mainstream UK citizens which the media often promotes in its address to the Northern Ireland public.

In these circumstances the shift towards bilingualism constitutes a conscious attempt to reinforce one's sense of identity. This phenomenon is in stark contrast to that of subtractive bilingualism whereby social pressures lead the individual to abandon one aspect of his cultural heritage in order to merge more fully into the 'national' scene (Lambert, 1977: 15–27). Bunscoil parents believed that their own Irish identity and that of their families would be reinforced by giving their children access to fluency in the language and by doing so within a functional context. Therefore, Bunscoil children were not the only beneficiaries of this decision. Rather, it was perceived that the 'Irish identity' of the whole family would be rendered more meaningful when one or more of the children began to attend the Irish school. The anticipation of this collective experience was partly due to the valuable and necessary participation of parents in the running of the Bunscoil. This role of parents was greatest during the early days of the school's existence.

Three fathers mentioned that they became aware of the importance of 'our own language' in relation to Irish identity while holidaying abroad. Another respondent commented that her job as a French teacher awakened her awareness of the link between ethnic language and identity. She became embarrassed because of her fluency in the French language and ignorance of 'our own language'. All of these respondents expressed a certain degree of shame because they lacked communicative ability in Irish. Bunscoil attendance was generally regarded as a way to strengthen the Irish identity of the child and the family. On a national scale, Irish is perceived as a fundamental component of cultural distinctiveness and ethnic identity. This basic belief forms the cornerstone of attitudes towards the language (CLAR, 1975). The view is not restrictive or exclusive. Rather these respondents embrace a set of values which is distinctively Irish and shared by others disposed to tap a rich natural resource.

'Cultural awareness' was closely associated with Irish identity by the Bunscoil parents, and was also frequently mentioned. It is apparent that respondents were referring to the desired diffusion of Irish identity and cultural awareness throughout the entire family and not exclusively in relation to the Bunscoil child.

An overall realisation of the position of the language and a commitment to its survival were also considered relevant. Some 26% of parents considered that the attendance of their children at the Bunscoil represented one contribution to the survival of Irish generally.

A relatively small proportion of parents was attracted to the Bunscoil specifically because of a perceived association with the Nationalist/Republican tradition. It was expected that this figure would be higher because slightly over one quarter of the fathers had learned Irish in prison. However, 'Irish identity' and 'quality of education' were the main advantages discussed by these respondents. Attendance at the Bunscoil was not seen as a way to fulfil a single aspiration. Rather, it was perceived on a wider plane. 'Irish identity' represented a broader context with which to express the attraction of the Bunscoil.

The Bunscoil's reputation for high educational standards was the factor which most respondents cited as either the first, second or third advantage which they had discussed. For many parents, the favourable pupil/teacher ratio was an important characteristic of the school. A few also expressed disillusionment with other schools in the area, especially those whose older children had attended a different primary school.

When respondents were asked to describe how their interest in Irish had been awakened or re-awakened, the replies often corresponded with the choice of 'advantages' mentioned. Some parents developed an interest in Irish only after deciding to enrol their child at the Bunscoil. However, many stated that the sociopolitical atmosphere of Belfast had engendered an awareness of Irish identity. Others were inspired by the increased variety of language classes and cultural events in their locality. Some said that they felt ashamed of their own lack of Irish after they had overheard young children chatting in the language. Three other respondents recalled occasions upon which other non-Irish-speaking adults had expressed their sense of shame as they listened to the respondents' children conversing in Irish.

Disadvantages

Most of the parents had very clear ideas of the disadvantages which attendance at the Bunscoil might have for their children and themselves. Indeed, only 7% of those interviewed said that they had anticipated no disadvantage. Their own lack of Irish was seen as the principal problem by the largest group of parents. This group encompassed 32.6% of all parents interviewed.

Analysis of the survey results reveals a very interesting insight into the allocation of roles, to be played by fathers and mothers in the education of their children. Among those couples who anticipated difficulties arising from the lack of Irish on the part of the mother, no less than 65% of the fathers already had a reasonable command of the language. On the other hand, a father's lack of Irish was seen as a disadvantage by only 7% of these couples.

The realism of these implicit views about the respective parental roles is underlined by the answers obtained when couples were asked to look back and identify those difficulties which, in fact, proved most onerous. Fourteen per cent of couples retrospectively identified the mother's lack of Irish as a major problem. Among this group, all of the mothers had little or no Irish before their children were at the school. However, it is interesting that the majority of them did in fact improve their Irish dramatically. Where only 7% of them could read Irish beforehand, 64% could manage their children's textbooks, at least, at the time of the survey. These mothers had made even greater improvements in the other skills of understanding and speaking the language. Nevertheless they looked back upon their own problems with the language as the greatest difficulty which they had to tackle. Clearly, mothers who did not possess a reasonable amount of Irish had been under some degree of stress in attempting to fulfil their expected roles. Yet, their response to the situation was positive.

It is evident, therefore, that the primacy of the mother's role in helping the children with their education was recognised prior to and after the children's attendance at the Bunscoil. The couples believed that the mother's part would be the most crucial. Therefore the mother's lack of proficiency in Irish was often feared as a potential problem — by both mothers and fathers.

Another anticipated disadvantage was related to fears about the possible effects of bilingualism; 21% of respondents viewed this as a possible problem and feared that their children's ability to read English might suffer.

A significant number of parents said that they had regarded the attendance of their children at the Bunscoil as causing 'inconvenience'. In effect, this 'inconvenience' was related to the location of the school and to the fact that many of the families did not possess a car. Among the couples who considered that 'inconvenience' would pose problems, 71.4% of mothers and 57.9% of fathers were unemployed at the time of the interview. They may not have been unemployed several years previously at the time when they were deliberating about whether to send their children to the Bunscoil. Nevertheless, in the context of Belfast's economic situation, it is quite likely that they were either unemployed or occupied insecure or lowly paid positions. Many of these respondents lived too close to the school to qualify for travel allowance. Furthermore, many of them had to carry infants while accompanying children to or from school. The steep climb to or from the Bunscoil often dictated reliance upon public transport — particularly in inclement weather.

Another aspect of the situation which caused concern to some of the parents, when thinking about sending their children to the school, was the 'pioneering' nature of the enterprise. Eight per cent of couples cited this as their major source of anxiety and a further 13.3% considered that it was their second or third most pressing anxiety. These fears were very understandable at the time when parents were making the decision about whether or not to send their children to the school. At that time, the Bunscoil was neither officially recognised nor supported by the Education Authorities. It was natural, therefore, that some parents should be worried about the possibility of the school being forced to close before their children had finished their primary education. Additionally, the absence of any Irish-medium secondary education may have been seen as a possible future problem. Another disadvantage associated with the pioneering situation of the school was the degree of commitment and hard work required of parents. A number of these commitments involved responsibilities not usually expected in other schools. For example, regular fund-raising activities, attendance at numerous committee meetings and actual physical work performed on a rota basis have always been undertaken by the parents. Against this background, it is perhaps surprising that there was not more anxiety among parents about the pioneering nature of the enterprise upon which they were embarking. As it turned out, the vast majority of parents regarded the situation as a challenge and felt far more deeply involved with the fortunes of the school than would normally be the case. Far from being a source of weakness, as had been feared, the precarious situation of the school proved to be a source of strength since it stimulated a degree of responsibility, commitment and activity which was certainly unique in primary education within Belfast.

It is interesting to compare the hopes and fears of the Belfast parents with the corresponding attitudes expressed by their counterparts in Dublin, when parents there were making similar decisions. One of the factors examined in the report, *All-Irish Primary Schools In The Dublin Area* (Ó Riagáin & Ó Gliasáin, 1979), was the set of arguments which Dublin parents discussed when they were considering sending their child to an all-Irish primary school.

Certain fundamental differences between that report and the work upon which the present account is based must firstly be mentioned. The differences relevant at this point concern methodology and the socio-economic background of respondents. Although the questionnaires administered in the two studies addressed similar questions, they were differently worded. Also, Dublin parents had a range of Irish-medium schools from which to choose whereas the Bunscoil was the only Irish-medium school in the Six Counties when the Belfast questionnaire was administered.

It must also be noted that the socio-economic situation of the Dublin parents differs from their Belfast counterparts in a number of significant respects. The most remarkable difference relates to the occupational status of the husbands in the pupils' families. In the case of Belfast's Bunscoil families, 34% of fathers were unemployed, 38% were unskilled or semi-skilled and 15% were within the professional or managerial category. This situation contrasts sharply with the corresponding position in Dublin where no less than 65% of fathers fell within the professional or managerial category, only 8% were unskilled or semi-skilled and unemployment is not specifically mentioned in the Report. In Dublin, no less than 51% of fathers were state or semi-state employees. This marked divergence in socio-economic situation between the Dublin families and their Belfast counterparts makes a comparison of their concerns about Irish language orientated education all the more interesting.

Despite these differences mentioned, it is possible to highlight some key similarities and dissimilarities in outlook between the two sets of parents. Dublin parents were asked to list the arguments which had motivated them to choose Irish-medium education. (They were asked about their choice of a particular school in a subsequent question.) Reasons given divided into three categories:

(a) Language related reasons only   37%
(b) Non-language reasons only, i.e.   36%
       mainly educational reasons
(c) Language and non-language reasons   27%

Just over one quarter of the Dublin parents had been persuaded to opt for Irish-medium education by a combination of language and non-language arguments. In contrast, all of the Belfast parents gave a combination of language and educational reasons for sending their children to the Irish-medium primary school in Belfast. Even allowing for the differences in the two situations and in the two studies, this contrasting result is of interest.

Two of the factors which were of significance to the Dublin parents were not as relevant within the Belfast situation:

(a) Preparation for secondary schooling was one consideration which refers to the advantage enjoyed by the child when he progresses to either an English-medium secondary school where he will study Irish as a subject, or to an Irish-medium secondary school to which he will be assured entry. The latter facility does not yet exist in Belfast, or anywhere in the Six Counties. Children transfer from the Bunscoil to the local English-medium schools. Some of the Bunscoil parents did mention their belief that an early grasp of Irish would assist later endeavours to learn other languages. However, none of them had given much consideration to the child's advantage in Irish classes at secondary school. As the children themselves grow older they do develop an expectancy of excelling in their Irish exams. This was evident from casual comments made by the older Shaw's Road children who were at secondary schools. These comments were made in a very matter of fact manner. They didn't accept much credit for a high performance in Irish. It was simply taken for granted.

(b) A second factor which influenced some of the Dublin parents, but which was not as relevant to the Belfast situation, concerned parents' consideration of their children's future job prospects. If a high grade was achieved in the Irish exam it would certainly help a student's application for a job or for entry into third level education. However, we have seen that this fact did not feature among the arguments which the Belfast parents discussed when they were deciding on their child's primary education. Also, the functional value of Irish has not been developed to the stage where it bears much weight as an asset to the job applicant. Within narrow confines, the language may be vital or desirable for an advertised post. However, that situation is too limited to contribute to the language's status.

The decision about Irish-medium education in the Dublin area subsequently permits a wider range of considerations for parents. In Belfast, the basic quality of education which the parents believed they would be offered at the Bunscoil was of primary importance. Alongside this consideration were the factors related to the love of Irish. More pragmatic reasons were absent from the Bunscoil parents' motivations. At a glance, that fact may seem to imply that the Belfast parents were motivated solely by non-materialist and cultural aspirations. However, the more pertinent reality is the lamentable absence of an official cultural policy which would expand the range of possible advantages attached to learning Irish in Northern Ireland.

Bunscoil parents are clearly striving to 'give the children something which we never got'. Those words were reiterated so often by parents either in reference to their own trying experiences of learning the language as adults, or as teenagers in secondary schools. They saw an opportunity to help their children avoid that more difficult path by enabling them to acquire the language in a more natural environment from an early age. That 'something' which parents wished to give their children was not just another language. Rather, it represented a self-fulfilling experience of oneness with the Irish nation, drawing from a rich heritage, rooted in centuries of tradition. This manifest expression of identity would provide a source of strength which is of particular importance to a people whose culture is not equitably treated.

Accordingly, it is not surprising that the Belfast parents gave consideration to both language-related and educational factors during their early discussions about the Bunscoil as a possibility for their children. The lack of more practical gains, such as the ultimate possibility of economic or social advantages, obviously did not deter these parents. That fact should encourage speakers of lesser used languages elsewhere in the world where official bodies do little to improve the prestige and status of their language.

However, when viewed within the Northern Ireland framework, very serious implications are highlighted by that same fact. The conspicuous absence of anticipated advantages which would ultimately enhance the child's employment prospects or introduce him to a range of other educational and social opportunities reminds one of the refusal of the Northern Ireland Government to consider a package of incentives which would encourage more people to endeavour to learn Irish.

Until now, language enthusiasts have been campaigning for an official attitude to Irish which would justly reflect the existing level of interest in the Irish language and culture throughout Northern Ireland. If that request had been conceded, the list of advantages anticipated by parents in Belfast would have included a few other items, for example, being able to benefit from:

(a) Access to a range of educational and social facilities for young Irish speakers — youth clubs, summer schemes, exchange schemes with Gaeltacht Irish speakers.
(b) Educational programmes in Irish on television.
(c) The provision of enhanced facilities for the Bunscoil, matching those in English-medium schools — textbooks in Irish, computer programmes etc.

(d) An enhanced demand for Irish speakers in future jobs linked to initiatives
     in the areas of public information, communication networks, educational
     services (extending into the areas of professional counsellors for bilinguals,
     and other support services).

Of course, until these basic requirements for the existing Irish-speaking population are met, another responsibility remains unacknowledged, namely, the obli-
gation of governing authorities to form a language policy and to act positively to
encourage a favourable attitude towards the Irish language. A language policy
with this orientation would generate the resources required by an expanding
population of learners. Such an initiative would certainly add a few valuable
items to the list of considerations which motivate parents to consider Irish-medium education. It would also help cultivate a more educated attitude to the Irish
language throughout the entire population of the Six Counties.

8 Diffusion of Irish into the Home

A key aspect of the Bunscoil's contribution to the growth of the Irish language in Belfast lies in its direct and indirect influence upon the linguistic behaviour of the children's parents and their friends. Of course, the children's parents must necessarily have had a favourable attitude to the language, otherwise they would not have sent their children to the school. Therefore, in assessing the importance of the school's influence on its extended community, it is worthwhile distinguishing between the aspects of parental linguistic behaviour which stem from their role as Bunscoil parents and those other aspects which are part and parcel of the lifestyle of the average Irish language orientated resident of West Belfast. This chapter sets out to evaluate the role of the Bunscoil within the context of an examination of the increased use of Irish in the homes of Bunscoil parents.

It should be borne in mind that 'learning Irish' has been, to some extent, part of the life experience of the average Belfast Catholic for many decades. The young person usually encounters some Irish at school. Many young people will have spent some time in the Donegal Gaeltacht, attending summer courses. In addition to this there are numerous language classes, run by Conradh Na Gaeilge (The Gaelic League) and other cultural organisations, which they might attend as young adults. Yet, despite these measures, it is only in recent years that Irish has been projected into the community as a functional medium of communication. This breakthrough owes much to the precedent set by the Shaw's Road Community, when they consciously commenced the arduous task of constructing a network of social domains wherein the Irish language could be used by their families. They began with the home.

In the previous chapter, it was indicated that parents from the surrounding districts, who later came to send their children to the Shaw's Road school, experienced some difficulties because of their own lack of proficiency in Irish. The Shaw's Road parents did not experience any major language problems as their children progressed through school and became more fluent in the language. They did pass through the learning process as young adults and, consequently, are familiar with the difficulty of acquiring a second language in adulthood.

However, by the time they had founded the Bunscoil, when their children were of school-going age, the language had been more or less mastered by them. Bunscoil parents from neighbouring areas often found themselves without that advantage of a 'head start' on their children's development as bilinguals. Accordingly, their problems were different.

It is to this question of the diffusion of bilingualism among Bunscoil families that our attention now turns. As stated above, developments made in this process cannot be automatically attributed to the families' connection with the Shaw's Road school. Nevertheless, the very fact of their children's attendance at the school does demonstrate that their awareness of Irish in this functional sense was raised by the existence of the Bunscoil. A more accurate estimation of the role of the Bunscoil is made by comparing the linguistic patterns before and after the families' first child began at the school. At certain points during the survey administration, clarification was sought by addressing direct questions about any relationship between the children's Bunscoil attendance and the linguistic change being discussed.

Naturally, the emergence of active bilingualism in West Belfast cannot be attributed to any one solitary factor. Various factors operate upon this phenomenon, which can only effectively exert influence within a particular social, economic, political and historical context. It can happen, however, that one project or enterprise initiates a chain of events which, in turn, inspires a dramatic surge forward. The establishment of the Shaw's Road Gaeltacht Community was such a project. Its all-Irish primary school engendered a heightened consciousness of what could be offered to children in terms of national, cultural, educational and linguistic values. By no means was it the sole factor responsible for the increased spread of bilingualism. This chapter shows, however, that its role was nonetheless crucial.

In the case of the Shaw's Road families, Irish-medium education represented a natural and necessary extension to the home bilingual scene. In later chapters, when we focus upon the young people reared in the Shaw's Road Gaeltacht Community, it will become evident that the use of Irish at home becomes weakened when the children leave the all-Irish system. Firstly, however, we will examine a very different process which is in operation in the case of Bunscoil parents living beyond Shaw's Road. Bunscoil families, generally, tend to initiate the process of bilingualisation when they decide to enrol their children at the all-Irish school. Home bilingualism of varying degrees develops from there.

In order to begin to consider the linguistic profile of Bunscoil families it is necessary to take a detailed look at the parents' familiarity with the language, prior to their children's attendance at the Irish school. In the previous chapter, some general insights were given into the parents' command of Irish before their children were attending the Bunscoil. During the survey administration, parents were asked to assess their language ability levels for four skills, both retrospectively and at the time of the interview. These results are illustrated in Figures 6–9.

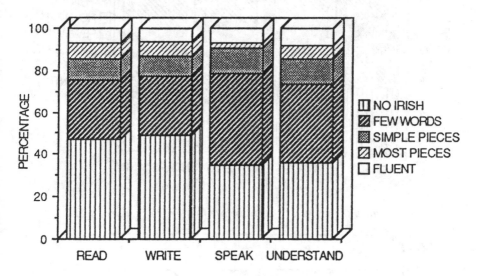

FIGURE 6 *Mothers' competence level (before first child at nursery school).*

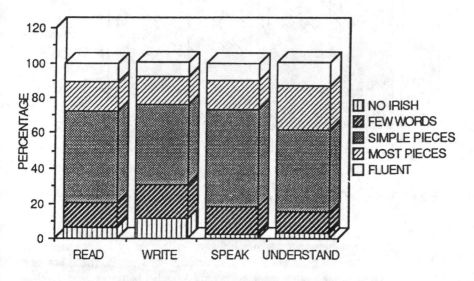

FIGURE 7 *Mothers' competence level (after first child at nursery school).*

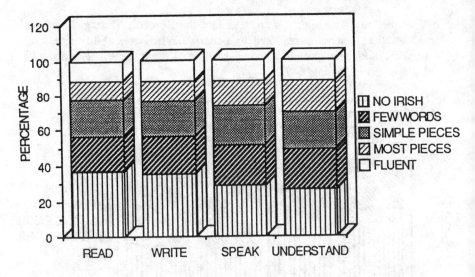

FIGURE 8 *Fathers' competence level (before first child at nursery school).*

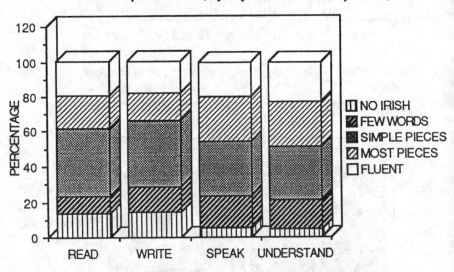

FIGURE 9 *Fathers' competence level (after first child at nursery school).*

These figures highlight a general change in the ability levels during the 'before' and 'after' situations. However, some disparity was also found between the language experience of mothers and fathers. Whether before or after the children began at the Bunscoil, the fathers were reported to be more proficient in

Irish than mothers. This fact is undoubtedly related to the type of disadvantage which some mothers encountered once their child began at the school. Fourteen per cent of couples considered that the mother's lack of Irish had proved to be the most troublesome difficulty associated with their child's attendance at the Irish school. Only one couple identified the father's lack of Irish as the principal disadvantage. (Although, a further 11% felt hindered by the language deficiency of both parents.) This lack of Irish was considered to be a handicap, to a certain extent, by those couples concerned. Pressure arose from two sources: the mothers' poorer command of the language, added to the belief that it was more important for mothers to acquire enough fluency to be able to support the child.

By the time of the interview, it was found that the language proficiency profile of parents had altered dramatically. That tendency to cluster around the two lowest levels ('no Irish'/'a few words') faded. Most people had progressed beyond those stages. Increases are evident in each of the three higher categories. However, despite this improvement, ability levels did not shift forcefully into the upper fluency ratings. Rather the average response settles around the 'simple pieces' category. That rating signifies sufficient mastery of the language to be able to read the children's textbooks and to handle simple basic conversation in Irish. Accordingly, once children start at the school, parents tend to acquire just enough familiarity with the language to keep abreast of their children's progress — at least, during the first three or four years. Fewer parents advanced to levels of proficiency.

Regarding the particular language skills considered, mothers made most progress in the oral command of the language. On the other hand, fathers' comprehension skills showed most improvement. In general, however, mothers scored more highly than fathers in each skill. This does not mean that mothers acquired a greater command of the language, but that they had advanced further from their earlier ratings. The scores given in Table 6 outline the distance covered by both parents during their endeavours to acquire Irish.

TABLE 6 *Competence improvement level of parents — Wilcoxen Test*

Skill	Mothers	Skill	Fathers
Speaking	−7.461	Understand	−6.147 (Most improvement)
Understand	−7.414	Speaking	−6.020
Reading	−7.220	Reading	−5.909
Writing	−6.934	Writing	−5.585 (Least improvement)

It was apparent, from discussions with parents, that motivation for mothers to acquire some Irish was sharper than for fathers. These results also reflect that fact, although it should also be reiterated that mothers were less familiar with the language than their spouses, at the outset.

The ability levels of parents is only one area where the language's diffusion may be discerned. In the next chapter, the learning patterns of other family members and friends will be examined. It will become clear that Bunscoil attendance does encourage some acquisition of Irish by the Bunscoil child's siblings and by other relatives and family friends.

Of course, increased levels of ability are not synonymous with increased usage of the language. Nevertheless, some sort of proficiency is a necessary step towards usage. Shaw's Road parents had gained fluency in Irish before they built their community of houses and school. Prior to that time, they had socialised together as young Irish learners. Even so, some of them encountered difficulties when they first moved into the Community, with the firm resolution that Irish would be the language of the home. This was the case, most especially, for those who had resided in the outer English-speaking areas while their Gaeltacht Community was being constructed. Lack of proficiency was not the principal obstacle. Rather, it was the effort of realising a deliberate and conscious language shift in the home domain which was most demanding. Indeed, it is notoriously difficult to switch from habitual use of one language with a particular person to habitual use of another, in a one to one relationship. One Shaw's Road couple overcame the initial strains associated with such a conscious effort, by inviting an Irish-speaking guest to stay with them for the first few months after moving into the Community. The presence of a third person, with whom each of the couple was accustomed to speaking Irish, introduced a sense of naturalness to the use of Irish in the home.

The lack of proficiency in Irish, reported by most of the Bunscoil parents from surrounding neighbourhoods, indicates that they would certainly not have been using the language before their first child started at the school. After that point, when they report considerable advancement in their efforts to acquire the language, usage would become possible. This, however, could only occur in a phased sense, as proficiency developed. Any introduction of Irish into the home would, therefore, be very different from the case of the Shaw's Road families.

Information was elicited, from Bunscoil parents, about the home usage of Irish within the following contexts:

(a) Interpersonal usage; i.e. use of Irish between mother and father, mother and children, etc.

(b) Situational usage; i.e. use of Irish within particular domestic situaions such as storytime, mealtime, etc.
(c) Irish media in the home; i.e. exposure to Irish programmes on radio, television, etc.

Interpersonal Use

The pattern of interpersonal use of Irish in the home, before Bunscoil attendance began, is relatively unchanged from the pattern of usage in the parents' own childhood homes. In both cases, over 70% of families rarely or never heard Irish spoken in the home. The language behaviour of family members in the home, in the 'before' situation and at the time of the survey administration, is illustrated in Figures 10 and 11.

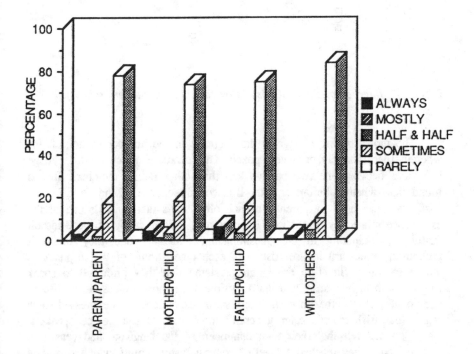

FIGURE 10 *Interpersonal use of Irish (before first child at nursery school).*

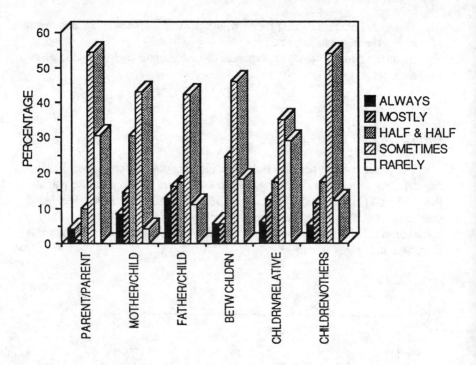

FIGURE 11 *Interpersonal use of Irish (after first child at nursery school).*

The most striking change is the decrease in the number of households wherein Irish is rarely or never spoken. That decrease affected the language behaviour between the two parents less than other family members. It was found that, whether before or after Bunscoil attendance of the child began, Irish was least used by parents to each other. This fact reminds one of the experience related by the Shaw's Road couple. Indeed, many of the Bunscoil families participating in the questionnaire, explained that they found it particularly unnatural to use Irish with each other. Some of the respondents who were quite fluent in the language stated that they preferred to speak English with their spouse, and that they found it almost impossible to discuss certain subjects together in Irish. These same respondents also expressed some regret that Irish classes cater generally for beginners and novice speakers. These parents felt that their own command of the language had ceased to improve once they reached a level of communicative ability which permitted them to handle everyday issues through Irish.

Nevertheless, the percentage of parents who used Irish 'sometimes' with each other, did increase from 17% to 54% after their child began at the Irish school. This level of usage may indicate that sometimes the couple used a little Irish together and the rest of the time they did not. Some parents explained that 'sometimes' signified that they used a little Irish together most of the time. The latter statements were qualified by a few parents with comments such as, 'We use as much Irish as we can' (i.e. as we have).

Some increase is also evident in the number of mothers who speak Irish and English with their children, in roughly equal amounts. In this 'after' situation slightly more mothers than fathers speak a fair proportion of Irish with the children. In both cases, the use of Irish increases after the child starts school.

In almost half of the households, children speak Irish together only sometimes. Eighteen per cent never speak Irish with each other at home. At the time of the survey, Irish was being used, between children and other family relations or friends, by over one third of the population.

The overall development of home bilingualism can be partly discerned from the fact that home usage of Irish showed some increase in 90% of households after the first child began at the Irish school. This would suggest that there must be a causal link between increased usage and Bunscoil attendance. Parents were asked to identify causal factors which they thought to be significant. Some of the parents (14%) claimed that the general climate of Language Revival had inspired them to try to use Irish at home. The attendance of their children at an Irish-medium school was one other aspect of that Revival. The vast majority of them did, indeed, state that the increased usage was a direct result of their efforts to support their children. A few of the parents attributed the change to the children's acquisition of Irish. Fifteen per cent of parents said that the language was used more at home in order to provide them — i.e. the parents — with the opportunity to practise. Some of the parents mentioned their willingness to use Irish with their children, in the home, as opposed to an unwillingness to speak Irish in other social contexts. These social inhibitions which operate upon the use of Irish are probed further in the following chapter.

Usage of Irish with the children and at home escaped many of the influences of personal and social inhibitions. Within this context, proficiency in the language was strongly influential in controlling language behaviour. Mothers who were fairly fluent tended to use some Irish with the children, both before and after they began at the Bunscoil. The language patterns of fathers were different. Of those who were quite fluent, only 12% used any substantial amount of Irish with their pre-Bunscoil child. However, in the 'after' situation, greater proficiency was likely to imply greater usage with the children. Indeed, at the time of the survey administration, over half of those fathers who commanded a

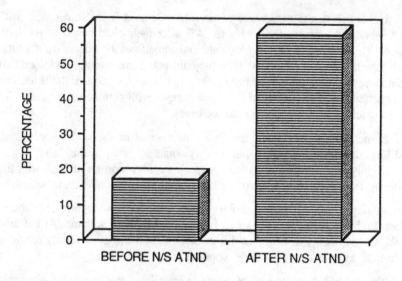

FIGURE 12 *Percentage of Irish-competent fathers using considerable Irish with their children.*

certain degree of oral fluency were using Irish frequently with the children at home. Figure 12 depicts this development.

Only four mothers stated that they never or hardly ever used any Irish with their children. These particular mothers had a very weak grasp of the Irish language. In addition, their attitudes towards their own prospects of learning Irish suggested a strong lack of self-confidence. They all hoped to learn Irish one day, but doubted their ability to do so. On the other hand, parents who speak mostly Irish with the children rated their language abilities as very high and, with a few exceptions, expressed positive views about their intentions to continue perfecting their language skills. Similarly, usage coincided with proficiency levels regarding parents who fell between these two extremes.

Just as the thrust of improvements to ability levels resulted in a clustering around the 'simple pieces' category, so also was this shift paralleled within the context of usage. In all of the interpersonal groups considered, the 'sometimes' rating was still the highest after Bunscoil attendance commenced. Accordingly, the process of bilingualisation is undoubtedly triggered by the children's introduction to Irish-medium education. However, this progress, which is widespread across families, is moderate in terms of degree.

Situational Use of Irish

Parents were asked to consider their language behaviour across a spectrum of domestic domains. Many people, particularly mothers, had expressed a diffidence about using the Irish which they did command outside the family setting. However, within the familiar context of the home, a pattern of some Irish usage was emerging. Nevertheless, that context did not escape the overwhelming pressure exerted against Irish usage, by the sheer force of English-language dominance. It became evident that the use of Irish was more easily incorporated into certain situations than into others. Situations wherein Irish could resist the pressure of English were still very much associated with the children's school life.

The most obvious example of a school-linked experience, conducive to some use of Irish, occurred at homework time. A substantial amount of Irish was used by at least one parent, in over 90% of households, while assisting the children with homework. A few parents were given extra help, in the form of tape-recorded versions of reading texts, in order to enable them to understand the children's work. At the time of the survey administration, some classes were still

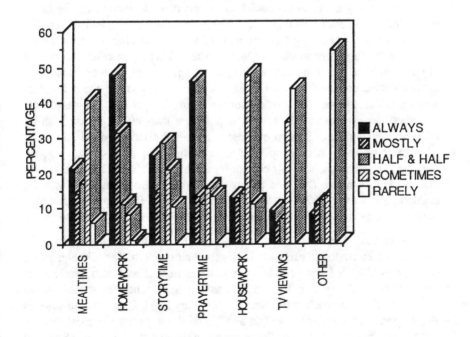

FIGURE 13 *Situational use of Irish in the home.*

quite small, so that teachers could make more time to respond to parents' needs.
That type of one-to-one support between parent and teacher has become a less
realistic possibility as numbers of pupils in the school and in each class multi-
plied. Additional pressures introduced by the Ministry of Education (extra working days, longer hours, mounting paper work and form-filling) have also played
their part in reducing the amount of time which a teacher can give towards
encouraging parents' efforts to use Irish with their children.

Figure 13 illustrates that other situations where some Irish tends to be spoken are found at storytime and prayertime. Again, these activities often involve
school materials, e.g. prayers learned by the children at school. Mealtime is
another example of an occasion where some Irish is likely to be introduced.
Certain phrases, learned by parents at Irish classes, can become standard modes
of expression in that type of situation. Indeed, in about half of the homes, at least
one parent used as much Irish as English at mealtimes. During those activities
where all the family tended to be together, parents seemed to make a special
effort to draw some Irish into use. This may involve informal chat and conversation. In the case of less proficient parents, it usually implied the use of certain
phrases and vocabulary items in Irish.

Some family activities conducive to the use of Irish come under the heading of 'other' situations, in Figure 13. 'Shopping' and 'family walks' were the
most common. It is no longer highly unusual to hear a mother address children
in Irish in the large supermarkets of West Belfast. This may be restricted to a set
of commands; however, it is more likely to be a feature of the more fluent and
confident speaker. The family walk is an example of a situation which is sometimes introduced specifically to encourage family use of Irish. Some parents
described the hindrances which were imposed on their efforts to use Irish by
television, visitors, etc. Several of these parents had established the custom of
taking family walks in order to have an opportunity to practise the language
together. The advantages of this custom for the bilingual family are also benefi-
cial in families where only one parent speaks the minority language with the
children. Saunders (1982: 238–9) refers to the merit of that parent arranging
occasional outings with the children, when the minority language is used.

Other parents referred to the journey to and from the Bunscoil as an occasion when they tended to use some Irish with their children. The school minibus
driver, who collected some children going to and from school, also remarked on
the children's habit of switching to Irish as they approached the school, and to
English as they approached the streets where they lived. One father mentioned
that he had tried to compel his child and Bunscoil companions to speak Irish in
his car, en route to school. Finally, he accepted the fact that his efforts were not
successful and refrained from telling them to 'speak Irish'.

The domestic situation least compatible with Irish speaking was when the family was watching television. This exerted a negative influence from the point of view of Irish usage. One or two suitable Irish language programmes are broadcast on the Southern channel, RTE. However, this coverage in Irish represents an insignificant proportion of programmes viewed. The detrimental effect of television in the bilingual situation in Belfast arises, firstly, because of the lack of Irish-language output and, secondly, because of the number of households where television and video viewing constitute the main leisure time activity.

The overall pattern of Irish usage in these domestic situations was found to be related to the age of the eldest Bunscoil child. This relationship operated at different levels. For example, in three families, the eldest Bunscoil child had transferred to a local secondary school by the time of the survey administration. In these families, Irish was the dominant language in each of the above situations discussed. Although the families did not reside in the Gaeltacht Community at Shaw's Road, they had participated in the early days of the school's construction and development. Their children had been among its first pupils. The parents' commitment to the language, and proficiency in it, had a head start on the younger families who were drawn to the language when the Bunscoil officially opened its doors to families from the surrounding areas. In general, a trend was found to exist towards some greater usage of Irish in relation to the children's age. Most of the eldest Bunscoil children in the families interviewed were aged between five and eight years. Irish was spoken more by the families of the older children, in every situation, with the exception of 'housework' (see Figure 14).

Therefore, home usage of Irish did seem to increase as the children continued their education at the Bunscoil. Whether that pattern would continue as the eldest children progressed towards the final year at the Bunscoil (at eleven years) cannot be taken for granted. That assumption would be particularly unwise in light of the tendency of progress to falter, after reaching a certain stage, in other areas — for example, regarding parents' improved ability levels or the development of interpersonal usage of Irish towards the 'sometimes' category.

In the following chapter, we will consider the effect of certain social restraints upon the parents' use of Irish outside the home. For these people, the home can provide the right balance of informality and security required to encourage some usage, in accordance with the stage of competence reached. Over half of the mothers and 40% of fathers, who reported that Irish was spoken as much as English in the various domestic situations, were not happy about using their Irish in all situations with their Irish-speaking friends. Obviously, a

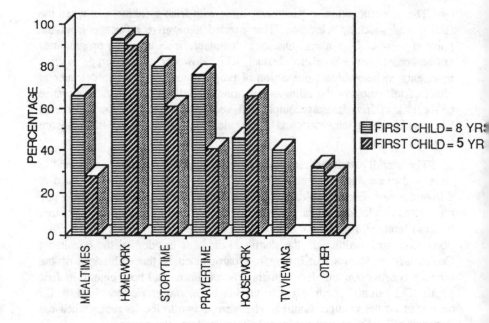

FIGURE 14 *Age of family's first Bunscoil child and situational use of Irish*
(> 50%).

fair degree of proficiency had been achieved by these people, yet the home still
provided an environment which was considerably more conducive to Irish usage
than elsewhere.

Irish Language Media in the Home

We have already referred to the generally negative influence of television
upon efforts to speak Irish at home. Television is one area of the media which
has not progressed in terms of provision for Irish speakers and learners in
Northern Ireland. The survey of viewing potential for programmes in languages
other than English, commissioned by UTV in 1985, is the closest that the broadcasting company has travelled in that direction. Nevertheless, the output of Irish
language material in the media, generally, has expanded somewhat in recent
years. At the time of the survey administration, two weekly language programmes were being broadcast on the BBC radio. The daily newspaper was
being published and other Irish language magazines were in circulation. The

parents' limited exposure to Irish in the media was — and still is — governed by this restricted range. In consideration of the scarcity of materials available in the media, compared with the wealth of English language output, the percentages recording use of existing resources were quite high. Sixty-seven per cent brought an Irish newspaper or magazine into the house, at least once a week. Irish language tapes and records were listened to less frequently. A television programme was watched on RTE and over one quarter of the population listened to a radio programme, at least once weekly.

Many of the parents were ill-informed about the Irish language materials which were available in the media. Irish learners and speakers are not exposed to the existing material as they are exposed to English language material. Often, they must go out of their way to avail of existing resources. The advertisement of such resources is not very effective.

The introduction of Irish language into the home, via the media, is not an area which compares to other categories of usage in terms of increases after Bunscoil attendance began. For about half of the population, the amount of Irish delivered into the home on the media remained unchanged once the children were at the Bunscoil. The rest of the population reported most increased exposure via reading materials. Over three quarters of the parent population buy more reading materials in Irish — newspapers, magazines, books, etc. — once their children begin at the school. To a certain extent, this change reflects, primarily, the parents' willingness to support the Irish language rather than to avail of the information service. In some cases, the proficiency levels do not enable the parent to read and understand the magazine or paper. Indeed, 70% of parents who buy an Irish paper or magazine at least once a week cannot read a standard above the 'simple pieces' category. For some people, the efforts to understand certain articles, phrases, words in the paper, was also perceived as a learning activity. Other materials are purchased as a gesture of support and encouragement to the children.

Pressures Influencing Home Bilingualism

The overwhelming presence of English-language dominated media created a major obstacle to parents' efforts to encourage the use of Irish at home. Ten per cent of the population considered that the most detrimental influence upon these efforts was caused by television viewing. Other people referred to it as one of the various hindrances which they experienced. Many parents explained that it was impossible to think about stimulating the use of Irish while the family was watching television. Indeed, over three quarters of the households reported that Irish was spoken never or 'sometimes' while the television set is on. The vast

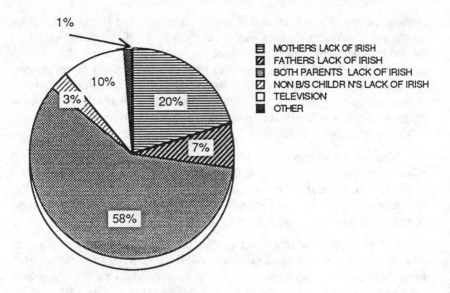

FIGURE 15 *Principal obstacle to use of Irish in the home.*

input of the English language via television, non-Irish-speaking visitors, etc. place serious restraints upon the use of Irish at home. However, the main diffi-culty was related to parents' competence levels. During the survey, parents were asked about the usage patterns within the context of their own capabilities, i.e. the extent to which they used the amount of Irish which they commanded. It became very clear that home usage was most inhibited by the parents' limited proficiency in the language.

When parents were asked to reflect upon the disadvantages associated with their children's attendance at the Bunscoil (Figure 15), just over one quarter of the population stated that parental lack of Irish had posed the most troublesome disadvantage. Yet, 85% of respondents identified one or both parents' lack of fluency as the main obstacle to home usage of Irish. This suggests that a consid-erable number of people did not regard limited home usage as a threat to the children's success at the Bunscoil. The importance of attending classes and endeavouring to support the children's progress as bilinguals is conveyed to par-ents entering their children into the all-Irish system. The increased levels of home usage, after Bunscoil attendance begins, indicates that parents appreciate some of the value of home bilingualisation. It is doubtful, however, whether the potential benefits of home usage are fully realised by parents. The burdens and strains accompanying parents' efforts to improve their command of Irish and to increase the extent to which it is used in their home may come to outweigh those benefits. This situation is not helped by inadequate support services for parents and families.

The principal obstacle identified by 3% of the population, was not parental lack of Irish but the fact that the Bunscoil child's older brothers or sisters had been educated at English-medium schools and had not acquired Irish. Naturally, this would influence the language patterns of siblings. Generally, the use of Irish among Bunscoil children with siblings and friends showed some hopeful signs of resistance to the pressures from an English-dominant environment. A fair amount of Irish was spoken by approximately one third of the children who happened to have siblings. This leaves a sizeable percentage of children who used Irish 'never' or only 'sometimes' amongst themselves at home. More Irish was used by children with their Bunscoil peers. Almost 44% of the eldest children used a fair amount of Irish with school friends visiting them at home. This level of usage decreased according to the age of the child — with younger children using less Irish. However, whereas half of the eldest children play with Bunscoil friends once a week after school, that frequency is also lower for the younger children.

During interviews with parents, many people expanded on responses, or volunteered additional information, which provided more detailed insights into the children's language patterns. These observations were also recorded and quantified. A few parents commented that their Bunscoil child had influenced non-Bunscoil peers in their neighbourhood. Some of these friends now use a little Irish with the Bunscoil children. Usually, this type of observation referred to the friends' interest in Irish songs and rhymes learned by the Bunscoil child.

Parents' comments indicate a tendency for the child to use Irish when other visitors and relatives are not present. Some children use a little Irish quite naturally with the Bunscoil peer when they are playing alone. This type of behaviour would normally refer to a limited use of Irish. Indeed, a different tendency is encountered in the school playground; there, constant supervision is required to halt the children's tendency to turn to English. The presence of adult Irish speakers can check that inclination.

Even at home, the influence of school upon language usage was evident. Several parents explained that they would hear their children switch to Irish if they are 'playing school' — acting teacher with a class of dolls or peers. Many parents, asked when their children spoke Irish, stated that they would use Irish when they returned from school and were starting off an account of the day's events. They soon switch to English. School terminology would often be left untranslated from the Irish.

Thirteen respondents mentioned specifically that their children draw a very clear distinction between the language of school-related events and that for home and neighbourhood events. Sometimes this referred to the fact that the children used more Irish in the vicinity of the Bunscoil. One father explained that he spoke Irish with his child only in the school grounds because his wife had no Irish. In a different case, the child disliked Irish and was reluctant to speak it at home. His parents believed that this was associated with the child's general dislike for school. Another parent had noticed that her child associated Irish exclusively with school until he began to bring his school friends home to play.

A remark made by many parents was that 'he (she) lays down the rules'. For example, some parents stated that their child will occasionally initiate a conversation in Irish with them. However, the same children will resist the parents' endeavours to begin a dialogue in Irish with the child. This same view had been expressed by the father who eventually desisted from trying to force the children to speak Irish on route to school.

Examples of children determining the circumstances in which they are willing to speak Irish are abundant. Some of them refuse to speak Irish with their own parents but are quite happy to speak it with other Irish-speaking adults. Often, this type of reaction is temporary. Figure 16 illustrates the main factors operating upon this phenomenon. The school secretary related one incident which depicted such a case. The secretary met a Bunscoil mother (who was attending Irish classes) with her five-year-old child on a shopping trip. After greeting the mother she conversed briefly with the child in Irish. The mother expressed wonder at her child's knowledge of Irish, explaining that the child had been refusing to speak Irish with herself. She had concluded that her daughter had not yet acquired very much Irish. This behaviour may be partly explained by the young child's reaction to starting school. It is true that some children can be a little hostile to the mother when they first begin school, because of the enforced separation. However, all Bunscoil children attend the all-Irish nursery for about two years before entering the school. They are not unaccustomed to being apart from their mothers, therefore. Other mothers who described similar experiences attributed it to the child's lack of confidence regarding the use of Irish outside the school environment. As the children's grasp of the language develops they become happy to recite verses, songs, prayers etc. for parents and to chat a little.

A number of parents mentioned that their children had been happy to use bits of Irish as they were acquiring it at nursery school and in Primary 1 at the Bunscoil. A changed attitude emerged around the second year of primary schooling. At this stage, the children rejected the use of Irish outside school, or more specifically, in the home. One factor which contributes to this phenomenon is the child's growing awareness of the parents' linguistic limitations. Indeed, most parents struggle to 'keep one step ahead' of their child's progress in Irish; however, that task becomes more difficult as the child's command of Irish develops. Several parents said that they reduced their efforts to learn Irish when they realised that their child's educational progress would continue anyway. Most, however, expressed some concern about the fact that the children had reached or surpassed their levels of competence. This stage most often occurs around the end of the child's second year or the beginning of the third year. This realisation, by the child, of the parent(s)' limited command of Irish can evoke sharp reactions around that time. Seven couples mentioned that their child reached an awareness of one or both parents' lack of Irish and communicated this knowledge very clearly. In these cases, the children refused to allow the parent to continue helping with homework. This type of phase was generally more typical of the eldest children.

Many parents felt that their younger Bunscoil children enjoyed certain advantages over the eldest child. Over 20% of couples stated that their first child had experienced a rebellious period during which they refused to speak Irish outside school. In some of these instances the parents had become concerned about the children's linguistic progress. These people were assured by teachers that the child's linguistic development was, indeed, satisfactory. Less than half of these children had a younger sibling who passed through a similar phase. In the case of those younger siblings this behaviour also occurred most commonly around Primary 2. Several parents commented that their younger children were more outgoing and keener to 'show off' their Irish.

Parents gave accounts of various incidents in order to illustrate their child's comportment during this period of rejection of Irish outside school. Some described how they would address the child in Irish and be answered in English. Responses showed that the child had understood clearly. This reaction was not extended to other adult Irish speakers. As mentioned, this behaviour is often linked to the child's perception of the parent's lack of proficiency. However, other factors contribute to this behaviour, one of which may be the nature of the parents' linguistic repertoire. Commands and question/answer sequences are often the first structures taught at adult language classes. When respondents gave examples of their own usage of Irish at home and when they addressed the children in Irish during the interviews it was most often in the form of brief commands e.g. gabh tseo (come here), bí ciúin (be quiet), tabhair dom an — (give me the —). It is possible that repertoires restricted to commands may evoke some negative response by causing the children to equate home Irish with orders.

The child's own developing personality is another factor which plays a role in this temporary rejection of Irish outside school (and sometimes in a more

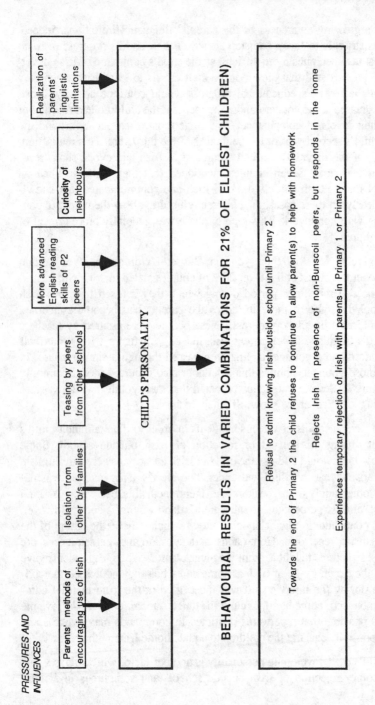

FIGURE 16 *Causal and resulting factors involved in some children's temporary rejection of Irish outside the Bunscoil.*

long-term rejection of Irish usage with a parent whose command of the language is inferior to the child's Irish). According to parental reports, one fifth of those eldest Bunscoil children who expressed a rejection of Irish were quite timid generally. The reaction of other local children to the bilingual child can also influence his attitudes towards the use of Irish in the home. Some Bunscoil children (especially the younger ones) enjoy chanting verses and songs to friends. However, quite a few parents described incidents where their child had been upset by the teasing of peers. A few children asked their mothers to stop using Irish phrases such as 'gabh tseo' (come here) and 'tar isteach' (come in) when calling them in from play. One child threw a tantrum in hospital because her mother addressed her in Irish in the presence of other children. Very often, difficulties with peers are related to reading levels. Bunscoil children begin to read English language material towards the end of Primary 3. Some children feel inferior to non-Bunscoil peers who have more advanced reading levels in English, at this stage. The problem fades as the child's literacy skills in English progress to reach the same standard as those which he has developed in Irish. Many parents mentioned their children's sense of pride on beginning to read English language texts.

Ten per cent of respondents happened to mention that isolation from other Bunscoil families caused problems for their children. This isolation and lack of social interaction was a more significant variable than distance from the school. Some of these families reside in the peripheral areas of West Belfast; others live in the next street to Bunscoil families. Most families live within a radius of four miles from the school. Children who live furthest away do not speak less Irish with school friends. The important factor is whether or not other Bunscoil peers live close by. However, parents explained that their children chose playmates within the immediate vicinity, of the same age and, usually, of the same sex. Bilingualism was not a criterion considered when selecting friends. Isolation from other Bunscoil families contributed to various difficulties. Immersion in an English-speaking neighbourhood sometimes generated well-meaning curiosity. A few unfortunate children had been irritated by neighbours' persistent requests to 'say something in Irish'. (Again, the child's own personality often determines how he reacts to such incidents. More extrovert children might well enjoy this type of attention.) One poor child had been escorted around several houses in the street, by one neighbour, in order to 'show him off'. Other Bunscoil parents commented upon the fact that their children's bilingualism no longer attracted the attention and curiosity of neighbours. These people expressed some relief about this change.

Shaw's Road parents have frequently observed the same change in public attitude towards the use of Irish by their children. The original families, in particular, recall the surprise of other people as a habitual reaction which they had to accept. Other adults on public transport, passing by on the street or in shops would sometimes marvel at hearing children use Irish in such a natural and easy manner. Over more recent years, it has become more novel to hear people comment upon children and families using Irish. Indeed, it was this aspect of isolation in an English-speaking district which Shaw's Road parents aimed to counter when they built their own Community. Bunscoil children do not enjoy the benefits of living within a Gaeltacht Community, even though they attend the Irish-medium school. Nevertheless, the growth of urban Irish as a phenomenon has reduced some of the social pressures which the young bilingual experiences.

Some of the parents displayed imagination and initiative in the manner in which they had learnt to tackle the resistance which their child sometimes showed towards the use of Irish in the home. Parents who tried forcing the child to speak Irish usually failed. They had to accept the fact that the child determined when the language was appropriate or desirable. More success was achieved by subtle ways of encouraging the use of Irish without evoking a negative response. For example, one mother noticed that simple interjections by her, in Irish, into the conversation, sometimes triggered a switch to Irish. The use of particular phrases in Irish became so natural that the child did not think of them as 'out of place'. These phrases were not restricted to commands, e.g. 'cad é sin?' (what's that?); 'Ar mhaith leat — ?' (Would you like a — ?); 'Maith an cailín' (Good girl); 'An bhfuil sin ceart?' (Is that right?)

Other parents allowed the child to assume the responsibility for correcting parents' Irish. One mother reported that she had made a harmonious pact with her young daughter: the latter helps mother with the Irish and mother helps her with homework. Fourteen of the respondents mentioned that their children happily (even gleefully!) correct their parent's Irish. A further ten couples said that the eldest Bunscoil child had been persuaded to help younger siblings with Irish. In most of these cases the mothers had explained to the child that his or her assistance could compensate for the parent's lack of proficiency. This candid explanation and allocation of responsibility had been accepted by the children involved.

Clearly, the usage of Irish outside school involves a spectrum of difficulties. However, this tendency of the eldest children to experience certain reservations about the language usually passes after a year or so. Thereafter, the child's active resistance to the idea of using Irish in the home dissolves. Usage continues to be influenced greatly by the parents' lack of proficiency, along with other social pressures to speak English.

One fact, of which parents seemed to be unaware, was the extent to which their levels of competence were related to that of their child (Figure 17). Levels of competence was not the only factor involved in this pattern.

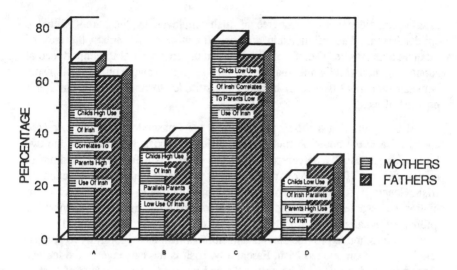

FIGURE 17 *Usage patterns (with friends), child by parent: correlations of levels of competence*

The parents' susceptibility to certain social and personal norms also correlated with the child's use of Irish outside school. The following chapter explores this subject more fully and discusses how parents' willingness to speak Irish is affected by certain social restraints. Some people, for example, are uncomfortable about using Irish in the presence of non-Irish speakers. It is pertinent to mention here that children of parents whose linguistic behaviour is least affected by such norms are, themselves, most likely to speak Irish with their Bunscoil friends outside school.

Almost three quarters of those mothers who claimed that they were happy to use Irish with their Irish-speaking friends at any time reported that their eldest Bunscoil child speaks a considerable amount of Irish with his or her own friends. A similarly high correlation existed between parents who experienced certain inhibitions about the use of Irish and the language behaviour of their children. This was particularly striking regarding mothers who were uneasy about using Irish in certain places and who felt unhappy about initiating a conversation in Irish. Children of these mothers tended to use very little Irish with Bunscoil friends outside school.

This relationship concerned not only parental attitudes towards the use of Irish but also the parents' language behaviour with their children's school friends. Accordingly, greater usage of Irish by the child with school friends usually coincided with the degree of Irish employed by the parent with the child's friends. This relationship was slightly more significant in the case of mothers than fathers. Therefore, although parents are aware of the importance of supporting their child's bilingualisation, they are not so aware of the relationship between their own use of Irish, and their attitudes to it, with their children's patterns of usage.

It is evident that a child's attendance at the Bunscoil leads to an increased use of Irish in the home. A fundamental difference exists between how the two languages are usually perceived. English is 'used' as a functional medium of communication. The 'use' of Irish, however, normally implies the 'practice' of Irish. Generally, it is not yet spoken in the home in order to convey or seek information etc. Rather, the principal purpose for speaking Irish is to support the child's bilingualisation, to bridge the linguistic gap between home and school environments and to provide parents and siblings with the opportunity to practise and improve their spoken Irish. Essentially, Irish is the language of the learner. Opportunities for use must be cultivated and protected. Home usage of Irish is approximated and strived towards. Most parents view the home within this supportive framework. Nevertheless, the ultimate goal for the children is indeed to use Irish in a natural and functional manner. So many parents made comments such as, 'We wanted him to learn Irish in a natural way without all the difficulties which we had', or 'We wanted him to have an opportunity which we never had'. This opportunity referred to the child's acquisition of Irish as a language which he could use naturally, without being consciously aware of it. The parents, on the other hand, are usually very conscious of their endeavours to use Irish and to introduce it — to some extent — into the home. Home Irish means hard work and concentrated effort. For most families, it is not a natural feature of family life but, rather, an exercise aimed at easing the children forth towards such a possibility.

The usage of Irish in each individual home was unique. Many of the factors and influences mentioned operated in a variety of degrees and combinations in each case. Clearly, bilingualism is being projected into the home domain. However, the degree of success in this area, as in others, reaches a plateau on which the majority of the population seem to rest. The challenge of injecting further momentum into this shift cannot rely upon the efforts and endurance of parents. At that point a supportive external network becomes most necessary. As the second Bunscoil establishes itself and the Irish-medium nurseries continue to expand, the need for some back-up service for families assumes a sharper urgency. This is only one of the facilities which could be provided by the type of centralised body referred to above.

This chapter has described the actual position of Irish usage in the homes of Bunscoil families and also highlighted some of the difficulties associated with the projection of Irish from school into the home. This process has worked in the reverse order from that adopted by the Shaw's Road families who established Irish-speaking homes and an Irish-speaking neighbourhood before founding the school. The importance of these two domains takes precedence over any other. The threat to usage of Irish in the home will be discussed later in relation to the transfer from the Bunscoil to English-medium secondary schools. The prospect of leaving the Irish-medium educational domain raises crucial questions about the bilingualisation process into which everyone involved has invested so much energy.

Firstly, however, the description of emerging trends in bilingualisation is broadened by looking beyond the home and school domains to survey the other areas into which the Irish language has penetrated. This material, dealt with in the following chapter, will complete the picture of the diffusion of Irish among Bunscoil families and friends.

9 Usage of Irish Outside the Home

West Belfast buzzes with activities for the Irish learner. We have already referred to the abundance of language classes for adults which form an important dimension to the social and cultural life in this part of the city. The usage of Irish outside the home is related to the learning process for most of those interested in the language. A substantial amount of fluent speakers will have been involved in giving classes to others, at some point. People endeavouring to acquire the language form links involving the use of Irish in the learning situation or in social situations connected with learning activities.

People attending these classes rate highly the contribution made by the Irish-medium school towards the Language Revival in Northern Ireland (Ó hAdhmaill, 1985). It is to be expected that Bunscoil parents, in particular, would be inspired to participate in language classes and related events. Irish is introduced into the home itself via the Bunscoil child — by the family's desire to support the child with his school work and to extend his language experience beyond the school domain. The infiltration of bilingualism into extended social networks would ultimately reinforce the demand for Irish-medium education itself and counter the effects of isolation from Irish-speaking peers, referred to in the previous chapter.

The nature of the Bunscoil's role in the diffusion of Irish throughout the surrounding community is particularly significant because of the fact that, after seven years, the child passes out of the primary education system. When all of the children in the family have reached that stage, contact with the school will, obviously, be reduced. Accordingly, it is important to consider the extent to which the usage of Irish, outside the home, is related to the Bunscoil, and to what extent families develop interactions with Irish speakers which have some degree of independence from the school. The Dublin-based study of all-Irish primary schools showed that the school was central to the maintenance of parents' Irish-speaking networks (Ó Riagain and Ó Gliasáin M. 1979: 103–5). The majority of parents — especially mothers — meet most of their Irish-speaking friends through the school. However, in Dublin, the possibility exists

132

for children to pass on into an all-Irish secondary system. This opportunity is not available in Northern Ireland. Until it does exist, it is all the more important for families to be able to continue social interaction with other Irish speakers while becoming less reliant on the primary school context.

The social contexts where families (particularly parents) use Irish outside the home may be divided into three categories:

(a) Irish learning activities.
(b) Activities associated directly with the Bunscoil.
(c) Other general social activities outside the home where Irish is spoken.

Learning Activities

It has already been shown that parents' command of Irish improved considerably after the first child began at the Bunscoil. Motivation to acquire some familiarity with the language is obviously high. Indeed, 90% of mothers and 78% of fathers made some attempt to learn Irish during their adult years.

Before the first child was attending the school, 40% of parents were attending language classes. Some of these people were also inspired to acquire the language in order to prepare themselves for the children's future bilingualisation. Once the first child begins school, there is a greater attendance at Irish classes by mothers (82%) than by fathers (64%). In fact, mothers participate more in learning activities generally than the fathers tend to do. This fact may partly reflect the fathers' higher competence levels in the first instance. However, it is also demonstrative of the greater sense of urgency which is attached to the mothers' familiarisation with the language and support for the child. The only exception to this overall pattern concerns those people who learned some Irish in prison. Only four mothers had learned Irish in prison, whereas 27% of the fathers had learnt some Irish in Long Kesh. (It should be noted that these prison terms were related to the particular political situation of Northern Ireland, including internment without trial.) This exception should not obscure the overall pattern whereby mothers become somewhat more involved than fathers in language learning activities once their children begin school.

The language classes attended by parents are usually held in local social and community centres. Some people had attended crash courses in Irish; generally, however, this type of course proved less popular because of expense. It was also more difficult to attend a class four or five nights a week and to keep up with study demands. Generally, people felt most comfortable about informal methods of learning the language. Usually, these methods were pursued in the individual's home. Nevertheless, it is more appropriate to refer to them within the present context. Over one third of the population had tried to teach them-selves the language at home, by listening to tapes and following books. Even more people had spent some time trying to learn the language from a friend, since their first child commenced the Bunscoil. This type of learning situation eliminated the inhibitions and fears which many people experience in more pub-lic situations, such as formal classes. Many individuals (mostly mothers) men-tioned their unease in that particular social context. Despite the fact that they did attend an Irish class, these people were diffident about their ability to acquire the language and dreaded being asked a question in the class. On two occasions the interview with parents happened to be arranged just before the parents' Irish class. On one of these occasions other adults arrived at the house, for a rota sys-tem was worked whereby the class was held in the participants' homes. In the other case, the parents left, after the interview, to visit a neighbour's house for the class. Such classes are more intimate and private than night classes held in clubs or schools.

The learning situation which proved most popular with parents involved the immediate family. Most people acquired some Irish by questioning and listening to their Bunscoil child. Mothers, in particular, picked up a fair amount of Irish from the children. They felt happy about asking the child to translate or explain a word or phrase. They also felt quite at home about being corrected by the child. We have already seen that many children pass through periods of impa-tience and intolerance regarding their parents' efforts to encourage the use of Irish. However, these phases are transitory. The sense of ease which many par-ents expressed about using Irish with their children and learning some Irish from them hinges upon the informal intimacy characteristic of the family situation.

The participation of parents in this spectrum of learning activities is illus-trated in Table 7. This table shows the extent to which parents participated more in learning activities once their first child had begun at the Bunscoil. It also highlights the most popular methods of acquiring Irish. The 'Irish class' is undoubtedly the most effective all-round means of learning the language which the parents consciously employed. Although many parents were most comfort-able about picking up the language from their children, this process occurred naturally and casually rather than as a part of a systematic learning programme. It was useful as a support to other efforts rather than as a conscious means of acquiring the language. It was irrelevant to consider information volunteered about prison-learnt Irish in terms of 'before' and 'after' the children had begun attending the Bunscoil. A few fathers were still in prison at the time of the sur-vey. All of the mothers were present at the interview.

Of course, attendance at classes or the act of following a self-instruction programme or, indeed, participation in the other learning activities cannot

TABLE 7 *Irish-learning activities of parents*

| Learning sources | Mothers | | Fathers | |
	Before (%)	After (%)	Before (%)	After (%)
Self-learning	16	45	18	40
Irish class	43	82	48	63
Crash course	4	17	7	11
Social functions	29	80	31	75
Friend	31	54	25	45
Bunscoil child	—	98	—	82
Prison	4	—	- 27 -	

always be equated with usage of Irish. Nevertheless, they do represent examples of occasions where contact with the language is thought to be of benefit to the parents' efforts to learn Irish. The degree and type of contact with Irish may range from simply being in the company of others who are using Irish, to a more active participation in drills or to practising the language during casual conversation.

Parents were asked about the type of facility which they thought would be of most assistance to their efforts to learn Irish. It was evident from the responses that most people perceive their learning objectives from the specific viewpoint of Bunscoil parents rather than from the more general perspective of learner. The most popular facility which would be appreciated by parents was a class which concentrated on school terminology. Irish language classes usually aim to cultivate a basic linguistic repertoire which will equip the learner to participate in conversation and to use the language in a variety of situations. However, Bunscoil parents feel the need of a class which would help them to become familiar with the language and specific terminology which their children are acquiring at school. This type of resource was ranked as a first preference. Some people explained that, as their children learn to handle specific concepts in Irish first, they find difficulty assisting the child by reinforcing these concepts when he is first introduced to them. One father referred to the fact that the child had begun to work with fractions and was, as yet, unclear about the subject. He suspected that he was perhaps confusing the child further during his endeavours to explain the concept in English because he was using terminology which the child was not yet accustomed to using. He felt a little frustrated by this situation. By the time the child was familiar with the usage of English terms, he would probably have overcome his early problems with the concept itself. Parents were most interested in gaining some familiarity with the fundamental terminology which their children were acquiring and using. The idea of arriving at that point by persevering at general language classes until they would be competent enough to handle most subjects through Irish, including subjects which their children explore, seemed unrealistic to many people. The short-term goals of assisting children with homework and discussing school matters with the child through Irish appeared to have a more immediate attraction than the possibility of becoming generally proficient in the language.

The aspirations of general fluency were reflected in the resource which was ranked as second in position of potential value. Parents felt that they would benefit from some support to their learning activities in the form of social occasions where they could practise Irish in accordance with their own limitations. The facility which was rated in third position was a class which focused on literacy skills in Irish. Once more, this choice demonstrates that parents were motivated towards the learning of Irish, principally, in order to be of assistance to their children's linguistic and educational progress.

The further participation of parents in learning activities, once the children begin attending the Bunscoil, augurs well for the bilingualisation of Bunscoil families. In addition, parents remained motivated towards further improvement of their competence levels. Both in the home and outside the home, the usage of Irish had been increased within the network of families. It may seem strange, therefore, that the parents' confidence about further improvement to their Irish was weak. Fathers were somewhat more optimistic than mothers about their language-learning endeavours. Almost one third of mothers and one half of fathers estimated that they will become quite fluent in the Irish language, without encountering any serious obstacles. However, that leaves a substantial amount of people who lack conviction about the likelihood of further progress. Indeed, almost one half of the mothers stated explicitly that they doubted that their future efforts to learn Irish would be successful, despite the fact that they sincerely desired to acquire Irish. These people felt intuitively that they had reached, or neared, a peak in their own achievement levels. That fact would suggest that their motivation to improve needed reinforcement. Practical support aimed at facilitating further advancement would also be required.

The overall pattern of results suggested that the widespread shift towards family bilingualism had made a dramatic development but had reached a plateau in that progress. The fact that many of the parents lacked confidence about their ability to significantly improve their Irish further was related to their usage of the language. The majority of fathers, who do not expect any serious obstacles to impede their acquisition of Irish, use a considerable amount of Irish with their own children. Conversely, only 17% of those who hope to learn more Irish, but who doubt their ability to do so, use the language frequently with the children. Motivation and encouragement of the fathers would most likely benefit the degree of bilingualism developed among family members. The results for mothers were not as significant as those for fathers. A high percentage of confident mothers use Irish frequently with the children. However, over 40% of the less confident mothers also use a considerable amount of Irish with their children. This fact reflects the sense of ease which mothers experience about using Irish with their children rather than in any other situation. Nevertheless, the relationship between confidence and usage remains valid and significant. In a more general sense, parents who believe that their endeavours to learn Irish will not be hindered by any serious obstacles tend to increase the usage of Irish with their children to a greater degree than those parents who express a less determined attitude.

Activities Associated Directly with the Bunscoil

The early years of struggle to keep the Bunscoil open and to develop its physical layout and educational objectives necessitated the complete dedication and co-operation of parents. Shaw's Road parents were committed to the maintenance and flourishing growth of their school as one fundamental dimension to their Community. This required much more than regular attendance at meetings — energetic campaigning to win official support and unending fund-raising initiatives to meet the financial demands which swelled as the school intake rose. It also demanded a willingness to take one's turn at the more laborious tasks, such as sticking translations on English textbooks, carrying out repairs to the schoolrooms or cleaning out the classrooms and toilets. These jobs had to be done. Only parents were available to carry them out.

When the fieldwork for this book was begun, the Bunscoil was funded by families and friends. The fund-raising campaign constituted a vital dimension to the parents' relationship with the school. Today, the Educational Authorities accept much of the responsibility for school maintenance and also finance the staff's salaries. Some of the parents themselves are employed to carry out particular duties. Fund-raising schemes continue to draw parents' support, although the rigorous financial commitments of the early years have been relieved somewhat. The management of the school changed dramatically once official maintained status was awarded, bringing it into line with English-medium primary schools. The nature and degree of parental involvement also changed at this point. A more formal system of organisation was introduced to cope with the rising intake numbers and larger classes. At the time of the survey administration, parents perceived advantages and disadvantages in relation to their responsibilities towards the school. Attendance at meetings and fund-raising duties were inconvenient. On the other hand, they created a bond between the families of Bunscoil children as well as between parents and the school.

Participation in school-related activities is particularly important because of the extent to which parents and children associate the language with the school. At the time of the survey administration at least one of the parents in most households did play a part in some of these activities. About one third had helped out for a while in the nursery school, when it relied more on voluntary help. Even more people had assisted with the preparation of teaching aids. Over one quarter of the population had helped out in some other way, such as doing repairs, cleaning, fitting shelves, etc. Almost all the parents had attended fund-raising events in aid of the school. Indeed, most had also helped organise these functions at some time. The school's dependence upon parental support for financial backing and practical assistance with maintenance determined the nature of parental participation in school life. Naturally, this role has changed as the school expanded, with both advantages and disadvantages associated with that development.

Apart from these various occasions when parents assist with some aspect of the school's maintenance, they also convene there, on a regular basis, to leave and collect their children. Mothers tend, generally, to be more frequent visitors to the school than fathers, whether picking up the children or attending meetings with teachers or other parents. One quarter had also attended some of the weekly language classes which were then held in the school. In addition, the majority of parents interact socially with other Bunscoil parents at least once every couple of months.

When the Bunscoil was a small community school Irish was the normal language to be heard among parents and visitors. However, once the school formally opened its doors to families from surrounding districts who did not speak Irish, then English was introduced at meetings etc. Today, most parents make an effort to use some Irish in the school. However, committee meetings and appointments with teachers tend to be conducted through English with people who are not fluent. In fact, 79% of mothers and 73% of fathers speak English when communicating with the teacher. Many of the parents qualified their responses to these language usage questions by expressing a general diffidence about employing the Irish which they did command with people whom they knew to be fluent speakers. They also expressed fears about misunderstanding the teacher or committee member if they introduced some Irish into the conversation.

Once more, it is evident that the degree of formality influences language behaviour. Official Bunscoil business, concerning parents, tends to be conducted through English. On the other hand the more informal situations, such as when the mother addresses the child or is attending certain social functions, generate a greater sense of ease about Irish usage. More than one parent commented that his fluency in Irish improved notably after a pint or two! At the time of the survey administration, several parents commented upon the fact that they found the Bunscoil to be more informal than schools normally tend to be. They felt happy about 'dropping in' to see the teacher without formal appointments and about spending time — when they had time to spare — in the school. However, the school environment does, nevertheless, create a formal social context. As it grows in size that intimate familiar quality, which parents appreciate, gives way to a more formal system of efficient management.

Parents would like to feel competent and confident enough to use the everyday school language within that social context. It is quite common for parents and visitors to begin a discourse with school staff by apologising for their lack of mastery of Irish. Many people, who have some command of the language, are unwilling to enter into a conversation through Irish in the school because they fear that the conversation may 'get out of control', i.e. pass beyond their comprehension levels.

Other General Social Activities where Irish is Spoken or Heard

Other social events where Irish was spoken or heard included the Irish-medium Sunday Mass. After the children begin at the Bunscoil some of the parents become regular participants in the Irish Mass while others visit on an irregular basis. Social functions such as dramas, festivals, and Irish language quizzes are attended with much less frequency than other events associated with the school. Over half of the families send their children to learn Irish dancing. Irish is spoken at some of these classes. Otherwise, parents referred to events such as *ceilithe* and *oícheanta airneáil* (evenings of Irish music and dance), the proceeds of which often went to the school.

The usage of Irish outside the home was usually related to the child's attendance at the Bunscoil. Parents' determination to support their children's educational and cultural development is the central motivating force which generates a shift towards bilingualism of varying degrees. This phenomenon is further facilitated as networks of Irish speakers and learners build up. We have seen that parents do interact socially with each other on a fairly frequent basis. However, the social networks extend beyond the Bunscoil families. Parents' social circles tend to include other friends and relatives, unconnected with the school, who speak some Irish. Only one respondent did not have at least one Irish-speaking friend. Eighty-two per cent of the population stated that their circle of Irish-speaking friends widened once their first child began at the school. Parents speak more Irish with these friends than they do in the formal school-related situations. Approximately half of the respondents use a little Irish with these friends. Over 40% use the language more often than that. The frequency of social interaction among these people is high; most meet and chat at least once weekly.

Norms Governing Use of Irish.

The willingness of parents and children to use Irish depends upon a complex of factors. We have already examined that phase which many children pass through when they are reluctant to use Irish with one or both parents. Adults are also influenced by the social situation and by the degree of fluency which the interlocutor commands. Mothers interviewed usually felt most comfortable about using Irish in casual familiar settings, particularly with the children. An entire spectrum of social and personal inhibitions affect the language behavioural patterns of the learner (see Figure 18). A full understanding of these factors is especially significant in urban centres like Belfast where Irish is very much the language of the learner.

Over one third of mothers said that they would only venture to use some Irish in certain places — usually the respondent's home. These mothers felt less vulnerable to embarrassment within the family setting. They had no objections to making mistakes when speaking some Irish with their children nor to expressing their confusion to family members. They also felt that they had greater control over the direction of the conversation within that familiar context. However, the prospect of asking questions and making mistakes in the classroom situation was extremely daunting. These adults had not come to terms with the fact that the successful learner of a second language is, at best, prepared to 'make a fool' of himself, or at least to wade through that phase of practising the language while in an imperfect or limited form.

The presence of non-Irish speakers in the general company causes approximately one third of the mothers to choose not to speak Irish. These respondents consider it discourteous to use Irish in this situation. Most respondents, however, are not discouraged from using Irish when non-Irish speakers are present in the group. Most of these people believe that it is socially acceptable to converse with one or two members of a group in Irish and to expect the others to listen or to communicate with each other in English. The significance of this point was highlighted in the CLAR Report (1975).

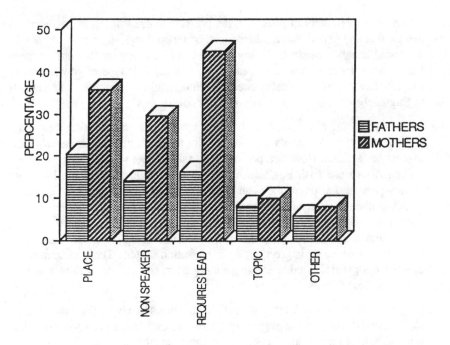

FIGURE 18 *Influence of social constraints on parents' use of Irish.*

Irish is a language which is very much on the defensive against the forces and influences of the dominant language in society. Its position is threatened in every respect:
— as a mother tongue in rural Gaeltacht areas
— as a mother tongue in the neo-Gaeltacht community at Shaw's Road
— as a growing component of incipient bilingualism, generated principally by Irish-medium nursery and primary education
— as the language of learners, many of whom desire to become active bilinguals.

In view of these pressures, the Irish language ought not to be exposed to the same code of social influences which normally operate. Survival cannot be jeopardised for the sake of common courtesy. Therefore, it follows that, regarding the language behaviour of the learner, social restraints should be dispensed with, as far as possible, and the learner given every encouragement to use his Irish at every opportunity. This is not a simple blanket statement. Learners can be discouraged and intimidated by a situation where some parties are conversing fluently in Irish. Yet, the pressure to use English in Belfast is so intense that any opportunities where it can be resisted should be grasped. Within the social contexts where Irish may be used, it often happens that one or more people are present who do not speak the language. This type of situation is so frequent that it would inevitably check the bilingualisation process should a shift to English be considered necessary in that context.

Other factors also inhibit the parents' sense of ease about using their Irish. Of course, proficiency levels exercise a major influence upon the speaker's willingness to use Irish. However, parents were asked about limited usage, i.e. their willingness to use Irish in situations where they could avail of the linguistic store which, at that point, they had built up. The dominant factor which influenced mothers' usage of Irish concerned the introduction of Irish into a discourse or conversation. Almost half of these people would use some Irish if the other speaker introduced it. However, they would not initiate a conversation in Irish, nor introduce it via greetings or conversation starters. These same mothers expressed a general timidity about speaking Irish, particularly with people who were not close friends or relatives.

The factor which least governed language choice was the conversation topic. This was somewhat surprising, given the fact that so many parents had rated a 'school terminology' class as the most valuable method of encouraging their progress. Nevertheless, the conversation subject was not considered to be a main factor which curbed the speaker's willingness to use Irish. Some respondents commented that they would just introduce loanwords or switch to English if they were not comfortable about the topic in Irish.

As mentioned, mothers were more susceptible to the strains of these personal and social norms than fathers. More fathers than mothers were prepared to use some Irish in any situation — over one half of the fathers and under one third of the mothers. The difference between male and female responses to this group of questions was generally considerable. For example, over twice as many mothers as fathers expressed a need for the other speakers to introduce some Irish before they would use any. This timidity adds to the sociolinguistic profile of the mothers which emerged, showing them to be less confident learners and users of Irish than their husbands. Mothers were less optimistic about the prospect of reaching proficiency and more inhibited about the use of Irish. Although their participation in learning activities had generally increased more than their partners' and their motivation for learning was greater, they reported lower competence levels. In addition, the percentage of women who expressed a desire to become proficient speakers and who doubted their ability to do so was striking. Susceptibility to social inhibitions emerged as one major factor which contributed to this situation.

The significance of these social norms is also related to the role which parents play in the introduction of active bilingualism into the home. The language behaviour of the Irish-speaking child is influenced by his parents' attitudes to the use of the language in social situations. Although the bilingualisation process depends much upon the parents, it often extends to other family relatives and friends. The Bunscoil child also triggers a greater tendency to acquire some Irish among siblings and social contacts. When the eldest child is attending the Bunscoil, younger pre-school siblings pick up a little Irish in 90% of households. Sometimes they become familiar with the Irish songs and verses which the young Bunscoil child is learning. Parents also tend to use some phrases and simple conversational terms with the infants. In those cases where older children had not attended the Bunscoil, 60% of them acquire some command of the language once the younger child begins the Irish school.

Many people are impressed and charmed when they hear a young child speaking Irish. About 40% of the respondents said that at least one relative, outside the immediate family, had begun to attend Irish classes when their child began at the school. Similarly, half of the parents knew some friend or friends who had taken this step. The social network of the Bunscoil families usually embraced other learners, once the connection with the school was established.

In some ways, the relationship between Bunscoil attendance and the diffusion of bilingualism is obvious. One example concerns the younger siblings. All of these parents intend to send the younger children to the Irish-medium nursery and primary school in the future. Some were already enrolled at the school and attending the nursery. This fact clearly motivated parents to introduce some Irish to the younger members of the family. Other cases could be more ambivalent as the relative or friend may have become interested in the language anyway, inspired by the same factors as other learners (Ó hAdhmaill, 1985). Parents were therefore asked to gauge to what extent some of these acquaintances were influenced by their children's acquisition of Irish at primary school. One quarter of this population considered that other factors had motivated their friends or relatives to begin learning Irish. Some had been persuaded to do so by other Irish-speaking friends; some had decided to send their own children to the Bunscoil in the future and were preparing themselves for this step; other people were simply responding to the general climate of Irish Revival. However, over one half of the population believed that the fact that the respondent's children were at the Irish school had constituted a major influence upon their friends' or relatives' decision to learn some Irish themselves. In some cases that belief was based upon direct comments made by the learners expressing their sense of shame and inadequacy when they heard young children conversing in Irish while they could not communicate at all in that language. The rest of the parents considered that a

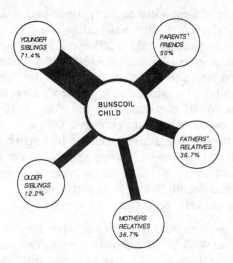

FIGURE 19 *Language diffusion diagram.*

combination of factors were in operation, including their child's attendance at the school. (See Figure 19.)

We have already referred to the fact that the children's usage of Irish outside school is related to their parent's attitudes towards the use of Irish. This fact merits consideration within the framework of planning a back-up service for parents. Indeed, much of the data derived from the study would be valuable within such a context. Often, it is the interrelationship of various facts which is most interesting. As one might expect, for example, language usage patterns were connected to parents' vulnerability to social norms. Whereas one fifth of mothers who speak only a little Irish with their Irish-speaking friends stated that they are generally free from such restraints and are content to use their Irish in any situation, this same view was expressed by twice as many mothers who do actually use a considerable amount of Irish with these social contacts. Similarly, in the case of fathers, a high percentage of those who were accustomed to using some Irish with friends showed a greater resistance to social and personal restraints than those who used little or no Irish. Competence levels were also related to the parents' susceptibility to these norms. The more proficient the individual is, the more likely he or she is to resist these social pressures. On the other hand, no significant relationship was found to exist between susceptibility to these pressures and the individual's confidence about further improving his or her Irish. Fathers, as

we have seen, were less likely to be influenced by considerations such as, who
initiated the conversation in Irish; where the conversation took place; whether
non-Irish speakers were present, etc. However, most mothers stated that their
willingness to use Irish was inhibited by such factors — regardless of which
attitude they expressed about the possibility of improving their Irish.

Clearly, parents who manage to reach high levels of competence in Irish
are happier about using the language with their Irish-speaking friends. Greater
mastery of the language also exercises some control over the speaker's
resistance to social pressures. However, it is equally certain that proficiency
will only improve with practice and that the range and quantity of that
practice is restrained by those same pressures. Even the most optimistic and
hopeful learners are subject to these influences. Their usage of Irish is
restricted by them, thereby reducing the likelihood of further improvement.
The importance of educating the learner about using his or her Irish and
equipping him or her to be able to handle the pressures upon the aspiring
bilingual gains weight and credence.

Another valid point, pertinent to these findings, received some attention in
the CLAR Report. Not only is practical support needed by the learner, but the
more proficient speakers of the language must also be taught to accept the
'novice' speaker's efforts and, at the same time, to respect and encourage them.
The learners' fears about being perceived as foolish, or about suffering embarrassment if the conversation passes beyond the level of their linguistic repertoire, could be eased and ameliorated somewhat by a positive, encouraging
approach on the part of the fluent speaker.

Conversely, the inhibitions of the learner can distort his perception of the
fluent speaker's attitudes towards him. A couple of the parents made references,
during the interviews, to their impressions about the Irish-speaking families at
Shaw's Road or to other fluent speakers. Although their admiration was evident,
they also interpreted their language behaviour as a little exclusive. One parent
referred to some fluent speakers as displaying a 'snobbish' attitude towards the
use of Irish. These parents dreaded the inevitable penetration of mistakes into
their Irish during those early learning stages, fearing mostly the reaction of
others. They were not personally familiar with the Irish speakers concerned.
However, they had heard them discussing or conversing freely in Irish with
other people, or perhaps had encountered them in a more authoratative role
when they were organising some function. Undoubtedly, this criticism is valid in
some cases. However, I found it particularly interesting that the Irish-speaking
families of Shaw's Road were drawn into this generalisation. As people who
learned the language in adulthood themselves and experienced the same learning
difficulties as these parents, many of the Shaw's Road families have made

considerable personal sacrifices to help and support the learning activities of others. Several of them provided series of language classes in their homes, another lady gives an adult dancing class for Irish speakers and learners. Other members have implemented countless schemes and initiatives aimed at promoting the language throughout the wider Belfast population. Yet, it is understandable that the timid learner, unfamiliar with these facts, could misinterpret the fluent speakers' attitudes.

This reaction to the language behaviour of fluent speakers is of further interest, in light of the suggestion that learners should be taught to use their Irish at every possible opportunity. If such a code of social values became more widely accepted then the possibility of this type of misinterpretation would be reduced. At present, this dimension of the diffusion of Irish is missing from adult teaching programmes generally. Much work remains to be done in the area of adult education in order to overcome these restraints upon language usage.

This chapter describes a further dimension to the pattern of bilingualisation which is consistent with other aspects discussed in previous chapters. The diffusion of Irish, generated by connection with the Bunscoil, is extensive throughout the associated families. Its usage is strongly related to school events and situations. Still, it spreads beyond the immediate family, with other relatives and family friends being inspired to learn the language. Once the family has a child at the Bunscoil, family members also use more Irish outside the home. Some people become fluent and regular speakers of the language. The majority, though, seem to falter in their progress, once a certain level of achievement is attained. As in the case of competence levels, usage patterns show a fair increase across the entire population; however, the increase stops short of balanced bilingualism. Nevertheless, the degree of progress achieved by parents on their own initiative, without any substantial support or official assistance, must encourage other communities, elsewhere in the world, which share a similar aspiration. This shift, in West Belfast, has been realised from a state of monolingualism towards a stage where the language has taken root within the family units themselves. The children are the vehicle and the hope; they open the door to the use of Irish. Parents' sacrifices are carried out with the next generation in mind. The bilingualisation process remains, for most adults, at the 'practice' stage; the learner takes advantage of opportunities to practise the language, and his network of Irish-speaking friends is mainly composed of fellow learners. His endeavours to facilitate further usage of Irish are made on behalf of the children. They are given access to Irish, as a functional and natural medium, within at least one major social environment. The parents do not, generally, have a real grasp on the same goals for themselves and their peers. If they can be persuaded of the benefits of moving some distance towards those goals, that 'plateau' stage could be left behind with greater ease. Parents do tend to desire more for their children than they have themselves. Much of the Irish usage outside the home is, accordingly, generated by that parental instinct — for example, the learning activities of the parents. However, having made considerable successful efforts to learn and use the language, during the early years of the child's attendance at the Bunscoil, progress wanes. The overall diffusion of Irish outside the home reflects a similar pattern. The establishment of networks of Irish speakers, mainly connected with the school, is extensive. Practical support is required to facilitate members to bridge that gap between basic, simple conversation in Irish, and everyday interaction in Irish without demanding any arduous, conscious effort. Furthermore, that process should incorporate the communication of a social code, equipping learners and fluent speakers with the freedom to avail of every possible opportunity to use and enjoy using Irish.

10 The Irish of Belfast: Parents' View

The early chapters of this book described the emergence of an Irish-speaking community in an environment where cultural independence was neither encouraged nor favoured. Those chapters dealing with the dynamic diffusion of Irish throughout the wider population of West Belfast provide insights into the strong feeling of loyalty to the Irish language which guides that development. This growth of Irish as a spoken medium is not confined to West Belfast; Derry, Newry, Downpatrick and other towns and cities of the North display a keen interest in grasping any chance to establish access to the language and to promote its use. However, West Belfast represents a concentrated force in this thirst for self and community expression of 'Irishness'. One senses that, there, Irish has established its roots and will continue to thrive. Or, is it, perhaps, that it must continue to thrive? In an area where so many have suffered harsh blows in recent decades, the propagation of Irish offers a sign of hope. Some good flourishes amidst so much pain. The Irish language will not be allowed to fade away, for lethargy is not a problem in this community.

Later chapters went on to explore the actual phenomenon of bilingualisation as it emerged among families and friends of Bunscoil children. The establishment of an Irish-speaking community in Belfast opened a door to other families who wished to introduce Irish into their homes. Irish-medium education offered them this possibility, along with the virtual guarantee that their children would become competent Irish speakers with relative ease.

Chapters 8 and 9 examined the usage of Irish in the homes and outside the homes of Bunscoil families. Evidently, the attendance of a child at the Bunscoil acts as a powerful motivating factor in the increased usage of Irish. Some shift towards active bilingualism was found to be occurring in every home visited. The nature of this shift was limited in many cases. Nevertheless, the achievement involved is quite remarkable regarding three specific aspects of the situation: (a) the extensiveness of the bilingualisation process throughout the school community; (b) the degree of bilingualism reached, given the general monolingual state of the families only a few years previously; and (c) the weight of factors compelling exposure to English and discouraging the use of Irish.

The story of Irish in West Belfast, and in other places in Northern Ireland, is a success story. Against so many odds, an Irish-speaking community created the social and educational conditions in which it could survive and grow. Incipient bilingualism bubbles with energy and determination. The Shaw's Road initiative has generated much of this energy and was proven to bear constructive, positive results. As the learning of Irish spreads and the possibility of using the language pervades more and more social domains, it becomes pertinent to raise the question of the type or variety of Irish which is emerging.

Three main dialects of Irish are spoken in Ireland. Learners of Irish tend to approximate, as far as possible, the dialect spoken in the nearest traditional Gaeltacht. Belfast learners base their Irish on the Ulster dialect; Irish-speaking pockets in the Six Counties lasted into the twentieth century. However, the remaining stronghold where Ulster Irish survives as an unbroken tradition is in County Donegal. Visits to the Donegal Gaeltacht are encouraged in those secondary schools throughout the North which teach Irish. Many Irish teachers from the Six Counties also spend a month or two of the summer teaching in one of the Irish Colleges in Donegal. In third level Irish language courses, annual field trips to the Gaeltachts usually constitute a compulsory feature of course work. The aim of these visits is to improve the students' command of the spoken language and to awaken an appreciation of the rich linguistic reservoir which has not yet faded away among older native speakers. Some of Belfast's older Irish speakers, interviewed in relation to their own endeavours to raise children with Irish in the city, recounted tales of their own visits to the Gaeltacht during their earlier days as young Irish learners. The value placed by these people upon visiting the Gaeltacht and, in a broader sense, upon campaigning for the preservation of traditional Gaeltacht has already been discussed. Indeed, some of Belfast's Irish-speaking families went to live in the Donegal Gaeltacht, including one of the founder members of the Shaw's Road Community.

Cultural organisations, such as Comhaltas Uladh and the Gaelic Athletic Association, encourage young people to spend time in the Gaeltacht by offering them scholarships to Irish Colleges. One of the main motivations for this work has been in providing the student with the chance to 'practise' his Irish. This opportunity was especially important during those years when teaching methods were guided by a grammatical approach which did not lay emphasis on situational use of the language. In order to 'use' the language in natural surroundings, the learner had go to the Gaeltacht where it was the normal medium of communication. As the language flourishes in Belfast, the sharpness of these distinctive roles fades. The association of urban learning centres solely with the study of

Irish and of rural Gaeltachts with the practice and use of that language becomes weaker. The creation of an urban Gaeltacht Community at Shaw's Road presented second language learners with conclusive evidence of the functional relevance of the Irish language in a modern urban setting. Irish-medium education offered the public easy access to the city's Irish-speaking community and the world of active bilingualism. Children who use the Irish language as a medium of communication at school, at Sunday Mass, in the home or on certain social occasions are acquiring a sense of the language's value in everyday life. Gaeltacht trips add one further dimension to that range. However, they no longer represent the main means of using the language as a communicative tool during everyday interactions.

Within academic circles, immersion in the traditional Gaeltacht is still encouraged among students of the language. Indeed, many students view this as the most enjoyable aspect of course requirements. The practical considerations concerned are, of course, reasonable. Grants and travel expenses are provided for a limited number of visits. Most of the students have few arrangements to make concerning the trips. These visits offer students the opportunity to speak Irish with native speakers as opposed to communicating exclusively with learners and second language speakers.

In Irish, a standard spoken dialect does not exist, although considerable work has gone into the development of a written standard. Therefore, the learner can check any grammatical or lexical feature, about which he is uncertain, with relative ease, by consulting a grammar book or dictionary. The native sound system of Irish, in many ways, poses a greater challenge. The most efficient and successful way to master the phonological system is by spending as much time as possible in the company of native speakers. Apart from this advantage, the rich reserve of idiom in the Irish of some native speakers is more easily appreciated and tapped during discourse with the speaker. Insights into the potential flexibility of the language are also gained in this way. Other practices such as extensive reading and listening to recorded materials reinforce the learners' efforts. Essentially it is the linguistic values associated with tuning in to the Irish of native speakers more than the functional value of practising the spoken language in real-life, natural situations, which attracts the student of Irish to frequent the Gaeltacht. Oral proficiency in the language can be advanced in this way. As rural traditional Gaeltacht communities continue to decline, the importance of using this source, from the learners' perspective, assumes a sense of urgency.

These values do not receive the same emphasis outside academic settings. Other objectives operate at higher levels on the scale of priorities. Concerns about the qualitative nature of the language, as it settles and expands among urban communities, are much less immediate than the need to firmly establish and fortify that pattern of bilingualisation and to promote usage of the language as it is acquired. As the popular Language Movement emerges, the variety of Irish being spoken remains of secondary importance to the fact that it *is* being spoken. Strategies for encouraging a propensity to use the language in basic everyday interactions take precedence. Previous chapters examined the correlation between linguistic competence and patterns of usage. However, the picture of language behaviour was much more complex than that and a range of other factors influenced the usage of Irish among Bunscoil families.

This fact is identified and discussed in a report on current language-related issues in the Twenty-Six Counties (Coiste Comhairleach Pleanála, 1986: XXXVIII–XL):

> State policies in the past tended to concentrate more on generating *competence* (e.g. through the schools) than in maintaining the climate within which bilingual *behaviour* could be generated and sustained (e.g. in the public service) ... It appears to be at the level of usage that the most intensive policy efforts are now needed. To say this is of course not to suggest that continued efforts to improve proficiency are no longer important, or that policies for Irish should concentrate in future on providing services only for existing user groups. As we have seen, the patterning of current usage in loose and changing social networks depends upon the existence in the population of a much larger pool of bilingual competence from which these networks can draw. But the converse of this point also needs to be stated: it seems increasingly likely that unless more people use Irish in their daily lives there will be a serious decline in the numbers of the population who see any point in acquiring facility in the language.

The Irish language enthusiasts and the population of learners in Belfast are primarily concerned about the need to swell the overall input of Irish in a spectrum of domains, to increase the numbers of those who participate in the wider Irish-speaking community, either as beginners or as more competent speakers. Plans for enriching the quality of the language in the city and for maintaining some proximity to the variety of Irish spoken in traditional Gaeltacht districts have not been considered on any satisfactory scale. Energies focus upon generating and sustaining the momentum of interest in the language at community level. Creating more extensive facilities for learners receives attention and the provision of Irish-medium educational facilities for children spearheads the current development. The idea of examining and monitoring linguistic changes in this eruption of urban Irish is generally perceived, as yet, to be of a lesser priority.

People favouring Irish, or actively participating in the shift towards bilingualism, are far from complacent or nonchalant about the standard of competence which they achieve, or to which they aspire. At the same time, among the growing population of learners and, indeed, among others who place value upon the language, the most important signs of progress are derived from seeing the language being used naturally in more situations and by more people. The fact that two people exchange greetings in Irish or carry out some negotiation through Irish — each understanding the other — carries more significance than the degree to which the quality of Irish used may be diluted by interference from English.

This value system is reinforced by another consideration — the limited nature of any resources for exercising control over the variety of Irish emerging in popular usage. The practical advantages enjoyed by third level students of Irish are not generally available to the average family man who is attending night classes in an effort to facilitate some introduction of Irish usage into his home. In many respects, Belfast is isolated from the rest of the country. From a geographical perspective, it is probably the most unlikely home of a neo-Gaeltacht community. Irish speakers in Derry, for example, have easy access to the Donegal Gaeltacht, in comparison with Belfast people. Access to Irish on the Southern-based media is insufficient to compensate for this lack of contact. Another factor which influences these restrictions is the low car ownership ratio in the city; West Belfast, in particular, has a lower level of car ownership than the average in the rest of the city, or within the wider UK context. Consequently, the idea of establishing regular contact with Irish speakers in other areas involves some expense and inconvenience. This isolation reduces the demands placed upon the communicative and linguistic flexibility of residents. As long as the language can function adequately, as a communicative tool, within that location the primary goals are met.

However, whether it is of primary or secondary importance, the variety of Irish emerging in Belfast, and in other urban centres, is inevitably shaped partly by such factors as:

— the degree of exposure to Irish achieved by learners and fluent speakers within social networks in the city
— the isolation of Belfast from other Irish-speaking areas
— attitudes which would ideally balance tolerance and encouragement of learners' efforts within the learning process with the pursuit of high linguistic standards

Unlike many other bilingual communities, Belfast's Irish speakers are using the language with others who have acquired it as a second language, or who are in the process of learning it. Elsewhere in the world, even in places where prowess in one of the relevant languages is flawed, either because the language is moribund or in other situations where it has not been completely mastered, it is, nevertheless, often used with native speakers. Nancy Dorian's account of the Gaelic spoken by East Sutherland's 'semi-speakers' is an example of the former (Dorian, 1981). An example of the 'nonfluent bilingual', within the latter context, can be found in Quebec where Francophones and Anglophones employ their second language during inter-group interactions with native speakers.

Sustained communication with native speakers does represent one way in which some checks can operate on the rate of linguistic diversity entering the nonfluent speakers' system. That check is not readily available to Belfast's Irish speakers. Meantime, the Language Revival in Belfast does not hold its breath, awaiting the introduction of promotional measures which could give direction to linguistic developments. Linguistic change and diversity is therefore, in itself, a healthy sign of a community's determination to sustain a brisk rate of growth and self-assertion in cultural terms. However, the degree of diversity being realised is an issue which deserves to be monitored and controlled. Contact with other Irish-speaking communities — in particular with native speakers — is one way of implementing such measures.

Chapter 12 will explore the nature of linguistic changes occurring in the Irish which is emerging in Belfast and discuss the implications of this phenomenon. Deviation from traditional standards is usually perceived as a sign of informality and casualness or as a flawed command of the language. In formal situations, in particular, the speaker is aware of the degree of 'correctness' which he maintains. This standard is usually based (either directly, or indirectly through the Irish of the classroom) upon the Irish of a native speaker. In many situations, therefore, deviations from the norms of native Irish can trigger feelings of inadequacy. This fact explains the mothers' sense of ease about practising Irish in the home, with their children. The speaker's evaluation of his own linguistic competence and language variety influence his self-esteem and confidence about using the language. In a situation where bilingualism is just emerging with remarkable vitality and resilience, the learners' impressions about the language are of considerable significance.

The survey which was administered to Bunscoil parents contained one section which addressed this issue. I felt it would be useful to probe the question of language variety with the parents. After all, not only were many of them learning the language, but their children were beginning to acquire and use Irish at three and four years of age. Did they form any impressions about the variety of Irish which was becoming the communicative norm? Had their contact with the Irish-medium school encouraged or influenced relationships with traditional Gaeltacht areas? In previous chapters, we saw that the families' exposure to Irish was usually associated with the Bunscoil, either directly or indirectly through learning activities. Did they consider this to be adequate, or was there a need for extended language contact with other Irish-speaking communities? Parents were not addressed as linguists. Yet, as the people giving momentum to the current bilingualisation drive, it was considered appropriate to consult them, in an informal manner, about this aspect of the ongoing language shift.

Questionnaire Results

Regarding visits to the Gaeltacht, it transpired that three-quarters of the population had rarely or never been to the Gaeltacht during the years before their children were at the all-Irish school. Several people were unsure about the term, 'Gaeltacht', associating it with a school-trip to Donegal. Once the children were attending the Bunscoil, visits to rural Gaeltacht areas showed no significant increase. Seventy-four per cent of mothers and 64% of fathers had not visited the Gaeltacht since the children began at the school. Some increase did occur in the number of older children who spent time in Gaeltacht districts, reflecting facilities at secondary school for organising summer vacations in Irish Colleges.

Among those people who did spend time in the Gaeltacht before their children were at the Bunscoil, half of them used some Irish while they were there. Of those who were at the Gaeltacht since that time, a further 30% were employing some Irish during the visit. Therefore, Gaeltacht visits were increasingly perceived as an opportunity to use and practise the language by those who did participate in them.

The majority of the population, who never or seldom visited the Gaeltacht, tended to be dissuaded from doing so by practical considerations. For example, financial restrictions was the main factor influencing 39% of the families. Almost one quarter of respondents had commitments to other places during spare time. Some had access to holiday homes elsewhere — perhaps owning a caravan. Almost another quarter of the population mentioned transport difficulties as a restricting factor. Parents were not suggesting that they would certainly have visited Gaeltacht areas if these problems had not existed, neither did they express any dissatisfaction about their situation. However, certain real difficulties did impede their mobility or their opportunities for contact with traditional Gaeltacht areas.

Other people cited non-practical reasons for their lack of contact with the Gaeltacht. These parents were simply unconvinced that visiting the Gaeltacht would assist their endeavours as Irish speakers or learners. Five of the families felt that no language-related advantages existed in traditional Gaeltacht areas which were not already available in Belfast. These people felt that they had access to language classes and to an Irish-speaking community in Belfast. They had no real desire to immerse themselves in another Irish-speaking community for the sake of the language.

It is interesting that 17% of the parents stated that they were discouraged from visiting the Gaeltacht by language obstacles. They were inhibited by their own lack of proficient Irish or by their difficulty in understanding native Donegal Irish. Some of these people had encountered native Gaeltacht Irish without actually visiting the Gaeltacht. They listened to Irish language output on Southern-based television and radio programmes, or had met native speakers who were staying in Belfast. Others had been to the Gaeltacht some years previously and had experienced problems understanding locals' Irish. A few parents referred to unfortunate experiences where locals had refused, or shown a reluctance, to speak Irish to them. This kind of experience is not uncommon in some places until the visitor is accepted in the community. The Irish of the visitor is, naturally, the language of the learner. Often, he is still reliant upon the classroom register and has not had the opportunity to familiarise himself with the range of skills and styles which the fluent or native speaker employs. Some degree of patience is needed to encourage the learner's attempts at using his Irish in these real situations — or at least not to discourage them. The initial comprehension difficulties can only be overcome as the learner improves his proficiency levels and communicative skills. Progress towards that stage is frequently impeded by social restraints which can become acute if the learner encounters a few embarrassing experiences when he does attempt to use his store of language, during those early social interactions. These types of situations can just as easily arise in the urban context as in rural Gaeltacht areas. In both localities there is an abundance of Irish speakers who inspire the learner's efforts, either because they have passed through the same stages themselves and sympathise with him, or because they have become accustomed to interacting with learners and respect their endeavours. However, a diffident adult learner can be discouraged from using Irish by one or two isolated incidents which deflate his self-confidence. Fortunately, most learners survive those early difficulties. However, in a language revival situation, every potential speaker counts. The fact that a few people were discouraged from pursuing their language learning activities in the Gaeltacht by this kind of experience is, therefore, worth mentioning.

This question arose during an RTE radio broadcast of a programme discussing the Irish language ('Live-line', 3/2/89). One of the debators referred to the need to cultivate 'language awareness' in Gaeltacht areas, pointing out that the difficulties faced by learners who are trying to be understood could be alleviated if local native speakers were enlightened about those difficulties and made aware of the importance of their own contribution to the Irish language.

The value of the language from other perspectives, not only cultural and educational but commercial as well, should also be developed alongside the development of an awareness of those values. Educational and cultural bodies as well as the state should carry that responsibility. It was thought that this building of language awareness would help the learner from outside to use and practise his Irish in the Gaeltacht with greater ease and confidence. These suggestions make considerable sense.

This subject of language variety arose in the early 1970s when Shaw's Road parents were mounting the first classroom on the Bunscoil site. They were faced with the task of finding and employing a suitable teacher for the school. The question of whether to appoint a native Donegal speaker or a local Irish teacher was not unanimously agreed, although it was never a major issue. Obviously, the presence of a native Gaeltacht speaker would ensure some input from Gaeltacht Irish. As we saw in an earlier chapter, the first teacher to be employed at the Bunscoil was, indeed, a Donegal Irish speaker. Thereafter, however, local teachers have always been appointed. (A native speaker from the Donegal Gaeltacht was appointed again in 1988. From the teachers' point of view, the presence of a native speaker is very much appreciated, on those numerous occasions when the latter can help clarify points of uncertainty concerning the language.) At the time of the survey administration, all of the teachers were Irish speakers from the Six Counties.

Survey results showed that only 10% of Bunscoil parents preferred their child to be taught by a teacher who was a native speaker from a traditional Gaeltacht. Over one half of the respondents expressed no preference about the teachers' backgrounds, 'as long as they're good teachers'. A few people mentioned that they thought a non-native speaker would have a sharper understanding of learning difficulties which they would probably have experienced themselves. Twenty-nine per cent of the parents would rather that their child was taught by someone from the locality, or elsewhere in Northern Ireland, who was reared with Irish at home. This choice demonstrates a loyalty to neighbouring areas more than a consideration of language-related factors. The findings also illustrate that only a small percentage of the parents placed a high value upon the language background of the teachers. The dedication and competence of teachers were clearly issues which they had taken into consideration. However, the choice between a native speaker from the Gaeltacht, a local person raised with Irish and a teacher who spoke Irish as a second language, did not evoke any strong response.

During interviews, the subject of language variety was discussed with those parents who felt that they had formed any opinions about Belfast Irish or Gaeltacht Irish, from the perspectives of learners and Bunscoil parents. Previous questions had prepared respondents for this more open-ended type of question. Nevertheless some 32% still felt that they had nothing to say on the subject because they were unfamiliar with native Gaeltacht Irish. To these people, the salient fact was that 'it is all Irish'. They did not know, nor did it seem relevant to them, whether any linguistic variations existed between the two.

The rest of the population had some comments to make about this subject. Seventeen per cent of these parents believed that a separate, unique variety of Irish was emerging in Belfast. Most of the responses, though, strayed from the specific issue of language variety, although their comments still shed some light upon the respondents' perceptions of the language. About half of those who answered the question believed that the striking difference between the two varieties of Irish was that Belfast Irish was easier to understand than Donegal Irish. Three respondents believed that Belfast Irish was more 'correct' than Gaeltacht Irish. These three families were regular and consistent visitors to the Donegal Gaeltacht. They expanded upon their comments with references to the degree to which English had entered the Irish being spoken in those areas which they had visited. Obviously, they still thought it worthwhile maintaining their relationship with the Gaeltacht. However, 26% considered that Belfast Irish was less accurate than Donegal Irish. Usually, this comment was not made as a criticism. Indeed, considering that the 'less correct' or non-standard features of the Irish popularly spoken in Belfast are often those same elements which simplify the system and render it more easily managed by the learner, it is not surprising that this feature was not referred to disparagingly.

Twenty-three per cent stated that Belfast people were more enthusiastic about the language, some of whom suggested that this was because they had to strive to acquire the language. They thought that Belfast people probably appreciated their Irish more because of those difficulties which they had to tackle. In general, parents were expressing a strong sense of loyalty to the fact that Irish was thriving in Belfast. Even those parents who stated that the Irish being spoken in Belfast was less accurate than native Donegal Irish, sometimes added defensive comments about the Irish of Belfast. Love of the language superseded considerations about linguistic diversions from traditional Gaeltacht Irish. The latter could not be isolated and discussed. The fact that Irish was being acquired and being used during everyday interactions was so laden with meaning for these people that the question of which linguistic direction the emerging language followed could not be viewed outside that context and, so, waned to relative insignificance.

Bunscoil parents are not, generally, concerned about contact with the traditional Gaeltacht and the exposure of the emerging language in Belfast to the influence of native traditional Irish. Most people have no particular feelings

about the potential value of contact with Gaeltacht Irish. The frequency or infre-
quency with which the families visit the Gaeltacht is largely unconnected with
any social, economic or educational characteristics of the families. Rather, the
above responses were broadly shared across the population of parents, whatever
their background. The degree of contact with the Gaeltacht was examined in
relation to a spectrum of other factors in order to discern any possible patterns:
no striking correlations were found. For example, one might expect to find some
correlation between Gaeltacht visits and the following variables: (a) employment status of parents; (b) parents' attendance at Irish classes; (c) Irish studied
by parents at secondary school; (d) Irish studied at third level.

The fact that almost 40% of parents had mentioned pecuniary restrictions
as a reason for infrequent Gaeltacht visits would suggest that employment status
might be relevant. However, Gaeltacht visits were found to be unrelated to the
class of the fathers' employment, and indeed, to whether he was then employed
or unemployed. In the case of mothers, it was found that professional women
were more likely to visit the Gaeltacht. This is probably explained by the fact
that many of these women were teachers and, therefore, aware of Gaeltacht visits as an aspect of learning the language because of school visits to Irish
Colleges.

Nevertheless, having studied Irish at secondary school does not significantly increase the likelihood of Gaeltacht visits by the parents with their families.
Regarding third level study of Irish, most fathers concerned visited the Gaeltacht
at least once a year since their child began at the Bunscoil, although this was not
the case for those women who had studied Irish at college. Parents who attended
evening classes to learn Irish showed no greater tendency to visit the Gaeltacht
than other people. This fact suggests that, apart from the practical difficulties
associated with Gaeltacht visits, Irish language classes did not stress any value
associated with trips to the traditional Gaeltacht.

Visits to the Gaeltacht represent the only activity, traditionally associated
with the learning of Irish, which did not substantially increase once the parents
became directly involved with the Bunscoil. Every other main aspect of language learning behaviour and usage patterns showed marked increase once the
children began to attend the Irish-medium school. The fact that this isolation of
the learning community in Belfast leaves its mark on the linguistic system itself
was not widely recognised by the parent population. Nor was it lamented by
many of those who were aware of it.

In the following chapters, it will become clear that the most significant feature of the linguistic changes characteristic of the Irish being spoken in Belfast
is the hectic pace at which these are occurring. This pace corresponds to the
dynamic momentum which propels the revival of Irish itself in parts of the Six

Counties. Changes in a linguistic system are widely acknowledged as a positive, healthy sign of language use. 'Pure' forms of language which adhere to standard norms cannot be wrapped up and stored in a safe place like an inanimate relic. Ultimately, the moths will do less damage to the cloth which is used and worn and subjected to the elements. Ó Cuiv (1971: 39) refers to the 'wear and tear' of speech. When a language ceases to incorporate variations and innovations, then it is perhaps beyond resuscitation.

However, Ó Cuiv also refers to the slowness of this process of change throughout history, with particular regard to the penetration of linguistic changes into written form. This subject is discussed in the context of dialectal developments. A time-span passes before the majority of popular changes occurring in speech reach the written form. A further lapse must pass before some of these changes become accepted as standard forms. The uniformity or diversity of changes across geographical areas and the rate at which they enter the spoken (or written) language are matters which are determined by a range of circumstances. At present, we are concerned with the deviations from traditional norms in the spoken language which have erupted, in Belfast, with a relative suddenness.

It is understandable that Bunscoil parents, and language enthusiasts generally, should be much less concerned with this phenomenon than with the continued drive towards active bilingualism in their neighbourhoods. Indeed, in the preceding chapter, we referred to the degree of tolerance which must be cultivated and developed towards the 'novice speaker' (a term used in the CLAR report). Therefore, any focus upon language variety has to be sensitively and dextrously handled. This requires striking a balance between encouraging the community to approximate, as far as possible, the target language, and at the same time inspiring social norms which attract more people to join the population of learners who use their Irish comfortably and freely, according to their own limits at any particular time. This ideal situation does not preclude giving priority to the latter goal while, at the same time, recognising the importance of the former.

The Irish commonly spoken in Belfast, among people who still consider themselves to be learners of Irish as a second language, ideally aspires towards the linguistic system which survives as an unbroken tradition in some rural areas. For most of these people their command of the language is still at that intermediate stage, somewhere between 'tabula rasa and the target language' (Ó Baoill, 1981a: 75). Under the umbrella of this overall target language, individuals and communities identify their own objectives. The lowest goal is always the acquisition of a functionally communicative system, so that the speaker can be understood and can communicate satisfactorily, in accordance with his own needs. If the speaker never intends to interact with speakers from other areas, or if he desires only to use Irish within certain domains, his functional requirements are obviously reduced. In relation to the learner, initial goals must be realistically accessible in order to permit a sense of achievement and to maintain learning motivation. The overall target language, on the other hand, takes other factors into account, for example, the need to secure some degree of stability within the linguistic system itself.

The Irish popularly spoken in Belfast is, as was already mentioned, based upon the Ulster dialect. However, the tradition of Ulster Irish in the east of the province was severed during colonialisation. Isolated Irish-speaking families carried on a tenuous thread of continuity by refusing to die out completely. However, the resuscitation of Irish in the mouths of living urban communities is a phenomenon which must be seen within the metaphorical context of the phoenix. Every possible source of assistance and reinforcement must be tapped in order to ease this process of bilingualisation. The spontaneous and unrestricted nature of the input into this process by the Irish-speaking Community at Shaw's Road is, in itself, a sound enough reason for availing of any possible support. Exposure to the rich linguistic reserves of native Gaeltacht Irish cannot be experienced while the community are largely unaware of its value. Of course, practical considerations must be thrashed out. In addition, other means of introducing some controls which would guide, without dictating, linguistic developments must be identified and sought.

Until now, closer contact with other Irish-speaking communities has been discussed in terms of the effect which it would have upon the variety of Irish being spoken in Belfast. Another dimension to this consideration is worth a mention. The Belfast situation is quite unique. A number of families built up their own Gaeltacht Community in order to create the circumstances which would allow their children to grow up, as Irish speakers, in natural favourable surroundings. They also adapted the educational system which they developed so as to make the language accessible to other families from the surrounding areas. The pool from which they draw more members is, of course, English-speaking. The rest of the city is English-speaking. The administrative, economic and commercial interests in Belfast also reinforce the dominance of English. However, other Irish-speaking communities, in Gaeltacht and in Galltacht districts experience the same pressures and disadvantages associated with the constant intrusion of the English language from neighbouring areas and from the media. Lessons learned from the common experiences of these different communities cannot be fully productive unless they are shared. During the early days of the Shaw's Road initiative, members did maintain contact with other Irish-speaking families and communities through the organisation 'Teaghlaigh Gaelacha' (Irish-speaking families). Inter-community contact is not very active today. The survey findings, summarised above, indicate that Bunscoil parents are, as yet, generally uninformed about the advantages of establishing close links with other Irish-speaking communities, in Gaeltacht areas as well as in other urban centres.

This chapter has explored only one factor which influences the language: isolation from other Irish-speaking communities, in particular those situated in traditional Gaeltachts. It has looked at the attitudes of Bunscoil parents towards the variety of Irish in common usage in Belfast. As we have seen, they express a strong loyalty to the Irish of Belfast, without any real awareness of, or significance attached to, the linguistic moulding of the language as it grows. Chapter 12 will focus attention upon the main trends within that linguistic system. Already we have alluded to reasons why this attention is indeed desirable. Hopefully, that will be fully justified before the concluding pages.

This story of the Shaw's Road Gaeltacht Community has followed its historical background and, subsequently, its creation and influence upon the shift towards bilingualism within surrounding neighbourhoods. The young people who were reared in the Shaw's Road Gaeltacht Community and passed through its all-Irish educational system have developed that functional communicative competence to which Irish learners aspire, including those families whose children attend the Bunscoil today. Their linguistic repertoire has been shaped by all the forces to which the families of Bunscoil children today are exposed. The attitudes of these Shaw's Road children to their own linguistic make-up reveal certain sharp insights among this group of young people. In the following chapter, these observations and insights are examined, before considering the results of the linguistic analysis in chapter 12.

11 Our Own Language: Views of the Community Children

Undoubtedly, there are many aspects of the unique language situation in Belfast which make a dynamic contribution to the linguistic moulding of Irish, as it spreads throughout some areas in the city. Many examples of these have already been mentioned. Clearly, one of these aspects is the geographical position itself. This physical distance between Belfast and traditional Irish-speaking areas is, to some extent, reflected in the distance between popular and standard norms within the linguistic system. The attitude of learners in the city towards the growing language is another factor. In the previous chapter, it became apparent that the expanding population who favour the language are most interested in the language's future welfare in terms of increased numbers of speakers and increased usage of Irish. The nature of broad linguistic trends attracted little interest. However, this very attitude exerts some influence upon those same trends.

Historical distance is as important a consideration as geographical distance. Indeed, in most of the country, particularly urban areas, the Irish language, as a spoken tradition, was extinguished under the pressures of colonial rule. As Ó Cuív points out in his book on Irish dialects, the variety of Irish which is spoken as a first language in cities today is not directly connected with the dialect of Irish which was spoken there some centuries previously (Ó Cuív, 1971: 35). It is to be expected that the time gap, or the broken tradition, will leave its mark.

Another factor which is significant within this context is the fact that so many dedicated, committed adults give up their free time in the evenings to teach adult language classes, without the support of training programmes in established educational institutions. Some of these people are already trained school teachers. Many, however, acquire the language informally and begin to teach it in response to the growing demand for classes, but without back-up resources to assist them.

Accordingly, the nature and degree of exposure to Irish, not only determines the strength of the bilingualisation process, but also, in turn, influences the nature of the linguistic system itself. In this way, the circumstances in which the language spreads into popular usage and the linguistic shape which evolves are inextricably linked. This chapter, like the previous one, focuses on material which clarifies the nature of that link.

As explained in the introduction, in this part of the book attention is directed at the Irish spoken by the children of the Shaw's Road Community. These are the young people whose parents were motivated to learn Irish themselves and to raise them with Irish as the family tongue. They live in the Shaw's Road Community and attended the Bunscoil. Several of them also attended the Irish-medium secondary school while it was operating. Most of the children were still at the Bunscoil when the research for this book commenced. However, during the years of fieldwork many of them passed on to secondary schools. When the Irish-medium secondary school closed in 1980 three of the young people transferred to an all-Irish secondary school in Dublin, travelling home at weekends. The rest attended local English-medium secondary schools. These young people were mature enough to participate actively in discussions related to the language.

Other Bunscoil children from surrounding districts, whose parents have limited Irish, were too young at the outset of this study to participate in recording or observational sessions. Although an analysis of their language skills would be invaluable in the investigation of language acquisition, their contact with the language had not, at that point, been intense enough to yield information about established bilingual patterns. Other reasons for this decision not to focus upon Bunscoil children from neighbourhoods outside the Shaw's Road Community were discussed in the introduction.

The Shaw's Road children, on the other hand, had the fluency of people raised with Irish. Their exposure to the language had also changed over the years. The experiences of these young people would have a particular significance for the hundreds of children attending the Bunscoil who had not yet passed through the system. They would also be of value to other young people throughout the country who were raised with Irish or were being educated through that medium.

The idea of carrying out a linguistic analysis of this urban Irish as a separate exercise, without delving into the heart and mind of the Community, never appeared justified. The language variety itself always seemed to be of secondary importance to the fact that a cultural revival was under way with such promising results. A clinical account of linguistic phenomena would give no insight into the remarkable achievement which the Shaw's Road project represented, nor the contribution which it made to the quickening momentum propelling the language forth, 'i mbéal an phobail' (in the mouth of the people). Nor would it afford any understanding of the social factors which are responsible for the development of that particular variety of modern urban

Irish. A more meaningful description of the Irish necessitated getting to know the young people of the Gaeltacht Community and earning their trust. It has already been stated that any presentation of their Irish, divorced from an account of their own relationship with the language, would have painted a distorted, unbalanced picture of the language situation in Belfast. However, it would also have been much less interesting and enjoyable.

During the fieldwork for this study, I endeavoured to explore the language and language-related matters from the viewpoint of the young people in the community, rather than observing it solely from the perspective of researcher. Some sensitivity towards the children's perception of the language — its value and functional role in their lives — was always considered crucial.

The Shaw's Road children and young people (SRC) were quite articulate about their own awareness of the complexity associated with their bilingualism, which emerged as they grew older. The interaction of language usage and social settings became more complicated. This complexity is attributable to the pattern of linguistic compartmentalisation which is being constantly developed. The general trend has been the penetration of Irish into further domains. However, it has also withdrawn from certain areas in the children's lives, as they have advanced in years. This was expressed by one seventeen-year-old girl in the following way,

> Nuair a bhí muidinne óg ní raibh fadhb dá laghad agat. Labhair tú Gaeilge an t-am uilig. Fiú na daoine a bhí Bearla acu, labhair tu Gaeilge cionn is ní raibh Bearla agat! Ach, em, anois, tá sé ag éirí nios deacra ...

> (When we were young you had no difficulty. You spoke Irish always. Even with people who spoke (only) English, you spoke Irish because you did not have English! But now, it's getting harder.)

This speaker is recalling her earliest years as a monolingual Irish speaker. The pattern of language behaviour varied from family to family, within the Community (and, to some extent, from individual to individual). This was influenced by the degree of parental enthusiasm, the presence or absence of a television in the home, the frequency of visits from non-Irish-speaking friends and relatives, etc. Some of the oldest children in the Community were monolingual Irish speakers for the first five or six years before acquiring English. Others were introduced to both English and Irish from infancy. Yet, despite these individual variations, they all look back on a childhood where Irish was the dominant language. This world was linguistically straightforward in comparison to their present bilingual world, wherein communicative competence in relation to language use makes more exacting demands. The social experience of the young child is, obviously, more restricted than that of the teenager. While home and school constituted the environment where the young child spends most of his time, then the rules about language use were relatively simple. Irish was the first language in both of these domains. During the early years of the Community's existence parents were very conscious of the need to protect that Irish-speaking environment for their children. The aim was to project the language outwards into further domains and into surrounding areas. Infiltration of English from outside the Community was resisted. Considerable effort and energy was therefore invested by the adults of the Community towards this end. Accordingly, the older children were cushioned from any notions of complexity or oddness regarding their unique language situation. In this way, the establishment of the Community had succeeded in overcoming the disadvantages which many of that older generation, who had been reared with Irish in scattered localities throughout the city, had experienced.

The perception of the SRC towards their own particular language situation is most effectively presented within the context of four main areas of social experience: home, religion, education, recreation.

Home

Irish is more closely associated with the home than any other domain by the SRC. For most of them, it is the dominant language in that context while, for others, it has come to represent the second language. Some of the children did not identify Irish as being the dominant language but merely perceived it as one of the two languages which are used at home. Below, one seventeen-year-old boy describes how he sees the role of Irish.

Boy A: Ach anseo, like, labhraíonn tú Gaeilge sa bhaile agus corruair ar scoil (i.e. a local English-medium secondary school where he studies Irish as a subject) agus na háiteanna a luaigh muid. Ach cuir i gcás go ndeachaigh tu chuig lár an bhaile nó áit éigin, nó amach oíche éigin le slua mor ... b'é an Béarla ár céad teanga in sa cineál rud sin.

Researcher: An í an Ghaeilge an chéad teanga agaibh?

Boy A: Sa bhaile, yeah, ... Ach níl Gaeilge ag cuid mhaith de mo chuid aintíní agus uncalacha agus an cuid is mó de mo chuid cairde, so, bíonn orm a bheith ag labhairt i mBéarla leo.

(Boy A: But here, like you speak Irish at home and occasionally at school and the places we mentioned. But say you went into town or somewhere, or out at night with a big crowd ... English would be our first language in those situations.

Researcher: Is Irish your first language?
Boy: At home, yeah. But many of my aunts and uncles and most of my
              friends don't speak Irish, so I have to speak English with them.)

Some of the SRC consider Irish as the language more specifically associated
with younger members of the family. As teenagers, they have become more
exposed to the English language and naturally associate new experiences with
the language through which they were encountered. The tendency to use English
with peers mounts accordingly.

Boy A (sixteen years old): Labhraíonn mo mháthair is m'athair, ar scor ar
              bith, i gclann s'againne, nó na páistí, trí Gaeilge an t-am uilig.
              Ach cuid den am suím mé síos le mo dheifiúr mór agus
              labhraím i mBéarla ...
(Boy A: My mother and father speak Irish in our family, anyway, or the
              children speak Irish all the time. But sometimes I sit down with
              my big sister and I speak in English ...)

These young people expressed an awareness of the need to protect existing
opportunities for using Irish, particularly in relation to the younger children.
They realise that the home is the nucleus of their Irish-speaking world and that
so much depends upon reinforcing their grasp of the language before the young
child, too, becomes more directly exposed to those same pressures. The conversation above continued as follows:

Researcher: An labhraíonn sibh níos mó Gaeilge leis na daoine beaga?
Boy A: Labhraíonn, i bhfad níos mó.
Researcher: Cad chuige sin?
Boy B (sixteen years): Duty.

(Researcher: Do you speak more Irish to the younger children?
Boy A: Lots more.
Researcher: Why?
Boy B: Duty.)

Quite a few of these older members of SRC related temporary experiences when
they felt inclined to reject Irish at home. This phenomenon was associated
exclusively with the teenagers. Nevertheless, it is not dramatically different from
those periods of rejection which Bunscoil parents described, concerning their
six-year-olds. In the latter cases, a degree of tension had entered the language
situation from various sources, at a time when the children were not yet confident and certain about their linguistic environment. The Shaw's Road teenagers,
who described a similar phase when they questioned what was expected of them
in terms of language behaviour, were able to go on and explain those fleeting
phases of resistance.

Boy (seventeen years): Ní tú rudaí difríocht. Má deir do mhamai leat, 'gabh ansin', ní théid tú ansin, théid tú an bealach eile ...

Girl (seventeen years): Linne is cuid den teenage rebellion atá ann in Gaeilge fosta. Mar, i gcónaí bíonn na tuismitheoirí, ní bhíonn siad ag brú ort, ach sin an rud ba mhaith le na tuismitheoirí thú a dhéanamh. Agus daoine eile, b'fhéidir go ndeachaigh siad thart le punk hairstyles ... Muidinne, stopaimid ag labhairt Gaeilge le cur isteach ar do thuismitheoirí.

(**Boy:**	You do contrary things. If your mammy says to you, 'go there', you don't go there, you go the other way.
Girl:	With us, it's part of the teenage rebellion. For, your parents are always, not pressuring you, but that's the way they would like you to behave (i.e. speak Irish). And other people might go round with punk hairstyles. We stop speaking Irish — to annoy the parents.)

The above speaker had recognised this type of behaviour in six or seven of her peers. It was accepted as one aspect of a phase which teenagers passed through and left behind them. One or two of the older members still believed that some parental pressure was being applied during a particular period. One of these only overcame this feeling upon leaving the family home. This young person was only interviewed on a couple of occasions and preferred to be interviewed in English rather than Irish. I sensed that this reflected a basic lack of ease about the presence of the tape recorder more than anything else.

It is notable that these experiences are so much milder and more temporary than the accounts related by several members of that older generation of people who were raised with Irish in families scattered throughout the city. Neither were those latter stories typical of all the people involved. Nevertheless, those members of the earlier Irish-speaking families who did describe such experiences were expressing hostilities which were quite deeply rooted, the repercussions of which influenced their relationship with the Irish language for some years. That serious note was generally absent from the descriptions of the teenaged SRC's rebellious moments. Indeed, the latter seemed quite humorous and natural to those who reflected upon them retrospectively.

As the SRC grow older, they tend to introduce more English into the home. This process occurs as contact with non-Irish speakers expands. Friends from surrounding English-speaking neighbourhoods and from the local secondary schools bring English, not only into the Gaeltacht neighbourhood, but into the homes as well. Exposure to English in new spheres of activity infringes upon the dominant position which Irish enjoys at home. The attendance of the young Irish speakers at English-medium secondary schools represents the most serious threat to the relative stability of the bilingual situation which exists while the children are still at the Bunscoil. Yet, ironically, the security of Irish at home becomes all the more crucial as the teenagers enter those English-medium domains. The home's position as the focus of their Irish-speaking world strengthens. Therefore, if the use of Irish at home weakens somewhat, its significance spills over into other areas. When English makes any serious incursion into the home from outside it becomes all the more imperative to strengthen the home situation in order to be able to resist those sources of the incursion.

When dealing with the fate of East Sutherland Gaelic, Nancy Dorian stated, 'The home is the last bastion of a subordinate language in competition with a dominant official language of wider currency' (Dorian, 1981: 105). In the Shaw's Road Community, where language revival rather than language death is the issue, the home is recognised as the *first* bastion of the subordinate language. It acts as a springboard, from which Irish is propelled into other areas of usage. The tenacity of Irish in the home is rendered vulnerable by the dominance of English in certain other domains, in particular that of secondary education. In light of this fact, it is appropriate to highlight the need to establish active bilingualism more firmly in the homes of Bunscoil families. If this could be achieved, the children would be better equipped to maintain their tendency to use Irish in later years when their exposure to English is intensified. Bunscoil parents are unaware of the full value of aiming at that more long-term goal.

Religion

For most of the SRC, religion is associated with Irish rather than English. One regular Sunday Mass is celebrated in St Mary's Chapel, situated in the city centre. Local churches only celebrate an Irish language Mass on occasion. St Patrick's Day, for example, seems to awaken that sense of cultural responsibility. Hence, on that day, the Shaw's Road children are in great demand to provide appropriate music. A rota system now operates, according to which other chapels take a turn in celebrating a Sunday Mass in Irish. However, the norm is for people to establish a sense of belonging to one parish. Accordingly, the Shaw's Road Community attend the regular Mass in the centre. A few of the families now opt for the convenience of attending local churches, even though English is the medium employed.

The younger boys serve as altar boys for the Irish Masses and other celebrations. Thirteen of the SRC participated in the Irish language choir during the years of fieldwork, and continue to do so. This involves weekly practices and occasional social bonuses such as excursions and seasonal parties. The choir leader, Éamann Ó Fagháin, learnt much of his Irish from the children and, in turn, inspired them by his enthusiasm for learning the language as much as by his love of music. The Irish choir has attracted other young people from outside the Community, including some who learnt the language once they became members of the choir. Senior Bunscoil children from neighbouring areas have also become involved in this activity. Considering the vacuum of social facilities and organisations which cater for Irish-speaking teenagers, this choir makes an important contribution.

The Irish choir represents one more example of cultural initiatives which have succeeded because of the determination and drive of a few individuals who share a unity of purpose. The choir leader and a few older members of the Community children invest a total commitment into the future of this project. Other examples of this same dedication and energy include the Shaw's Road Community project itself; the work carried out by individual Irish-speaking priests on behalf of the Community; the building up of an Irish language bookshop; the provision of an independent Irish language radio station; the daily publication of an Irish newspaper.

The penetration of Irish into the religious domain was achieved during the early days of the Community's establishment, when a group of the leading members, along with other Irish speakers, campaigned vigorously to have religious services provided through Irish. The co-operation and support of individual priests allowed the eventual expansion of services until the young Irish-speakers could experience all the sacraments through their first language. Accordingly, although the oldest children in the Community travelled to Dundalk in order to celebrate their Confirmation through Irish, subsequent children were able to celebrate First Holy Communion and Confirmation at home. By the time this fieldwork was under way the position of Irish in the religious domain was firmly established for the Community and Bunscoil children.

The extension of Irish into this area was particularly significant because of the official and formal character of the religious domain. The Irish language was already dominant in the informal setting of home and neighbourhood, at Shaw's Road. However, participating in the celebration of the sacraments afforded an official status to the children's mother language, which was absent in other official domains sponsored and controlled by the authorities. Outside the Shaw's Road Community the world of business, commerce, administration and mass media reinforce the dominance of the English language in prestigious domains. Education and religion are vital as proof of the viability of Irish as an efficient medium in formal settings as well as in the more casual familiar context.

Wherever a single society assigns particular roles to different languages, i.e. in a diglossia situation (for further explanations of this term see Ferguson, 1959: 330; Fishman, 1967: 29–37; and for a description of its relevance to a Gaeltacht community, refer Ó Gallachóir, 1981) it is commonplace for the

Church language to represent the prestigious learned language. Indeed, the official adoption of a particular language by the Church very often reinforces the perceived superiority of that language in society. In Friesland, for example, the vernacular Frisian is the language of home and neighbourhood; however, Dutch is the dominant language for more formal domains. Only 2% of sermons are delivered in Frisian. Similiarly, the tradition of Bible reading is a Dutch-medium activity, even in Frisian-speaking homes. This reduces positive impressions about the value of Frisian.

Founder members of the Shaw's Road Community recognised the importance of establishing Irish in the religious domain. Not only does it extend the range of settings where Irish is used naturally, but it also protects and supports already existing footholds. The dangers inherent in attendance at local English-medium secondary schools — which allow English to encroach further upon home use of Irish — would be just as active in the case of an English-prevalent or dominant religious domain.

Attendance at the Irish Mass also acts, to some extent, as a social event for the congregation. The habit of gathering outside the chapel, before and after Mass, creates another opportunity where social interaction is most natural through Irish. Attendance at the Mass also adds to the children's repertoire of verbal styles. The language of the liturgy, sermons, prayers, etc. is more formal and elaborate than the language used by the children at other times — during that informal gathering outside the church, for example. In this way the verbal repertoire and communicative competence of the children are extended. The priests who participate in the rota timetable for celebrating the Irish Mass come from various parts of the country. Consequently, the variety of dialects to which the children become accustomed also enriches their linguistic experience.

Education

Irish-medium nursery and primary education has revolutionised the Language Movement in Northern Ireland. The momentum for that development stemmed from the success of the Belfast Bunscoil. During the preparation of plans for creating an urban Gaeltacht Cummunity, the necessity of providing Irish-medium education for the children was accepted. Their goal of raising their children to experience full lives through Irish could not be realised without extending the use of Irish outside the home. Primary education had to be available to them in their home language if the language was to resist being marginalised and weakened by the dominant language.

Apart from the obvious language development which would be cultivated during those primary years, other considerations made Irish-medium education imperative. Much of the children's time is spent at school. They build up social networks around their school friends. At home they find it most natural to discuss school-related events in the language through which they were experienced, rather than depending upon translation skills. When the Bunscoil was founded SRC were able to enjoy those advantages. The primary school was, essentially, an integral part of Community life. This was *their* school. Their parents had physically constructed it, employed their teacher, financed its running costs, cleaned out their classrooms, etc. The children played outside it after school hours. The school was also used for other purposes, such as meetings. All of the parents were involved, in some way, in its operation. Therefore, until the children reached eleven years old, education represented an extension to home life. Indeed, even in a physical sense the Bunscoil is situated virtually in their back gardens.

The transference to secondary school implies a shift from a predominantly Irish-speaking world into a predominantly English-speaking world. The first few children who crossed this bridge into an English-medium educational system found the experience quite disturbing. Today, the transference of Bunscoil children to local secondary schools is an annual occurrence which elicits the usual feelings of anticipation among the children. The path is now well trodden. However, the first of the Shaw's Road children to make this move had not this advantage. For the first time, they had to make a break with the Community, travelling on buses or in taxis to the new school. In addition, the first couple of pupils involved were transferring from a little community school to what was the largest school in the city. The language represented just one more dramatic difference. Today, these factors have lost their significant stature.

This move to a local English-medium secondary school was originally made after the Irish-medium secondary school closed. For two years the first pupils to pass through the primary system carried on their education through Irish, on the same site. These pupils were taught by uniquely dedicated teachers, who were employed in other local secondary schools but who gave up all their free classes, as well as time before and after the normal school day, to offer their professional services to the 'Méanscoil' (Irish-medium secondary school). This system was in operation from 1978 to 1980 and terminated when the additional strains on the Community became too heavy. At this point, some children transferred to local English-medium schools. However, two families decided to continue the Irish-medium education of their children in the only way that remained possible, at that time. They enrolled their children at a Méanscoil in Dublin. In all, three girls attended the Dublin Irish-medium secondary school. Obvious practical reasons impeded others from following this course. It was found, during the years of fieldwork, that these three girls were the most confident and fluent speakers in their age group. This feature was also observed by their parents, in comparison to siblings who had attended local English-medium schools. These girls used Irish more frequently than their peers, even outside the domain of formal education. One of the teenage boys in the Community, who was attending a local secondary school, identified a difference in the language behaviour of these girls and in his own language behaviour when in their company.

Boy 1:   Bhuel labhraímse in Gaeilge leo cionn is níl siad siud anseo ó Dé Luain go dtí Dé hAoine, right? ... Ag an am sin (i.e. when they first went to Dublin) bhí muinne just ag toiseacht ar gabhail chuig Naomh Mhuire (the local boys' Grammar school). Bhí muid just cleachtaithe le labhairt in Gaeilge. Níl muid cleachtaithe le labhairt i mBéarla. So, tá mise cleachtaithe le labhairt in Gaeilge leothusiúd, so labhraím Gaeilge leo.

Boy 2:   Labhraíonn X (one of the girls) an t-am uilig in Gaeilge leat.

Boy 1:   Agus má (tá) tusa ag labhairt i mBéarla le X tabharfaidh sí freagra duit in Gaeilge.

Researcher: Cad chuige a ndéanfadh sí sin?

Boy 1:   Ní rud éigin atá ann go bhfuil sí a gabhail a rá léithi féin go bhfuil, tá mise a gabhail Gaeilge a labhairt. Just sa subconscious, ye know, just, labharfaidh sí Gaeilge leat.

(Boy 1:   Well, I speak Irish to them because they are not here from Monday to Friday, right? ... At that time (when the girls first went to Dublin) we were just beginning St Mary's. We were used to speaking just Irish. We aren't used to speaking English (together). So I am still used to speaking Irish with them, so I speak Irish.

Boy 2:   X always speaks Irish to you.

Boy 1:   If you speak English to X, she answers you in Irish.

Researcher: Why would she do that?

Boy 1:   It is not something that she says to herself, 'I am going to speak in Irish.' Just, in her subconscious. ye know, just she will speak Irish to you.)

This boy realised that his friend did not consciously decide upon using a particular language within a particular setting, but that she instinctively felt it more natural to use Irish with her neighbours. This speaker's insights into the situation are quite astute and perceptive. The girls who attended the all-Irish school in Dublin were not subject to the same linguistic pressures and influences as their Community friends who had transferred to local schools. The latter would be taught through English, would meet new school friends who did not speak Irish and would bring these friends and the common language back into the Community and into the home. The girls who were educated at the Dublin Meánscoil were not exposed to these changes to the same degree. They therefore expected their linguistic relationship with Community peers to remain based upon the patterns of their childhood — i.e. using Irish together more naturally than using English, particularly within the Community. The observation of Boys 1 and 2 point to two salient facts: firstly the detrimental influence which transference to English-medium secondary schools exerts upon use of Irish in neighbourhood and home and, secondly, the impact of one's perceptions of others' expectations upon language use.

Both of these boys estimated that they tend to speak English for approximately three quarters of the time since beginning to attend the local secondary school. SRC are also aware of the fact that the quality of their Irish is affected by the reduction of time and occasions when they can use the language. A few of the young people expressed admiration for their parents' command of Irish. One of the factors to which they attribute this is the extended range of domains in which these parents employ Irish. Many of the Shaw's Road parents use Irish in their place of work. However, the teenagers felt that their own usage of Irish was drastically diminished when they passed into an English-medium secondary school system.

Boy (seventeen years old): Tá Gaeilge ár gcuid tuismitheoirí níos beachta ... Bíonn siadsan i measc Gaeilge, Gaeilgeoirí níos minice ná mar a bhímse.

(Our parents' Irish is more correct ... They are in the company of Irish (i.e.) Irish speakers more often than I am.)

The same relationship between reduced exposure to the language and mastery of the linguistic system is commented upon by another teenager whose younger siblings did not attend the Bunscoil, but who went to a local English-medium primary school. This speaker observed certain difficulties which his younger siblings had expressing themselves through Irish.

Tá (sé) deacrachtaí acu Gaeilge a labhairt cionn is go bhfuil siad in, ah, gach duine thart orthu ar scoil ag labhairt Béarla. Ní bhíonn seans acu Gaeilge a labhairt ansin.

(They have difficulties with speaking Irish, because they are, ah, everyone around them at school is speaking English. They don't have a chance to speak Irish there.)

The SRC who attend local secondary schools encounter both positive and negative attitudes to Irish at school. One member described the disadvantage which Irish suffers in relation to science subjects at his school. (Note also in the following extract, the extent to which English phrases and terms enter the speaker's Irish when he happens to be discussing the English-medium secondary school.)

Ní amharcann daoine, múinteoirí nó na science teachers uilig nó na career teachers ... nó. Má tá tú a gabhail teangaidh a dhéanamh, déan teangaidh usáideach, go dtig leat, b'fhéidir, eh, interpreter a dhéanamh nó rud éigin mar sin, ye know. Rud éigin that will get you money. Ach Gaeilge — dead language, forget about it. Agus anois i scoil s'againne tá sé optional. I mean, fa choinne bliantaí agus bliantaí bhí ort Gaeilge a dhéanamh.

(People don't consider (Irish as a useful language) — the teachers nor all the science teachers nor the career teachers. If you are going to do a language then choose a useful language which will enable you to be an interpreter or something like that, you know. Something that will get you money. But Irish — dead language, forget about it. And now it is optional in our school. I mean, for years and years Irish was compulsory.)

This speaker laments the fact that Irish has lost its compulsory status throughout his school. The attitude which he describes threatens Arts subjects generally. This development has filtered down from third level establishments and ultimately from Government's structuring of society. Commercial viability enjoys a supreme position in the hierarchy of values. Other areas of educational development lose out. Indeed, for a while it seemed that the latest curriculum changes, announced by the Education Minister, would have the effect of further deteriorating the position of Irish, not just more than any other Arts subject, but also more than any other language, in Northern Ireland secondary schools. Policy makers, in particular, should be informed about the inevitable effect of this reduced status upon young people's perception of their language's relevance and the degree to which it is respected at official levels.

Despite these restraints, SRC are aware of the growing enthusiasm for Irish at community level. This is also perceived within the context of school, from time to time, when peers communicate their impressions about that phenomenon.

Boy 1:   Tá gach duine ag foghlaim Gaeilge ...
Boy 2:   Aye, I know. Chan cionn is gur mhaith leofa 'O' leibheal in Gaeilge. Ba mhaith leo Gaeilge a labhairt. Agus déarfaidh siad, ye know, tusa a suí sa scoil, ye know ...
Boy 1:   Ní thiocfaidh siad suas i Fraincis agus déarfadh siad, ye know, 'fág cuid de sin dom' i Fraincis. Ach déarfaidh siad in Gaeilge, 'fág toit dom'.

(Boy 1:   Everyone is learning Irish.
Boy 2:   Aye, I know. Not because they want an 'O' level exam in Irish.
             They would like to speak Irish. And they will say, you know,
             (when) you are sitting in school, you know ...
Boy 1:   They won't come up to you and say in French 'leave me some of
             that'. But they will say, in Irish, 'leave me a smoke'.)

Therefore, this speaker recognises the cultural relevance of Irish, as opposed to
any other language, in their lives. He also realises that his school peers share this
view. It is natural for them, particularly in the present cultural climate wherein
Irish thrives among the West Belfast community, to employ even simple turns of
phrase in Irish which they would not think of casually using in French, for
example. Ironically, this preferential cultural status, which is instinctively appreciated by some children, is not vigorously encouraged in schools generally.

One of the minor difficulties encountered by SRC when they transferred to
local secondary schools concerned their unfamiliarity with school terminology
in English. The scale of this problem is not comparable to that experienced by
the first couple of individuals who left the Shaw's Road Meánscoil.
Nevertheless, even the younger members find that they have to acquaint themselves with features of the verbal repertoire which — it is taken for granted that
— all children have. This challenge is not only very short term, but is also very
manageable for the children.

B'fhéidir tiocfaidh an form master isteach agus deir sé, 'Right, déarfaidh
muid an Our Father agus an Hail Mary'. Agus deir se, 'Right, abair tusa é,
abair tusa é.' Agus nuair a deir se leata — 'Sorry, I can't'. Agus amharcann
sé ort, 'What?' 'I can only say it in Irish.' 'O.K. then abair in Gaeilge.'
Agus i ndiaidh sin, 'O bhuel, fíor mhaith!' ... Agus you're sort of the focal
point of the class. Gach duine ag amharc ort. Chuaigh mise amach as mo
bhealach le paidir agus seo agus siúd a fhoghlaim i mBéarla, agus cinéal,
rinne mise dearmad ar an Gaeilge.

(Maybe the form master will come in and say 'Right, we'll say the 'Our
Father' and 'Hail Mary'. And he says, 'Right, you say it. You say it. ' And
when he tells you to recite it, 'Sorry, I can't'. And he looks at you, 'What?'
'Sorry, I can only say it in Irish.' 'O.K. then say it in Irish.' And afterwards,
'O well, that's very good!' ... And you are sort of the focal point of the
class. I went out of my way to learn prayers, etc. in English, and I sort of
forgot about Irish (i.e. in the school domain.).)

Younger members of SRC are unlikely to have to make these initial adjustments
to the same extent because of their greater exposure to English. Most of their
school friends at the Bunscoil are not raised with Irish as the first language of

the home. Therefore, Bunscoil children have a natural tendency to introduce English into their communicative exchanges, which teachers and supervisors constantly monitor and discourage. The younger SRC are present in this scenario and influenced by it. They have more opportunity to speak English than their older siblings did. In addition, older siblings, at secondary schools, have already introduced them, indirectly, into their English-speaking world at school, by talking about it and describing their own experiences. The teenagers who referred to their 'duty' towards younger siblings were conscious of the wider exposure to English which the latter experience.

The language behaviour and linguistic systems of all of the SRC, both younger and older, are influenced by their transition to English-medium secondary schools. Even though they may study Irish to an advanced level, their usage of the language decreases. During conversation, shifts to English and the incorporation of English lexical items become more frequent. Parents and older siblings also commented upon these changes. Several parents related how their children's repertoire in Irish had weakened, even during the first year at secondary school. Both parents and teachers mentioned that the local secondary schools did not take into account the Irish-medium background of SRC. First year classes are generally directed at children with very little, or no Irish.

A further point which affects the language habits of the SRC outside school also results from the norm of speaking English at school. Bunscoil children who transfer to secondary school soon become accustomed to using English together rather than Irish. Accordingly, even when these SRC are not in the company of non-Irish speakers, it becomes natural for them to continue using English together. English becomes the medium of communication while walking home from school, for example. One mother described how her son does not switch back to Irish until given a kindly reminder, such as 'an bhfuil Gaeilge agat, a mhic?' (Can you speak Irish, son?)

Recreation

While the children are still attending the Bunscoil their recreational activities are based within the Community and associated with Bunscoil friends. However, as they grow older their social life extends into English-dominant areas. This development is attributable, partly, to the lack of facilities for Irish-speaking teenagers.

The dominance of English in the media also exerts a powerful influence upon language behaviour. Television is the most dynamic medium, in this respect. Some families did not have a television for many years because of the impact which it has on children — including the custom of using Irish at home. This reductive effect which television viewing exerts upon home use of Irish was also evident in the homes of Bunscoil families. A vacuum also exists under the heading of Irish 'literature' suitable for young people, including both light reading material and more serious works. At the time of this study one of the Shaw's Road youths was involved in the production of a magazine for young Irish speakers, under the auspices of the *Lá* team. More recently, another has become a full time member of the team. Adult and young children's literature in Irish is not prolific in comparison with the bulk of material available in English; nevertheless, these categories offer a much wider range than exists in the field of teenage literature. A serious gap in the market exists in this area. One seventeen-year-old boy expressed his dissatisfaction with the dearth of 'fashionable' material:

> Léann siad níos mó ná mar a léimse, ó thaobh litríocht na Gaeilge ar scor ar bith. I mo chás féin, níl mise rothugtha do litríocht na Gaeilge. No creidim go bhfuil sé uilig mar an gcéanna. Tá sí uilig faoi feirmeoir eigin thuas ar an sliabh agus a cuid ba agus a chuid gabhar agus a chuid caora ...

> (They (i.e. his parents) read more than I do — Irish literature, anyway. In my own case, I am not very fond of Irish literature. Or I believe that it is all alike. It is always about some farmer up on the mountain and his cows and his goats and his sheep.)

There was a note of mischievous humour underlying the comments by this speaker. He was uninformed about the few writers who do direct some of their literary material at teenagers, such as the Co. Fermanagh writer, Micheál Mac Canna. Nevertheless, he does express a valid point about a limited choice for his age group. The literature which he had studied at school or read at home was rural-based and, as he stated, unrelated to his experiences of life. This young person did praise the work of a local writer, Liam Mac Carrain, who writes humorous short stories and amusing accounts of his own experiences of life in Belfast. The speaker mentioned that he enjoyed reading that author's corpus of light material.

The central force which determines a shift towards dominance of English, in the area of recreation, is also the English-medium secondary school system. School friends of SRC at secondary schools are usually non-Irish speakers. Some of these friends learn Irish as a school subject. A few school friends were influenced by the SRC to use the language; one of these friends described his desire to use Irish when visiting his Shaw's Road friend at home. As mentioned, the Community youth choir also attracts other young people who are motivated to learn and use the language. However, the majority of friendships made through school involve the use of English, exclusively. Social events enjoyed with these peers, which in turn expand the network of monolingual English-speaking contacts, are also English-based. The patterns of social interaction, whereby school friends and other contacts visit the SRC at home, or spend time in their Community with them, creates the habit of automatically switching to English, which subsequently decreases the overall tendency to use Irish.

Researcher: Abair go bhfuil sibhse ag caint le chéile agus tagann duine isteach nach bhfuil Gaeilge aige. Cad a tharlaíonn?
Girl 1 (sixteen years): Athraím go Béarla.
Others: Béarla
Girl 2 (sixteen years): Sin drochmheas.
Girl 3 (seventeen years): Agus tá daoine ann — ní maith liomsa daoine a théann ar aghaidh ag labhairt Gaeilge.

(**Researcher:** What happens if you are chatting together in Irish a a non-Irish speaker joins the company?
Girl 1:   I change to English.
Others: English.
Girl 2:   That would be disrespectful. (i.e. to continue speaking in Irish)
Girl 3:   And there are some people — I don't like people who go on speaking Irish.)

These same views, on the social requirement of switching to English upon the arrival of a non-Irish speaker into the company, were expressed by almost one third of the Bunscoil mothers from surrounding districts. Sensitivity towards this type of situation is, naturally, more intense when a solitary non-Irish speaker enters the company. However, even in the case of a group of non-Irish-speaking acquaintances joining the company, pressure to switch immediately to English is perceived as a sign of courtesy and friendliness. Considering the increasing frequency of this type of social situation, particularly when the children grow older, the use of English during recreational activities assumes dominance for many of the SRC.

The association between the English language and peers of teenage SRC establishes a corresponding association between that language and subjects discussed with those peers. As a result, the SRC develop the habit of employing English when they are discussing particular subjects, even among themselves. The language behaviour of Shaw's Road parents, on the other hand, was less inclined to be influenced by the conversation topic than by other factors. The SRC come to consider English as a more suitable or natural medium for particular conversation topics and, accordingly, Irish is designated 'inappropriate'. Expressions and terms relevant to these topics are not developed in the children's repertoire of Irish and the existing repertoire is considered inadequate. In the following extract, some teenaged girls described subjects which they tend to discuss in English rather than Irish.

Girl A: Gasúraí nó rud ar bith mar sin, like.
Researcher: Sin níos fusa i mBéarla?
Girl A: Tá.
Girl B: Bhuel chan, ... linne, linne —
Girl A: Na foclaí a deir tú, 'Oh, I'm madly in love with him', you know, mar sin. Cad é, cad é an dóigh a deirtear sin in Gaeilge? Oh, tá mise i ngrá leis'.
Girl C: Agus fiú rudaí cosúil le nuair a théid sí sa sráid, deir sí, 'oh he's gorgeous looking', nó rud éigin. Níl, 'Oh, tá seisean go h-álainn'.
Girl A: Sounds really, oh my God!
Girl C: Uggh!

(Girl A: Boys and things like that.
Researcher: That's easier (to discuss) in English?
Girl A: Yes.
Girl B: Well not, ... With us, with us —
Girl A: The words you use. Oh the way girls say, 'Oh I'm madly in love with him', you know. How do you say that in Irish? — 'Oh, tá mise i ngra leis'.
Girl C: And even things like when she is going down the street, she says, 'Oh, he's gorgeous looking!' — or something. Not, 'Oh, tá seisean go h-álainn'
Girl A: Sounds really, oh my God!
Girl C: Uggh!)

The girls realised that their association of English with particular topics was strongly influenced by the media. One of them explained this tendency as:

> Sin cionn is gur tógadh sin on teilifís. (That is because it (i.e. the terminology) is picked up from television.)

Consequently, regarding this particular subject area, the Irish language is perceived as antiquated.

> Agus níl an Gaeilge trendy. (And Irish is not trendy.)

When the older members of the SRC reflect upon their childhood, they recall a more varied range of recreational activities through Irish than those which they now experience. While still at the Bunscoil, they participated in cultural festivals throughout the country. The social life which they enjoyed, as members of an Irish-speaking community, was more detached from that of the surrounding English-speaking community. The Gaeltacht Community draws more people from surrounding areas, for various reasons. Many are motivated in favour of Irish. However, Bunscoil parents and relatives use both Irish and English. Secondary-school friends of the older siblings tend to trigger a shift to English. Accordingly, the younger Community children are exposed to more English than the older children were. Conversely, in one of the Shaw's Road families, the parents explained that they deliberately encouraged their children to participate in recreational activities, such as youth clubs, outside the Shaw's Road Community as well as within the Community. Their reasoning for this decision was based upon a fear that their children would otherwise feel alienated from peers in surrounding neighbourhoods.

As Irish speakers, the teenaged SRC are not provided for socially. The children themselves described their own attempt to set up a youth club by 'commandeering' one of the mobiles which had been secured for the school. A variety of problems accompanied this move and, as a result, their attempt was short-lived. Currently, some of the teenagers are, once more, involved in an effort to introduce youth club facilities, based in one of the Gaelic League Branches. On this occasion, the participants are motivated by a desire to introduce an Irish-medium social and recreational dimension in the lives of senior Bunscoil children who approach the teenage years. They are also aware of the need to furnish past pupils of the Bunscoil with opportunities to continue using Irish in a functional and enjoyable way. The personal experiences of these SRC and their Irish-speaking friends, whereby they missed that social dimension themselves, have sharpened their sensitivity to the needs of younger Irish-speaking children.

The parents at Shaw's Road, as well as other local Irish speakers, are aware of the need for attention to be given to this social area. For over a decade, the running of the Bunscoil required a constant and demanding input of energy and resources. Similarly, for two years, the Meánscoil monopolised much of the Community's efforts. Catering for the social needs of teenagers seemed a less exigent priority. Discussions are presently being held, among interested Irish-speakers and supporters, to explore the most effective and expedient means of reintroducing secondary Irish-medium education and a supportive Irish-medium environment for children leaving the Bunscoil.

Attitudes to Linguistic Uniqueness among SRC

The SRC convey a sense of pride in their parents' achievement and in their own language. They realise that their linguistic situation is unique. Regarding the variety of Irish spoken, the older members of SRC consider that their parents' command of Irish is more grammatically correct than their own. They give three reasons for this opinion:

(a) Many of the parents use Irish across a broader spectrum of domains, e.g. at work.
(b) Their parents read more Irish literature than they do.
(c) Their parents had to strive laboriously to acquire Irish in adulthood and are, subsequently, more careful of grammar.

The validity of this opinion varies from family to family. In some cases, parents share some of the non-standard features of speech with their children. Other features are characteristic only of the children. Conformity with grammatical norms is not a cherished ideal of these young people: communicative competence, fluency, functional value are among the goals which the children do appreciate. Grammatical regularity is considered important in relation to exam success and, to a lesser extent, formal oral situations. The SRC can, themselves, identify some of the linguistic features peculiar to their own variety of spoken Irish, which they would tend to avoid in written material.

Researcher: An bhfuil difear idir labhairt agus scríobh na Gaeilge?
Girl A: O caithfidh tu athrú.
Girl B: Deir muidinne na mílte rudaí — 'tabharann' mar shampla. Deir muidinne 'tabharann' an t-am uilig, agus níl a leithéid de focal ann mar 'tabharann'.

(**Researcher:** Is there a difference between speaking and writing Irish?
Girl A: Oh, you must change.
Girl B: We say thousands of things — 'tabharann' for example. We say 'tabharann' all the time and there is no such word as 'tabharann'.)

In that particular example, the girls referred to a feature which is not in fact unique to their variety of Irish. They identified it as such because it is not accepted as a standard form. However, it is heard in some traditional Gaeltacht communities just as it is in the learner's repertoire.

The three girls who received secondary education in Dublin were particularly aware of vocabulary items which they did not hear from school friends nor from teachers, although, very often, the examples given were not peculiar to Belfast Irish only, but characteristic of various Ulster dialects. They chatted amusedly about words they used which their peers were less familiar with, e.g. 'móraí grandmother': 'alpóg flú' (cf. Lucas 1979: 50). These dialect differences lead to good-humoured teasing by school friends, where the latter tune in on English words similiar in pronunciation.

... agus an foclóir — 'doiligh' agus rudaí mar sin — dilly-dally, agus seo uilig.
(... and the vocabulary — 'doiligh' (hard) and things like that — *dilly-dally* and all this.)

... agus (nuair a dúirt mise) 'amharc air sin.' 'What? ONC? Agus bhí gach duine (ag rá) ONC, ONC, ONC, — muc.
Agus deir mise — amharc, amharc.
(... and 'amharc air sin' (look at that). 'What? ONC? And everyone (was chanting) ONC, ONC, ONC, — like a pig, And I said, 'amharc, amharc, (look).)

A couple of the younger members of SRC had become aware of their own linguistic distinctiveness while attending summer Irish College courses in Carlow. These members described how they sometimes adapted their own variety of Irish, at first, in order to be understood more easily. After a week or so, however, they also demanded that their fellow students made some effort in this regard! The SRC have the linguistic flexibility to enable them to cope in this type of situation. However, more importantly, perhaps, the children are confident as fluent Irish speakers. This is the area where many learners and non-fluent speakers encounter difficulties. Their confidence about using a limited repertoire, in the company of more fluent speakers, is as yet vulnerable. The Shaw's Road children who visited different Gaeltachts expressed surprise at the proximity of their own variety of Irish to that of Donegal.

Boy (twelve years): ... agus bhí sort iontas orm faoi dtaobh dó sin. Shíl mise go mbeadh sé (i.e. Donegal Irish) mar, cosúil le, em, na daoine a bhfuil a conaí síos i Baile Átha Cliath agus Ceatharlach agus áiteanna mar sin. Ní raibh. So bhí sé i bhfad níos cosúil le an Gaeilge a labhair muidinne.
(... and I was a bit surprised about that. I thought that it (i.e. Donegal Irish) would be like, em, people living down in Dublin and Carlow and places like that. It was not. So it was much closer to the Irish that we speak.)

The SRC expressed a very positive attitude towards linguistic diversity. Their respect for other dialects of Irish is no greater or less than their respect for their own variety of Irish. Linguistic differences do not create communicative problems for them. During my stays in Rannafast with the children, it was apparent that their conversation with locals was uninhibited. I joined the children after three or four days. The children (aged eleven) described to me how they made an effort to adjust to the Donegal accent during those first couple of days. Little misunderstandings, at first, qualified as lively anecdotal material.

In amannaí déarfadh, bheadh sí a rá, 'An bhfuil tú ag iarraidh milseán?', nó rud éigin. Agus ní thig leatsa tuigbheáil. I ndiaidh sin deir tú, 'No'. Agus nuair a gheibh tú amach bíonn tú ar mire.'

(Sometimes she would say, she would be saying, 'Would you like a sweet?'
— or something. And you can't understand. So you say, 'No'. And when
you find out, you are raging.)

The children recalled these types of incident with a great sense of fun. They
enjoy their own variety of Irish and its interaction with other varieties. The
younger children, in particular, were often playful in their handling of the language. In the following extract a group of eleven-year-olds were discussing hobbies. Boy 1 mischievously bewilders his peers with his direct translation of a
word. When his friends work out what he means, they burst into laughter and he
goes on to tease them about how long it took them to grasp his meaning:

Boy 1:	Éistimse le téapeanna.	I listen to tapes.
Researcher:	Cén sort téapanna?	What sort of tapes?
Girl:	Popcheol?	Pop music?
Boy 1:	No, chan popcheol go díreach, no iarann, iarann trom.	No. Not exactly pop music. Metal. Heavy metal.
Boy 2:	Eh?	Eh?
Girl:	Heavy metal. [laughter]	Heavy metal.

The next extract also illustrates, not only the children's sense of fun in general,
but also the amusement which they derive from the wider notion of linguistic
diversity. Here, the same group of eleven-year-olds are recounting tales to each
other about their holiday experiences in France.

Researcher: Ar labhair sibh Gaeilge no Béarla sa Frainc?

Boy 1: Fraincis! [acompanied by a well deserved derisive laugh.]

Boy 2: No, bhí X an cuid is mó ag labhairt. Bhí sise ag foghlaim
Fraincise an Bhliain sin agus bhí sí, em, nuair a bhris mo, mo
dheadaí síos, — chuaigh poll sa roth — bhí uirthise caint agus eile
faoin roth.

Researcher: Agus an raibh sí abalta?

Boy 2: 'Sé

Researcher: Maith sin.

Boy 1: Bhuel is cuimhin liomsa, bhí máthair Y ann, bhí sí sa Frainc agus
chuaigh sí ag an siopa seo. Agus dúirt an, — ní raibh Fraincis iontach maith aici — agus dúirt sí, 'punta tratai' i Fraincis. Agus
chonaic sí an bean sa siopa, an mála mór, iontach mór, ag cur a lán
trátaí, a lán, a lán trátaí ann. I ndiaidh sin dúirt sí, 'no, níl mé ag
iarraidh sin.' I ndiaidh sin taispeáin sí an leabhar díthe agus thosaigh an bhean ag caitheamh iad uirthi. [laughter] Ag caitheamh
na trátaí.

Boy 2: Sure, mo dheadaí, bhí muidne ag gabháil sa supermarket agus
caill muid a céile. I ndiaidh sin bhí mo dheadaí ag cuartú do, do

cipíní. Agus ní thiocfadh leis labhairt Fraincis agus bhí sé ag gabhail (mimics a gesture with fingers to lips, meant to suggest a cigarette). Agus shíl an fear go raibh sé i grá le duine éigin! [laughter]

(**Researcher:** Did you speak Irish or English when you were in France?
Boy 1: French! [laughter]
Boy 2: No. X was speaking (French) mostly. She was learning French that year and she was, em, when my daddy broke down — the wheel was punctured — she had to talk and all about the wheel.
Researcher: And was she able?
Boy 2: Yes.
Researcher: Good.
Boy 1: Well, I remember, Y's mother was there, she was in France and she went into this shop. And she, — she couldn't speak much French and she said, 'a pound of tomatoes' in French. And she saw the shopkeeper, a great big bag, putting a huge amount of tomatoes, a huge amount of tomatoes onto it (i.e. the bag). So she said, 'no, I don't want that.' Then she showed her the book (Tourist guide book) and the woman began to throw them at her. [laughter] Throwing the tomatoes.
Boy 2: Sure my daddy, we were going into the supermarket and we lost each other. Then my daddy was looking for matches. And he couldn't speak any French and he was going ... (mimics a gesture with fingers to lips, suggesting a cigarette). And the man thought he was in love with somebody! [laughter]

Like Bunscoil parents, the SRC expressed a sense of loyalty to the Irish language, as one fundamental and major dimension to their individual, community and national 'personality'. The older members, who had studied in Dublin, conveyed that same sense of loyalty to their birthplace.

Sin an rud a dhéanann gabháil ar shiúl go Baile Átha Cliath, (or) óir beidh tú ag iarraidh ar an bhomaite teacht ar ais agus do cuid eile do shaol a caitheamh anseo. Nó, tá difear ann, like. Seo an dara cathair is mó in Éirinn like, agus tá siad iontach cairdiúil thuas anseo. Tá daoine a rá i mo rang — 'Béal Feirste, bhí mé thuas, like, b'fhéidir uair amháin. Tá siad uilig chomh cairdiúil.

(That's what going to Dublin does to you, for you want immediately to come back and spend the rest of your life here. No, there is a difference (i.e. between Dublin and Belfast) like. This is the second largest city in Ireland, like, and they are friendly up here. People in my class say, 'Belfast — I was up there, maybe once. They are all so friendly.')

For the SRC language loyalty is part of loyalty and trueness to self. Irish is simply one aspect of life in Belfast, for the children; the English language is another aspect. Once they move into the English-speaking environment of local secondary schools, with their associated recreational activities, complexities inherent in their bilingualism become evident. Even at this stage, the Irish language is perceived as the main factor which ascertains their cultural distinctiveness. They have an intuitive grasp of the sentiment expressed below: 'Only Irish can prevent us from being levelled into an indistinguishable conformity with the rest of the enormous culturally panmictic population that surrounds us on both sides of the Atlantic' (Brennan, 1964: 263–77).

The younger members of SRC referred to their deeply rooted attachment to the Irish language with the phrase, 'tá mothú ann' (i.e. they have a special feeling for it). The older children described their sharpened sense of value of that living heritage within the context of visits abroad. This same view was also related by some of the Bunscoil parents. Two teenaged Shaw's Road girls give an example of their appreciation of the Irish language, as an expression of cultural distinctiveness, in the following extract:

Girl A: Nuair a théann tú hostelling agus rud éigin mar sin, tuigeann cad é chomh maith ... mothaíonn tú go bhfuil rud éigin agat. Tá teangaidh agat.

Girl B: Má labhar(ann) tú Béarla mothaíonn tú, sort, go gcaithfidh tú a mhíniú d'achan duine go bhfuil tú i d'Éireannach. Ach linne, ní gá dúinn cionn is go bhfuil muid ag labhairt (Gaeilge).

(Girl A: When you go hostelling and things like that, you understand how good ... You feel that you have something. You have a language.

Girl B: If you speak English you feel sort of, that you have to explain to everyone that you are an Irish person. But we don't need to (do that) because we speak (Irish).)

This degree of language loyalty, like everything else, varies from individual to individual. However, a certain fundamental appreciation of it was shared by all the SRC. These children love their language.

12 Linguistic Trends in the Irish of Community Children

In the previous chapter, focus was directed at the children of the Shaw's Road Gaeltacht Community, presenting their perceptions of the social role of Irish. Having earlier looked at the history of the Community and at its influence upon the bilingualisation process in Belfast, it only remains to examine the linguistic system itself, as it is evolving in the city.

The children of the Shaw's Road Community are first introduced to Irish in their homes and neighbourhood. It would be interesting to conduct a linguistic analysis of the Irish spoken by other bilinguals in the city — children from outside the Shaw's Road Community who acquire Irish at the school, people who learned the language as a school subject only, or at an adult evening class, in prison, at university, or who picked it up from their children. Nevertheless, it is hoped that some reliable insights into overall ongoing linguistic developments, within this growing bilingual setting, can be gained from material presented here.

Despite the fact that the Irish of the SRC is their mother tongue, it is still the language of lesser currency within the society in which they live. Consequently, although Irish dominates in certain domains and forms an integral part of their identity, it is the lesser used language in their city and country. When they leave the Bunscoil the children are faced with the conflicts and tensions consequent upon their immersion in an English-speaking environment. In consequence, the linguistic system is exposed to a stronger impact from English. In this sense, Irish may still be considered as the target language — the language which the city's bilingual community strives to fortify and assert. So, although Irish is the language of the home, in the case of the SRC, English retains its prevalent position within the wider framework of society and, as such, it is also the language which the children master most confidently.

If Irish represents, in this wider sense, the target language, how should English be perceived in this bilingual environment? Within the context of second language teaching, the terms 'target language' (TL) and 'native language' (NL) are commonly employed. In the case of Irish language learners, the target language is Irish. However, even though the stronger language of wider currency is English, the term 'native' language, in this instance, would be rather confusing. The parents of Bunscoil children most frequently referred to Irish as 'our/their own language' and secondly, as the 'native' language. Identification with the Irish language is not restricted to those who have mastered some degree of proficiency in it. Therefore, even though some people may be monolingual English speakers, they would tend to perceive Irish as the 'native' and the indigenous language of the country. Accordingly, in Belfast's community of bilinguals, including fluent and novice speakers, English is perceived as the dominant language (DL) in common usage, as opposed to the NL.

During the process of acquiring the first language the child passes through various critical learning periods. However, for years afterwards people normally continue the process of perfecting and expanding their command of that language, as well as their communicative skills in general. In adulthood, literature can be one of the most challenging and, often, enjoyable means of becoming aware of the potential of the mother tongue. In the unique situation experienced by the SRC, their acquisition of Irish begins in infancy. However, the process of developing a command of the linguistic system is not assisted by the many influences which the DL enjoys. On the other hand, the learning process is subjected to a range of other factors — environmental, social, political, psychological, as well as inter-linguistic — which mould the linguistic system as it develops. Therefore, although Irish is the first language, it will probably always be the language which needs to be defended and promoted, always the TL. It was in order to render that TL more accessible and resilient to pressures from the DL that the Shaw's Road Gaeltacht was founded. Strong measures will always be needed to protect the language of lesser currency from the intrusions of the DL.

As with the second language (L2) learner, the Irish of the SRC may be described as a system which operates somewhere between TL norms and the DL. The children draw from their entire cultural and sociolinguistic background as an expression of their reality. As in any bilingual situation, the two linguistic systems are not isolated into completely separate structures; rather, the DL exerts considerable influence upon the TL. This same phenomenon presents a constant challenge to school teachers, whether they are teaching Irish as one subject on the curriculum or teaching through the medium of Irish. In this sense the L2 may be described in terms of an 'Interlanguage', (Ó Baoill, 1979a). This analytic tool allows the linguist to describe the L2 learner's linguistic system, including the many irregular features which would seem peculiar to a traditional native speaker. The interlanguage of the learner may closely approximate the native speaker's system. On the other hand, it may have reached a more intermediate point in its development towards the TL, or, indeed, it may be at a very incipient stage. The interlanguage system is usually characterised by a degree of instability and fluctuation between linguistic forms, regular and irregular. Nevertheless, it is a system which is governed by its own code of rules. Nonstandard elements can usually be explained by one of the strategies employed by the L2 learner (Ó Baoill, 1981a).

Interlanguage as a descriptive concept is just as relevant to the urban scene where a language is being reintroduced into common usage. Accordingly, it bears some relevance in this consideration of the Irish of the SRC, just as it does to the L2 learner's command of Irish.

Language Norms

The centre of gravity for progression towards the TL must, of course, depend upon the identification of the linguistic norms themselves. For example, a university student will be expected to expose himself to rural Gaeltacht Irish when trying to master the phonological system and to obtain a firm grasp of standard grammatical structures. That objective, as we have seen, is not considered relevant by many of the Bunscoil parents. Adult learners in West Belfast look to the language of their teacher and fluent Irish-speaking neighbours as their goal. The norms of some will be influenced by Irish writers whom they study on exam syllabuses. School children also base their Irish upon that of their teachers, with their experience in Donegal Gaeltacht Colleges exerting some influence upon the developing linguistic repertoire. To whom can teachers turn? Third level courses will have steered them towards considerable proficiency levels. Nevertheless, they often lack confidence in certain areas and find themselves at a loss for resources which could assist them. In particular, this applies to teachers who have studied the language as a subsidiary subject, or perhaps who have not formally studied it at all. One such area of ambiguity concerns the native Irish phonological system. A person who is uncertain about a grammatical or lexical item has easy access to standard forms in a grammar textbook or dictionary. Pronunciation cannot be checked so readily. Indeed, teachers are much more hesitant about correcting pupils' phonological errors than grammatical or lexical ones. (Ó Baoill, 1981b: 40)

Several problems arise, therefore, when deciding what is the 'norm' which should control the linguistic output of the L2 learner or of the child being raised or educated through Irish. This linguistic analysis of the Irish of the SRC identified, as the TL, the Ulster dialect of Irish. County Donegal has survived as the home of the only remaining Gaeltacht area where the tradition of speaking Ulster Irish as the mother tongue has remained unbroken. Standard grammatical forms which are not often heard by native Donegal speakers, but which the SRC encounter in their textbooks, also represent obvious norms for them to assimilate and were taken into account. When I refer to traditional or 'standard' forms in this account, the above definitions apply.

Clearly, however, the interlanguage system which is found among Irish speakers in Belfast is at a disadvantage. There is no locally based and clearly defined standard (especially of pronunciation) to which learners have easy access. Without such an accepted local standard, the Irish spoken in Belfast is vulnerable in the degree to which it is susceptible to influence from the DL.

In chapter 9, a couple of the Bunscoil parents were reported as estimating that Belfast Irish was more 'correct' than that spoken in the Donegal Gaeltacht. These comments reflected the fact that the native systems also show considerable influence of English. Therefore, a great many characteristics of the SRC's Irish which I refer to as irregular, can be heard from native Donegal speakers of all ages. During this chapter it will become apparent that the tendencies and strategies developed in the Irish of the SRC are not restricted to the children. The movement away from traditional norms is an ongoing process which also affects the individuals and communities whom urban revivalists look to as long-standing guardians of the language. Within this context, the identification and preservation of norms becomes more difficult.

It is sometimes pointed out that the English spoken in Belfast contains many features peculiar to regions within that locale (Milroy, 1981). Some of these are modified in certain formal contexts, producing stylistic variations. In some respects, this phenomenon may be justifiably paralleled with the incorporation of irregular forms into the Irish of Belfast. However, the nature and degree of divergence from norms cannot be explained entirely as stylistic variation. As we shall see, many other factors come into effect.

The fact remains that whatever the linguistic goal to which the speaker establishes allegiance, the Irish spoken generally in Belfast, and most definitely by the children of Shaw's Road, serves their communicative requirements satisfactorily. A communicative norm has been developed which relieves some of the pressures which learners experience (CLAR, 1975). The impact of these pressures was discussed in chapter 9, in relation to Bunscoil families. A couple of the Shaw's Road parents mentioned their observation that the children always displayed a tendency to adopt what they called the 'lowest common denominator'. Whatever version most suited the communicative needs of the group was tacitly elected. Often that implied the adoption of a non-standard form directly influenced by the English system. Less frequently, it resulted in the broad acceptance of forms which were unique to the children, yet showed no connection with English. This fact was usually referred to as an inevitable strategy which children will employ in order to meet communicative exigencies. As in the case of the L2, when non-standard forms become fossilised in the children's Irish it is often because standard alternatives have become redundant in terms of today's communicative needs or because an item is being transferred directly from the DL.

Another factor which deserves attention when examining the Irish of the SRC, or of other Belfast Irish speakers, is the question of language loyalty. This factor does not usually require consideration in the study of L2. It is interesting, at this point, to recall the high degree of loyalty which the Bunscoil parents expressed towards the Irish commonly spoken in Belfast as opposed to the Irish of the traditional Gaeltacht. Like the concept of interlanguage, 'language loyalty' is a little complex in this particular sociolinguistic context. In a language contact situation, a standardised version of the language, free from a high level of interference, usually emerges as a defensive reaction to that language's vulnerable position:

> In response to an impending language shift, it (i.e. language loyalty) produces an attempt at preserving the threatened language; as a reaction to interference, it makes the standardised version of the language a symbol and a cause ... It is in a situation of language contact that people most easily become aware of the peculiarities of their language as against others, and it is there that the pure or standardised language most easily becomes a symbol of group integrity. (Weinreich, 1974: 99–102)

We have already glimpsed some of the factors involved in establishing linguistic norms in this particular urban situation. It is not a pure standardised form of the language which generates loyalty at community level. The degree of pride which the North's Irish speakers and learners feel concerning individual and community endeavours to rekindle a sustained interest in the language, against so many odds, leads them to respect every single attempt to use Irish. Indeed, the presence of irregular features in the novice speaker's Irish in some ways reflects the fact that this has not been an academic exercise, supported fully by all the possible services and resources that a sympathetic official stance could introduce. Rather, it has surged upwards through the community, propelled by an energy and determination engendered by themselves. Linguistic purity does not therefore operate in that high position on their scale of values, as it may in some other situations.

Consequently, although adherence to traditional norms is appreciated as the general aim, some deviation must be expected, especially at the level of phonology.

The SRC share that loyalty to their own variety of Irish. The Irish which is spoken around them and by them contains many features upon which academics might frown. Indeed, in certain situations the SRC might also display limited tolerance. At the same time, however, some traditional phonological and grammatical norms would be actively rejected by the children as 'not belonging' to the Irish of Belfast. Linguistic snobbery is just as likely to be rejected by the children as is the careless use of the language in formal situations. Loyalty to 'Belfast Irish' hinges upon a consideration of the circumstances of the language phenomenon to be found there. Irish is the language of the learner: the SRC frequently displayed a sensitivity to that fact. On the other hand they would also check each other's employment of aberrant structures in situations which, in their estimation, demanded a more careful adherence to standard forms.

This tension between acceptance of communicative norms which imply some deviation from formal norms, and the preservation of those features of a linguistic system which distinguish it from other languages, including the DL, poses a challenge which has not yet been faced in the Six Counties. At this relatively incipient stage of the revival of Irish as a functional, effective medium, it is possible that the people are not yet ready to consider the linguistic implications of this natural inertia. With respect to educational programmes for bilingual communities (more specifically, immigrant communities) Einar Haugen warned of the dangers of linguistic straitjacketting:

> It may be better to bend than to break. Acceptance of useful convergence between codes is better than a total rejection of the mother tongue, which is likely to result if one always and everywhere insists on rigid rhetorical norms of the academicians. (Haugen, 1977: 101)

This view is widely held among many of Belfast's Irish speakers also. Alongside them are a substantial body who advocate some stronger resistance to change and interference. Haugen's view does not suggest any merit to allowing the language to landslide into the system of the DL. Protective measures are required. However, it is also important to keep a firm grasp on the reality of what constitutes healthy, inevitable change within a particular set of circumstances. Within immigrant bilingual communities communicative norms often reflect the adaptability of the language in its new environment. A certain degree of stability is required in the speech community so that some checks can be imposed on the linguistic flexibility and, to some extent, unpredictability, preventing excessive cultural and linguistic assimilation. Striking a balance successfully is a delicate and, sometimes, precarious operation.

Resilience versus Fragility

One attitude to be examined questions the need for linguistic controls on a language variety which is emerging so dynamically and defiantly as the Irish language in Belfast. Loyalty to the achievements of that community is well deserved. In addition, tolerance of the problems encountered by learners may even represent the key to diffusing the language as a spoken, viable medium, more freely and successfully. Some linguistic impact from the DL, during this process, is inevitable and natural. The bilingual speech community in Belfast has displayed incredible strength, to have emerged and expanded to the extent which it has. The resilience of the linguistic system itself is demonstrated by the fact that it has survived in this urban centre, isolated from the traditional Gaeltacht and surrounded by an English-speaking society wherein the Irish language has been, often at best, officially disregarded. At the same time, however, the fragility of the speech community has become apparent in other respects, for example when the children of the Bunscoil pass through to an English-medium secondary system of education without any sense of continuity from their Irish-speaking environment. The linguistic system itself wavers in consequence. The degree of pressure imposed by the DL upon the TL makes a similar contribution.

Learner Irish

Further paradoxes are evident in the similarity between the linguistic system of the SRC and the systems of other vulnerable groups. We have already referred to the interlanguage of the L2 learner. Many of the non-standard forms which teachers encounter in their pupils' spoken and written Irish are also heard in the casual chatter and conversation of the SRC. Some of these features, though not all, are modified by the SRC in more formal situations when they believe that traditional structures are expected of them. The error tendencies identified by Ó Domhnalláin and Ó Baoill (Ó Baoill, 1979b; Ó Domhnalláin & Ó Baoill, 1978) in the written Irish of secondary school pupils in the Twenty Six Counties are also typical of the types of errors which teachers in the North encounter in their students' written and oral Irish. With a few exceptions, these irregularities appear, sometimes sporadically and sometimes more consistently, as features of the Irish of the SRC. One of the exceptions would be the use of the present habitual version of the present tense. In Irish the 'tá' form of the substantive verb is used to describe single moments in time, whereas the 'bíonn' form is used in a more continuous sense. Ó Domhnalláin and Ó Baoill reported the usage (or non-usage) of this form as a significant error. However, the SRC use the present habitual tense with relative ease and competence. When communicating through Irish they grasp a 'feel' for those occasions where it is natural and appropriate without having been taught explicitly to differentiate.

Similarities between the Irish of the SRC and the Irish of the second language learner are to be expected, despite the fact that the children are untypical in the sense that they have been raised with Irish as their mother tongue. The vast body of language input which they experience is from second language learners, whether adults or children. English was the first language acquired by their parents and teachers, some learning Irish at school themselves, others learning it as young adults. In addition, other children at the Bunscoil are usually acquiring Irish as a second language, even though it quickly becomes a medium through which they fluently and competently communicate at school.

Dialects in decline

Ironically, however, this language which is emerging with such determination in Belfast and in other areas, effecting a language shift in its own right, also bears much in common with another linguistic phenomenon: language death. Moribund dialects have been seen to pass through the same linguistic processes as this vibrant urban variety is currently demonstrating. Whereas the latter is tentatively, though forcefully, feeling its way, the former slip into decline and disuse. Both systems are vulnerable. The future faced by moribund dialects or whole languages has been evidenced again and again throughout the world, although one need look no further than the Celtic family of languages for examples. When considering this parallel, it is useful to bear in mind Dorian's warning about the folly of presuming that all seemingly moribund languages rigidly follow a pattern of decline and retreat towards ultimate extinction (1981: 111). The moribund dialect often displays some obstinate signs of resistance to the overall pattern. Indeed, the resurgence of Irish in urban 'Galltacht' areas indicates the possibility of reassertion, even when the endangered language had been hanging on by a thread for generations. The similarity which the incipient bilingual situation bears to the dialect which is fast slipping from its earlier position of strength is not restricted to linguistic phenomena triggered as the contact language extends its territory. The two very different language situations also share those more resilient characteristics which seem to defy the undertow.

The 'semi-speaker' in the East Sutherland dialect situation (Dorian, 1981) is endowed with remarkable skills as a passive speaker, which enable him to contribute to the conversation without any restrictions which impede comprehension. In this way, reduced proficiency does not cause a stilted communicative flow. In the case of the SRC, not only are the passive skills alert but the more active, productive language skills enable the children to communicate freely and fluently about a wide spectrum of topics. During the many hours of informal interviewing and social interaction in other scenarios I was very aware of the happy ease with which the children expressed themselves. Strategies such as borrowing from the DL assisted this uninhibited communication. Another significant factor, already mentioned, was the sense of self-assurance which the children had developed in their own identities as proficient Irish speakers. The custom of communicating their needs through Irish at home and at school laid the foundations for this process. However, another important contributory factor is the status which the children enjoy in the eyes of the wider community. Irish speakers in a declining speech community often perceive their language's status to be dwindling, as the most venerable members of their community die, leaving a gap with no *seanchaí* (storyteller), poet or scholar to reinforce the local pride in their language. The native language can be judged to be inferior to the 'high-prestige' DL. Left undefended, disregard of the language's predicament leads to a conclusion that it must, somehow, be unworthy or insignificant. Conversely, in Belfast the mood is one of optimism and the Shaw's Road children symbolise hope. They are aware that they have been the focus of considerable media attention over the years. In many ways they are in a prominent position to which other people aspire. Being raised and educated through Irish, the children took an active role in extending the functional potential of Irish in the North. The story of their Community is followed keenly by everyone interested in Irish and in language revival generally. They are the object of much good will. Their school and Community spearheads the Language Movement in the North in terms of a model for success and a source of motivation. The Shaw's Road children are quietly aware that they are important. This favourably reflects upon their ability and willingness to communicate without restraints.

Like the East Sutherland Gaelic speakers and other vulnerable speech communities, the SRC also share those signs of linguistic tenacity whereby they retain certain grammatical norms which might be expected to change. These linguistic categories themselves may not coincide; for example, consider the Sutherland semi-speaker's ineffectiveness at constructing the passive voice. Rathlin Irish offers another example of the decline of the passive; there, the passive was to survive only in a few petrified expressions (Holmer, 1942: 106). The SRC, on the other hand, showed competence in that particular area. Nevertheless, the same overall pattern holds, where a complex configuration of regular and deviant forms operate side by side within the linguistic system.

It may be reasonably argued that many of the aberrant forms which enter the Irish spoken in this urban neo-Gaeltacht Community, examined more closely below, reflect the pattern of historic changes which mould the language over a period of time as it adapts and responds to a changing environment. In one respect, such developments must be healthy and natural.

It is true that if the language was merely studied in the fashion of classical languages (a category in which some people, in the past, have chosen to view Irish) it might receive an instant immunity to change. However, it is precisely because it is in use that it can incorporate new features as it develops. This phenomenon is viewed by many of Belfast's Irish speakers as an inevitable result of the diffusion of bilingualism in the city. The question of effecting some controls upon that development is a subject which has not yet been tackled. Some future treatment of this issue must examine the tension between the degree of change which represents one healthy aspect of a living, functioning language and that which could ultimately trigger a linguistic avalanche in the direction of the DL.

In relation to the fate of Manx, Professor T. F. Ó Rahilly looked bluntly at what was occurring to the language:

> From the beginning of its career as a written language English influence played havoc with its syntax and it could be said, without much exaggeration, that some of the Manx that has been printed is merely English disguised in a Manx vocabulary. Manx hardly deserved to live. When a language surrenders itself to foreign idiom and when all its speakers become bilingual the penalty is death. (Ó Rahilly, 1972: 121)

This conclusion may appear extreme or severe at a first glance. However, consider the word 'surrenders'. Surely this implies the absence of any real measures aimed at halting assimilation into the system of the DL.

If, on the other hand, any language deserves to survive, it is the Irish language which is emerging in Belfast and in other urban centres with a new vigour. We have already mentioned that linguistic purity has for some time been allocated to a lower position on the scale of values. However, if that position is not carefully analysed and bolstered, balancing the emphasis on quantitative progress, we may find that something is surrendered before its significance has even been realised.

In his outline of the 'Characteristics of Irish dialects in the process of extinction' R. B. Breatnach concluded that moribund dialects were most susceptible to interference at the level of vocabulary. Morphological and phonological norms showed greater resistance. Indeed, borrowed items were generally adapted to the Irish morphological system, e.g. by fixing the Irish verbal noun ending '-áil' onto English verbs — 'fideáil', feeding; 'do mhiteáileas', I met. Syntactic patterns also reflected influence from English idiom and word order in the later stages of decline (Breatnach, 1964).

In the case of the SRC, phonological patterns closely follow the English system to which the children are exposed so intensively, while the impact of the DL is also very evident on the children's syntactic structures. Lexical borrowings do not have the clear lead in anglicising influences, relative to other aspects of the language, which Breatnach found to be the case in moribund dialects. Nevertheless, the children's vocabulary does reflect these influences to some extent. The degree of interference affecting various aspects of the language may differ, but the overall patterns of change appearing in the children's Irish have been influenced by the English system. Parallel changes occurred in dialects of Scottish Gaelic which approached extinction. Indeed, broader historic developments in Scottish Gaelic, which have not yet entered into the Irish language, may be found in the Irish of the SRC. One example of this phenomenon is the disappearance of the imperfect tense from the repertoire of the SRC. The conditional mood, on the other hand, is in common usage. In Scottish Gaelic the imperfect and conditional tenses have completely coalesced — a development which also reached an advanced stage in the Irish of Rathlin Island, before it became extinct in the early part of the twentieth century. The traditional form of the imperfect tense has become a redundant feature for the SRC. They function effectively without it. On rare occasions some tense confusion may result as a young speaker juggles with various forms in search of one which would express the sense of the imperfect. In the following extract the thirteen-year-old boy communicates his message lucidly, but the tenses become a mixture of past and present.

De gnáth, nuair a bhí mé ag an Gaeltacht, B'fhéidir gur glacfaidh (glac-fadh?) [glakha] mé píosa beag de blas s'acu siúd isteach chun — you know — sa dóigh is go mbeidh siad siud ábalta mé a thuigint. Ach ansin, just lab-hair me (le) mo blas fein.

(Usually when I was at the Gaeltacht, I might assume their accent a little, you know, so that they would understand me. But then, just, I spoke (in) my own accent.)

To some extent this example might even reflect the Belfast anecdotal style which can switch into the present or (less frequently) future tense when relating actual or proposed actions of the speaker.

Normally, the children communicate the sense of the imperfect with complete ease and clarity by drawing upon one of three other linguistic resources:

(1) Ba ghnáth leis ... + verbal noun = He used to ... e.g. Ba g(h)náth leis rith an bealach uilig chun na scoile. 'He used to run the whole way to school.'

(2) Past tense of the verb 'to be' + adverb of time + gerund, e.g. Bhí daoine i gcónaí ag teacht anseo le caint linn. 'People were always coming here to talk to us.'

(3) Adverb of time + conditional mood of verb 'to be' + gerund, e.g. I ndiaidh sin bheadh muid uilig ag ceol ... 'Afterwards we would all be singing ...'

However, as well as this broad historic type of change which has somewhat abruptly appeared in Belfast, other traits are more specifically characteristic of dialects in the process of extinction. One example of this would be the weakening of the nominal character of the verbal noun so that the personal pronoun becomes the object of the verbal noun, as it is in English. This development occurred in moribund Scottish dialects and in Manx. In Irish the conservative structure is found in: 'Tá sí do mo cheartú', 'She is correcting me'. However, the more likely version to be heard among the SRC would be 'Tá sé ag ceartú mé', with the pronoun stated explicitly at the end and the 'disguise' of mutation removed from the verbal noun. This syntactic change has become relatively stable in the children's Irish. It is becoming established more widespreadly, and is very commonly encountered in the L2 learner's repertoire.

An example of a change which is less predictable, but rather more sporadic and characteristic of only one group of children, is the use of certain emphatic personal pronouns in their accusative form instead of the nominative form which would be expected. These children would be just as likely to produce the conservative form:

Bhí *seisean* sa bhaile: '*He* was at home'

as the deviant form:

Bhí *eisean* sa bhaile.
Other examples of the latter are:
beidh *eisean* fiche *he* will be twenty
bhí *ise* tinn *she* was sick
bhí *iad* siúd ag teacht *they* were coming

This weakening of the nominative form of the pronoun is one of the historic characteristics of Scottish Gaelic and Manx, as opposed to specific traits associated with one or two moribund dialects. However, the forms 'iad' and 'í' sometimes replace 'siad' (they) and 'sí' (she) in the Irish of Tory Island. In Rathlin, the same trend occurred, influenced probably by Scottish, before the demise of the Rathlin dialect.

In an article entitled 'Linguistic trends in the terminal stage of Q-Celtic dialects', Professor G. Stockman (1988) highlights four trends which were common to Manx, Scottish Gaelic and Irish dialects, while on the brink of extinction.

(1)   Reduction of the case system.
(2)   Simplification of the phoneme system.
(3)   Loss of lenition.
(4)   English influence on vocabulary, morphology and syntax.

It could be added that these linguistic trends are to be found, to some extent, in every Irish-speaking speech community today. However, they are particularly advanced in the L2's system. The Irish of the SRC is moulded by these same trends.

The case system

As Stockman points out, the case system in Irish has been greatly reduced during the development from old to modern Irish. The dative case remains only in a few fossilised phrases. Similarly, the accusative is now obsolete and the dual form has also disappeared, leaving only a singular and plural. Nevertheless, today, learners still find the declension of nouns a fairly complicated exercise. The tendency is to reduce the whole system further. The SRC may or may not employ the vocative, for example. In some incidences the use of the vocative quite dramatically alters the sound of a name. Names which begin with 'F' are least likely to be heard in the vocative because the initial letter becomes silent when it is lenited.

The genitive case remains in modern Irish. However, this is another area where a great deal of modification is taking place in modern spoken Irish, especially in urban centres. Learners find it a difficult grammatical feature to master. Declension of a noun in the genitive requires attention to the word order, initial mutation and morphological alteration to the noun. Sometimes the SRC fulfil all requirements, although this occurrence lacks consistency. The most predictable and reliable instances of its usage involve petrified expressions, e.g.

mála scoile	school bag (i.e. bag of the school)
obair bhaile	home work (i.e. work of the home)
a cuid oibre	her work (i.e. her share of work)
Mí na Nollag	month of Christmas
deireadh seachtaine	a weekend (i.e. the end of a week)
teach an phobail	the church (house of the people)
ag guí chun Dé	praying to God
i lár na hoíche	in the middle of the night

Otherwise, a process of change is under way, whereby the traditional word order remains as an indicator of the genitive. However, its other two signals have come to be regarded as somewhat redundant; they may or may not appear. In the following examples only the syntactic norm survives. The nouns are unmutated and uninflected, where that would normally be expected:

fa choinne bliain	for a year
fa choinne siulóid	for a walk
i ndiaidh an cogadh	after the war

chun an Gaeltacht	to the Gaeltacht
doras na cailíní	the girls' door (i.e. door of the girls' room)

Sometimes, among these systematic changes which characterise the children's Irish, non-systematic irregularities sporadically appear. For example, mutation might be applied where it is inappropriate, or the feminine form of the definite article might be used with a masculine noun. These rare occurrences which deviate from the general pattern of change are indicative of the state of flux in which the linguistic system finds itself.

That general pattern of the decaying genitive was reported by Nancy Dorian as a feature of the Scottish Gaelic of East Sutherland (Dorian, 1981: 130–1) The same tendency, for the syntactic structure to resist change while mutational and morphological signals grew less reliable, was also described by Holmer (1942: 89) in reference to Rathlin. In the dialects of the more vulnerable Gaeltacht areas, in the past, this same process was in operation (Stockman, 1988). Similarly, in many of today's Gaeltacht areas, the inflection of nouns and their accompanying adjectives, according to the genitive, shows the same susceptibility to inconsistency and fluctuation.

The phoneme system

Breatnach (1964: 145) observed that modifications of the phonological system in moribund Irish dialects were much less dramatic than other changes which occur in the language. Conversely, the emerging sound system in the urban situation distinctly reflects anglicising influences. The English phonological system represents the substratum upon which the Irish system is built rather than the intrusive influence which acts upon the native system.

The principal difference between the two contact languages, which leaves its mark on the Irish of the SRC, on learners' Irish generally, and on some dialects in the process of extinction, is the correspondence of various 'neutral' English consonants to a dual system of palatalised and non-palatalised phonemes in Irish, e.g.

$$\text{English } /f/ \longrightarrow \begin{array}{c} \text{Irish } /f'/ \\ /f/ \end{array}$$

A similar dichotomy exists regarding the consonant phonemes, /p m b k g t d n/ and, traditionally, a correspondence of a single English phoneme to four Irish ones applies to 'l' and 'n'. Subsequently, for example, the 'l' sound in each of the following Irish words is distinctive —

fill /f'iL'/ (return)	mall /maL/ (late)
file /f'il'/ (poet)	mála /mal/ (bag)

Similarly, the final 'n' sounds in these words are phonemically different —

> ban /ban/ (of women)   banna /baN/ (band)
> bain /ban'/ (take)   bainne /baN'/ (milk)

However, even native speakers in the strong Gaeltacht areas no longer distinguish between all of these contrasts and, during the more vulnerable stages of declining dialects, further reductions occur. This becomes most evident in studies which examine inter-generational patterns (Ó Dochairtaigh, 1982).

The weakening of the 'slender/broad' opposition of consonants is one of the ways in which the phonemic system of moribund dialects has become reduced. Scottish Gaelic shows this same trend, and in Manx the distinction has disappeared altogether. This tendency towards neutralisation of consonants is strong in the Irish of the SRC. Where there is a likelihood of confusion, because of this process, compensation is made within the context of the sentence. For example, the nouns in the following examples are usually pronounced identically because of the loss of palatalised 'r' -

> a rothar: his bike
> a rothair: his bikes

However, ambiguity rarely results from this loss because of the opportunities to clarify the distinction in its context.

Lenition

Loss of lenition in the Irish of the SRC will be discussed below. This represents a phenomenon which is very characteristic of moribund dialects, as well as of learners' Irish. Lenition, the most common form of initial mutation to be found in Irish, occurs sporadically rather than consistently in the less robust dialects.

English influence on vocabulary, morphology and syntax

The influence of English is destined to make an impact on the Irish language of today. Its implications with regards to the Irish of the SRC will be discussed more fully below. Obviously, the extent of this influence is also intensified in dialects which are yielding as the DL further asserts itself. This phenomenon does not fully explain all the changes occurring in those dialects; however, it is a central factor which triggers so many other changes. In moribund dialects it ultimately governs the changing pattern of the linguistic system. Indeed, even in the stronger dialects, English is today the principal contributor to changes occurring within the linguistic mould. Breatnach described the lexicon as the area which most demonstrated this influence (1964: 141–5).

Transferred lexical items and borrowed roots, onto which Irish morphological segments are fixed, are quite characteristic of the Irish which is heard from native speakers in rural Gaeltacht areas. English idiom and word order are also commonly superimposed onto the Irish system.

However, it is the more vulnerable speech groups, including the L2 learners, whose linguistic system is most likely to be saturated by anglicising influences. Regarding dialects which fell into disuse, striking a balance between what Haugen called 'bending' and 'not breaking', usually proved inadequate under the weight of other, mainly sociolinguistic, factors. The newly emerging bilingual community has the advantage of its own determination and commitment as its principal security, for it is conscious of its own defensive position. However, it may not yet be aware of the specific threat posed by a sparsity of linguistic controls.

The four trends outlined above give some insight into the changing linguistic shape of dialects approaching extinction. In these speech communities English encroaches on language behavioural patterns in traditionally Irish domains as well as on the linguistic system itself. In urban scenes where the direction of the language shift is being, in a limited sense, reversed, many of the same characteristics prevail. We have referred to the fact that there is some degree of conformity between the nature of linguistic developments which have occurred historically and those which are precipitated more abruptly in moribund dialects. The difference in the two processes lies, not in the *nature* of the changes which are evolving, but in the *amount* of change (Dorian, 1981: 151).

In the case of the resurgent language, an additional factor comes into operation that is the *velocity* of that change. In the early chapters of this book, some account was given of the history of the Irish Revival in Belfast. The language shift which, in some parts of the city, is under way today has, nevertheless, come into effect quite dramatically. The Shaw's Road Community has been in existence since 1969. During the 1970s, the people of West Belfast became aware that, for the first time ever, a Gaeltacht Community was thriving in their midst. The North's first all-Irish school had been in operation for less than two decades at the time of writing. It represents the momentum of the growing interest invested into Irish-medium education, propelling the bilingualisation process forward most effectively. The diffusion of the language is facilitated through the extended network of families and friends. This dimension to the resurgence of Irish in Belfast and elsewhere in the North has erupted quite forcefully and relatively suddenly in the last couple of decades. A further indication of how recent this development is, is the fact that Irish can now be heard in West Belfast without attracting any surprise or curious attention, whereas even the Shaw's Road children can recall the well-meant observations of fellow passengers in taxis or fellow shoppers in local supermarkets. Even the emergence of adult evening classes has expanded from a handful of small classes scattered throughout West Belfast to a number in excess of 70, within a relatively short period of time. Political trends also influenced this rapid expansion of Irish speakers, learners and learning activities. For example, internment was introduced in 1971 and prison populations swelled accordingly. Many of these prisoners learned Irish during their period of arrest. The input of 'new' Irish speakers and others, motivated to learn the language, back into the community represented one contribution to the surge of intensity in the Language Movement. This relative abruptness of the shift towards bilingualism corresponded to an accelerated pace of change in the linguistic system itself. Accordingly, that development influenced the intensity with which a number of overall trends entered the Irish commonly spoken in Belfast and to be heard in the linguistic output of the Shaw's Road children.

The examination of those trends, which follows, underlines, to a large extent, the natural tendency towards which the language leans in the modern bilingual situation. These patterns are also evident to varying degrees in the Irish of native speakers and learners. As we have said, it is the amount and rate of change that govern the main differences between the various speech groups.

Linguistic Trends

Simplification of the TL

This process operates in the language of learners and in the declining language. At a slower rate, it also represents a natural inclination in the evolvement of languages generally. The SRC simplify conservative norms for a variety of reasons. However, one of the principal factors is the nature of the Irish to which they are exposed. So many speakers around them employ similar reductive strategies. Consequently, their exposure to certain 'standard' forms is limited to the Irish which is used by a few parents, some teachers, or some other language contacts. On occasion, linguistic features are simplified by the children in order to facilitate complete comprehension in the social group.

Any strategy which accommodates effective, uninhibited communication is likely to be adopted. The ultimate objective of contributing to the conversation cannot be jeopardised by a complex grammatical structure. A joke falls sadly flat if the enthusiastic speaker delays the punch line while he ponders grammatical accuracy. It is more convenient to employ simplified structures which become accepted as a communicative norm, as opposed to the standard orthodox norm.

LINGUISTIC TRENDS IN IRISH

This economising process is employed quite extensively by the children. Subsequently, its effects are evident across a considerable expanse of linguistic categories. Some of these categories have been already referred to because of the pattern of change paralleled in other speech groups, for example, the case system. The general tendency to simplify and reduce this system has been taken further in the Irish of the SRC. The overall pattern points to a movement in the direction of the nominative case, with the vocative disappearing and one signal of the genitive remaining, i.e. word order.

We have also referred to the levelling out of the palatalised and non-palatalised consonant opposition and to the weakening use of lenition. Holmer identified simplifications in the initial mutation system as among the first incidences of change in moribund Celtic dialects (1940: 36). The mutational system is so prevalent in Celtic languages that its collapse leads to the reduction or disappearance of other grammatical and phonological features. For example, the disappearing velar fricatives, corresponding to the orthographical representations 'ch' and 'gh' can slip out of the system, almost unnoticed, partly because of the loss of lenition. These sounds most frequently occur in grammatical environments traditionally requiring lenition, e.g. sa ghairdín/in the garden; an ghealach/the moon; oíche gharbh/a rough night; ceithre chat/four cats; mo chóta/my coat. Consequently, the omission of initial mutation greatly diminishes the need for the phonemes /x/ and /Y/.

Nouns resisting the omission of initial mutation in the children's Irish may be found in petrified expressions or terms, e.g. 'fear an phoist'/the post man; Bóthar na bhFál/the Falls Road; i gcónaí/always; i ndiaidh/after; i mbun/in charge; ár dteanga/our language. Other categories of nouns retain lenition within particular environments. Names of family members retain lenition after the possessive adjective: mo mhamaí/my mammy; a mhóirí/his grandmother; a dhearth(áir/his brother; do thuismitheoirí/ your parents. The second form of initial mutation, nasalisation, is less predictable in this category.

Attributive adjectives are traditionally lenited in particular instances, e.g. when qualifying a feminine noun, or following a preposition + masculine noun, e.g. an bhean mhór/the big woman; leis an pháiste bheag/with the small child. However, the SRC's treatment of adjectives has dispensed with initial mutation even more thoroughly than in the case of nouns.

Some grammatical categories show greater resistance to this change than others. Irregular verbs, for example, tend to retain traditional lenition in the past and conditional tenses, e.g. thiocfadh liom/I could; bheadh sé/ it would be; ní fhaca sé/he did not see; chuaigh me/I went; ní dhearna tu/you did not do. A few other individual regular verbs also demonstrate consistency, especially some verbs with an initial 's' or 't'. When lenited, these sounds are articulated as the glottal 'h'. The words 'shíl'/thought, and 'thit'/fell, are examples where appropriate lenition is rarely omitted.

The verbal system in general has experienced further reductions in the number of tense markers. For example, what has evolved as the negative particle preceding past tense regular verbs, 'níor', shows signs of being reduced to 'ní', the particle associated with irregular past tense verbs. However, 'ní' also precedes verbs in the present and future tenses. Therefore, in the examples,

'ní ith siad' (they ate): 'ní labhair mise' (I did not speak)

instead of the standard,

'níor ith siad': 'níor labhair mise'

the only remaining past tense signal is the lack of a present tense suffix ending. In more 'careful' speech the conservative particle would be used.

Regarding number, the imperative form remains in the second person singular. The plural form is rarely employed. Sometimes, however, the second person plural pronoun will precede the command, e.g. 'sibhse, tar isteach' (you (pl), come (singular) in. This reduction reflects the English imperative form. Further change in the representation of number in the verbal system is discussed below as a generalising rather than a reductive trend.

Outside of the verbal system, another area where reduction occurs is in the production of numerals. The construction of numerals in Irish is a complex procedure; learners find this a particularly difficult aspect of the language to master. Different systems exist for cardinals, ordinals and personal numerals. Not only do rules of initial mutation apply but syntactic norms also come into effect. Note the position of the nouns in the following examples:

trí *chapall* = three horses
trí *chapall* is fiche = twenty-three horses
an dara *lá* (de Mhi na Nollag) = the second day (of December)
an dóú *lá* is fiche = the twenty-second day

The pattern adopted by the children (and by many other Irish speakers today) has been a total simplification based on the syntax of numbers less than eleven, according to which the entire numeral precedes the noun. This parallels the English system. In addition, the noun is frequently produced in the plural, contrary to the conservative structure;

fiche a naoi gasúraí / twenty-nine boys
daichead a sé *tithe* / forty-six houses

There is a tendency for teachers to reinforce this adapted system. This observation is based on my own experience. Since beginning to teach young children through Irish I have been aware that this simplified form can 'slip' out in the interests of clarity, during mathematical exercises, even though the form is not naturally a part of my own Irish. The fact is that young children can be distracted from the concept being illustrated, if they first have to overcome grammatical barriers. The only way I could check this inclination during oral exercises was by couching the conservative structures in additional clarifying ones, e.g. 'Bhí sé bhó dhéag sa pháirc — sin sé déag, agus cheannaigh an feirmeoir trí chapall déag — trí dhéag de chapaill ...' (There were sixteen cows in the field — that's sixteen, and the farmer bought thirteen horses — thirteen (of) horses ...) Alternatives are to write the number on the blackboard or to produce pictures. Regarding ordinals, the lower numbers have persisted in common usage among the children. The higher numbers are quite likely to be produced as cardinals by some of the children, e.g. 'fiche a cúig de Bhealtaine' (literally = the twenty-five of May), instead of the standard 'an cúigiú lá is fiche de Bhealtaine'. Some of the children show a stronger resistance to this particular change and still usually adhere to the standard.

The reductive process does not only operate at levels where entire systems or structures are simplified. Abbreviations on a much smaller scale are also quite typical. For example, because the preposition 'chuig' (to) is generally pronounced by the children as [eg] it has coalesced with the preposition 'ag' (at). This feature is quite widespread in some dialects (Achill, Tory, Ros Goill). The SRC are beginning to represent this change in their written Irish. Another specific development might be paralleled to the reasoning of the hiatus. Normally, where prepositions terminating in a vowel precede another vowel, in a possessive adjective or the definite article, the two vowels are bridged with a consonant or else merged. This norm is frequently disregarded by the children in preference of the raw, uninflected elements

Standard	SRC
leis an / with the	le an
lena / with her	le a
lenár /with our	le ar
da / to his	do a

Another dimension to the reductive process in the linguistic system is its selectiveness. This involves the elimination of elements which have limited informational value. We have already seen examples of the reduction of grammatically redundant indicators, e.g. in the treatment of the genitive case. Features which do not add to the information being communicated are treated as semantically redundant and, as such, are quite likely to be omitted.

Naturally, the communicative flow does not suffer because other signals remain. Whether the speaker articulates the standard form of the comparative adjective 'is deacra' (harder) or leaves the adjective unchanged as 'is deacair', the sense is perfectly clear. In effect, the comparative/superlative form of the adjective is sometimes, but not consistently, inflected by the children. Certain adjectives are more traditionally treated than others, e.g. the common forms — níos measa (worse); nios mó (bigger); níos fearr (better); níos lú (smaller); níos deise (nicer); níos luaithe (earlier); níos minice (more often).

Any possible confusion, resulting from reductions is normally clarified within the context of the discourse. For example, the phrase 'ag bualadh na mná' translates as 'striking the woman', where the article and noun are in the genitive. However, if the structure follows the ongoing pattern whereby the word order is the only remnant of the genitive, then the phrase would be referring to 'the women'. It is the context of the sentence which clarifies any ambiguity.

Overgeneralisation

This trend is, as Ó Baoill points out (1979a), very characteristic of the interlanguage of learners, as well as the linguistic systems of other groups. Overgeneralisation occurs when the speaker extends the traditional application of one of the language's rules. One example of this concerns the construction of certain irregular verbs in the present tense. An overgeneralisation of the future tense forms of these verbs has established quite a strong foothold in the children's Irish. The standard grammatical construction is as follows:

Verb	Present (3rd person)	Future (3rd person)
to go	téann sé	rachaidh sé
to give	tugann sé	tabharfaidh sé
to get	faigheann sé	gheobhaidh sé
to come	tagann sé	tiocfaidh sé

In these cases the children show quite a strong tendency to add the present tense 'ann/eann' ending to the future tense stem, producing the following present tense forms: rachann sé (he goes); tabharann sé (he gives); gheobhann sé (he gets); tiocann sé (he comes).

This development is not unique to the children's Irish. The first two forms, 'tabharann' and 'rachann', can sometimes be heard amongst children in rural Gaeltacht areas and, indeed, among some adult speakers. This hybrid form is used alongside standard forms of the present tense. It is the latter which the SRC encounter in their school textbooks. In addition, they are also familiar with the distinctive Ulster dialect varieties of these verbs: théid sé (he goes); bheir sé (he gives); gheibh sé (he gets); thig sé (he comes). These three forms alternate in the Irish of the SRC. It is when their own self-monitoring systems are most relaxed, in casual, carefree situations, that the second form is most likely to appear. The other two 'standard' forms can be used, either sporadically or as a clarification of the tense. Consider the following extract of a conversation with a ten-year-old boy, during his stay in Rannafast (in the Donegal Gaeltacht). The boy is explaining that his Donegal peers are attending school every day, but that he is free from school until his return home:

Researcher: An dtéann siad ar scoil?
Do they go to school?
Boy: Sé. Rachann. Ní rachann muidinne.
Yes. They do (go). We don't go.
Researcher: Ní théann sibhse ar scoil anois?
You don't go to school now?
Boy: Ní théann. Chan go rachaimid ar ais go dtí Béal Feirste.
No (we don't go). Not until we go back to Belfast.

This speaker has chosen to use the non-standard form of the present tense, 'rachann', based on the future stem. However, where the speaker wishes to distinguish between the present freedom from school in Rannafast and the future return to school in Belfast, he draws on the orthodox form. As a result, although the present tense form would be expected after the conjunction 'go', the future tense is employed. This represents a confusion of tenses, according to standard norms. However, the speaker's choice is systematic, according to his own terms and rules of clarification.

Overgeneralisation is evident in the extension of the analytic form of the verb. According to standard norms, the first person singular and plural are expressed as a synthetic part of the verb in the present tense. The second person is also included in the verbal form of the conditional mood. The future tense has a first person plural synthetic form. However, the SRC tend to generalise the analytic form by always adding the personal pronoun. This leads to the introduction of redundant signals, as opposed to their elimination — e.g. feicim mé (I see); déanaim mé (I do); rachfá tú (you would go); ithim mé (I eat); thabharfadh siad (they would give). This seems to represent a transitional stage, approaching an overall shift towards a single form of each tense, followed by the pronoun as the only person-indicator. That tense form is being based on the third person form — e.g. téann mise (I go); déanann mise (I do); labharann muidne (we speak); ní íosfadh mise (I would not eat).

Another aspect of the verbal system which is being influenced by this process of overgeneralisation, concerns the standard syntactic structure whereby the infinitive normally comes at the end of the sentence, preceded by the noun, e.g.

Caithfidh mé an obair a dhéanamh. = I must do the work (literally — the work to do).

This structure often causes problems for learners, showing interference from the English syntax. An exception to this traditional word order occurs following the verb of motion;

Tá mé ag dul a dhéanamh na hoibre (I am going to do the work)

In this environment the noun is rendered in the genitive case, preceded by the infinitive form of the verb. It is interesting that the SRC have generalised the former structure, so that it is found in the traditional context, e.g.

Glacfaidh sé mí dó cailin a fháil. (It will take him a month to get a girl)
... ag iarraidh gual a iompar (trying to carry coal)
... an t-Aifreann a rá (to say Mass)

However, its function has been generalised to apply to the latter structure, following the verb of motion — e.g.

Tá siad ag dul an ceol a fháil. (They are going to get the music)
Bhí siad ag dul an cat a mharú. (They were going to kill the cat)

Further overgeneralisations in the syntax are based upon the traditional verbal noun structure:

ag déanamh; doing
ag imirt; playing
ag troid; fighting

This form is taking over the structure traditionally used to express certain states or positions, based upon use of the preposition + possessive adjective. Structures like 'i mo shuí' (sitting; literally, in my sitting), show clear signs of yielding to the 'ag' + VN structure.

Although the process of overgeneralisation is under way, it is still at an intermediate stage. Not only is the traditional structure present within the receptive repertoire, but it is also produced by the children in more 'careful' speech. Nevertheless, there is a strong overall preference being shown for 'ag' + VN. Consequently, a range of modifications to the traditional structure is possible, reflecting the graded steps in this transitional process. Firstly, the conservative structure might be produced: 'Tá tusa i do sheasamh' (You are standing).Other possibilities are:

(1) 'Tá tusa ina shuí' — where the role of the third person possessive adjective
is extended. Specification of person in the possessive adjective is redundant
because of the presence of the pronoun. Other persons are therefore identified by the pronouns, e.g.

Bhí muinne ina shuí. (We were sitting.)
Bhí mise, Una agus Maire ina shuí anseo. (Una, Maire and myself
were sitting here.)

This tendency towards generalisation of the third person (masculine) has
been evident in various dialects, for example, Tory, Ros Goill, Tyrone
(Hamilton, 1974; Lucas, 1979; Wagner & Stockman, 1965).

(2) 'Tá tusa a suí' — where the preposition 'i' (in) is eliminated. Although
the remaining 'a' originally represented the possessive adjective, it
becomes equated with the 'ag' + present participle of verbs. Other
examples are

... a bhí a luí (who were lying down)
... bhí mé a seasamh (I was standing)

This overgeneralisation of the verbal noun is occurring simultaneously in
rural Gaeltacht areas, among younger speakers.

Interdependence of linguistic changes

The erosion of 'i mo shuí' type structures has been reinforced by other
developments in the children's Irish. The general strengthening of the personal
pronoun exerts considerable impact upon this, as well as other, prepositional and
verbal structures, traditionally requiring the possessive adjective.

SRC	Norm
ar cúl iad (behind them)	ar a gcúl
i ndiaidh muidne (after us)	inár ndiaidh
fa choinne tusa (for you)	fa do choinne
in éadan iad (against them)	ina n-éadan
i mbun é (in charge of it)	ina bhun
ag bualadh mé (hitting me)	do mo bhualadh
ag déanamh é (doing it)	á dhéanamh
ag gortú iad (hurting them)	á ngortú
ag fáil é (getting it)	á fháil
ag foghlaim é (learning it)	á fhoghlaim

All of these developments reflect strong anglicising influences. As in English, the personal pronoun becomes the object of the verbal noun. In addition, these specific changes within the linguistic system influence each other, weakening other structures which share similar key features.

The above examples are also gaining some access to the Irish of the traditional Gaeltacht today. Naturally, the more vulnerable speech groups show less resistance. These particular changes have been noted as features of moribund dialects (Stockman, 1988). Ó Rahilly (1972: 136) describes this occurrence in Scottish Gaelic and Manx. Similarly, the interlanguage of learners is characterised by these syntactic irregularities.

Like so many aspects of the language, the above changes are reinforced by the impending collapse of the mutation system. The possessive adjective usually requires initial mutation of the noun. In the third person, singular and plural, this is the only indicator of person.

> a carr — her car
> a charr — his car
> a gcarr — their car

However, if mutation is omitted, the context usually includes a pronoun which can clarify the person. Compensation is also made by the increasing use of the prepositional form, 's'againne' etc. to indicate possession, e.g. hata s'aige — his hat (hat of his); madadh s'aici — her dog (dog of hers). The decaying mutation system is a key factor in the developing linguistic character. Its disappearance influences most aspects of the linguistic system.

Another feature, directly influenced by the relaxation of initial mutation, is the neutralisation of gender distinctions in nouns. This system has already been simplified, in a broader historical sense, by the disappearance of the neuter. Mutation is the principal indicator of gender, with feminine nouns in the nominative and qualifying adjectives being lenited. Usually, however, little significance is attached to gender signals and, consequently, the distinction is not consistently made. Feminine nouns may be lenited by the children, in accordance with grammatical norms, but its occurrence is no longer reliable. This development is most applicable to inanimate objects and to animals. The preservation of nominal gender distinctions remains more predictable in reference to people, e.g.

> D'aithin muid an *bhean* (We recognised the woman)

Similarly, corresponding masculine and feminine object pronouns remain:

> Chonaic mé *eisean*. (I saw him.) Bhuail sé í. (He struck her.)

The gender distinction between the masculine pronouns, sé/é, and the feminine ones, sí/í, is also well preserved. In traditional Gaeltacht dialects the phonological distinction is much weaker than that articulated in Belfast. This fact reflects the influence of written Irish in the urban scene.

The more common prepositional pronouns also tend to remain intact, in reference to people:

Bhí eagla orm roimhe. (I was afraid of him.)
Tá aithne acu uirthi. (They know her.)
Tá a fhios aici. (She knows.)

However, the gender of inanimate objects and animals is generally disregarded in pronouns as it is in nouns. In the following examples the feminine nouns are not distinguished from masculine nouns and pronouns correspond:

Sé an *Fraincis* an teanga is fearr leis na múinteoirí. French is the language preferred by the teachers.

... agus bhí mise ag amaidí thart le mo *bróga* is caith mé é amach an fhuinneog. Bhí sé, bhí sé, bhí sé, i lár an bóthar ...
... and I was fooling around with my shoes and I threw one (it) out the window. It was, it was, it was in the middle of the road ...

Therefore, even though initial mutation does not apply to pronouns, the latter are influenced by the relaxation of gender distinctions in nouns.

The linguistic developments described above result from the universal propensity to cast off superfluous items, deemed informationally redundant, and to extend the traditional role of remaining features. When key features are eroded, a mesh of other, related characteristics succumb. This may occur, in domino fashion, as in the case of gender pronoun neutralisation. On the other hand, changes also emerge which are influenced by various other developments simultaneously. Often, several interlinguistic influences are in operation. Consider, for example, the simplification of the phoneme system. As mentioned, the palatalised version of 'r' has not been incorporated into the children's Irish, as is the case, generally, in the city. Consequently, the two 'r's in the following phrase are pronounced identically;

i lár an bhóthair; in the middle of the road

However, this articulation can also be attributed to the simplification of the case system, whereby the genitive case has reduced its number of signals, including, in this case, palatalisation of the final consonant in the noun. Other reductions to the phoneme system are partly attributable to the relaxation of initial mutation, as well as to their absence from the English system.

Fluctuation between variations

The unique situation of the SRC places them in a position where they can draw on a wide range of linguistic alternatives, some regular and some irregular. The result can be viewed as colourful and satisfying the linguistic needs of the children. Simultaneously, that very intensity of colourful variation is indicative of the rapid state of flux which the Irish language is experiencing in Belfast. As seen above, the changes which characterise the Irish of the SRC, and that spoken widely in Belfast, can be set in the framework of the more global process of language evolution. Within this context, it becomes apparent that many of the changes to appear in the children's Irish can be identified, at various stages of development, in Gaeltacht areas where the tradition of Irish continues; in those areas where the language declined; and in the learning situation where Irish is being acquired as a second language. The range and acceleration of change, typifying the incipient bilingual situation, produces an additional trend in the children's Irish: the high frequency of alternation between 'standard' and aberrant forms.

In the case of the two verbs 'to be', the same degree of flux occurs between traditional usage and erosion of the two verbs' distinctive functions. In the following extract, the speaker switches from the substitution of the copula by the substantive verb to the traditional copula construction:

Girl (11 years old): Tá mise an duine is sine.
                   I am the eldest person.
Researcher: Tá tusa ar an duine is sine?
                   You are the eldest person?
Girl: Is mé.
                   Yes (I am).

Some changes are more firmly asserted and less susceptible to flux. This is particularly true of the sound system because of the substratum of English.

Phonetic articulation tends to be based on corresponding sounds in the English system. Accordingly, the levelling of palatalised and non-palatalised distinctions is well under way. Where corresponding phonemic distinctions exist in the English system distinctions are preserved in the Irish. Hence, the replacement of the traditional palatalised stops by affricates, e.g. the words

   tiubh [t'uh]; thick
   déan [d'an]; do
   tinn [t'iN']; sick

are pronounced the same as the English words 'chew', 'Jan', 'chin', respectively. This particular feature entered Antrim Irish, and is heard to a large extent in

Donegal Irish (Gregg, 1964; Wagner, 1959; Ó Searcaigh, 1925: 103–7) In the Irish of the SRC these affricates are firmly established.

Another example of phonetic developments which are entrenched in the children's system is the narrowing of certain diphthongs. In Irish, there is a wide range of distinctive diphthongs. Some of these are narrowed by the children or reduced to a single vocalic sound. Again, this development results from the tendency to produce sounds based on corresponding English utterances.

Traditional	SRC	like Belfast English utterance
d'iarr [d'i:ar] (asked)	[dziər] or [dzi:r]	jeer
síor [ʃi:ər] (eternal)	[ʃiər] or [ʃi: r]	sheer

Diphthongs show most resistance, in the children's Irish, in final position, for example in the words rua (red); luath (early); dóigh (way); léamh (reading).

Grammatical deviations are among the most tenacious developments, e.g.

(a) the articulation of numerals before plural nouns

> sé deag daoine: sixteen people
> fiche a naoi gasúraí: twenty-nine boys

(b) the extended function of 'cionn is' (because). This conjunction traditionally precedes a causal clause, e.g.

> cionn is gur ghortaigh mé é; because I hurt him.

However, the SRC employ this conjunction before nouns, prepositions, verbs, the definite article, as well as in its orthodox environment, e.g.

> cionn is níor smaoinigh mé; because I did not think
> cionn is na daoine sin; because of those people
> cionn is go bhfuil daoine ...; because people are ...
> cionn is le daoine ...; because, with people ...
> cionn is bíonn eagla orthu; because they are afraid

(c) object of infinitive precedes verb in future of intention, e.g.

> tá mise ag gabhail Gaeilge a labhairt
> I am going to speak Irish

(d)   pronoun as object of verb, e.g.

>   ag glanadh iad
>   cleaning them

One or two older members showed a preference for the conservative structure
(d), 'á nglanadh'. In these cases the irregular form was less frequently produced.
The following extract from the discourse of one teenaged girl shows fluctuation
between standard and irregular structures:

> Bhí fuath agamsa ar an Bhéarla, sure, agus mé á fhoghlaim. Shíl mise, tá a
> fhios agat an dóigh le teanga eile — Fraincis — Ba gnáth liomsa i gcónaí a
> rá le mo mhamaí — Bhí deacracht agam a(g) foghlaim é. Bhí fiche dá
> dheanamh é ...

> (I hated English, sure, when I was learning it. I thought, you know how
> with other languages — French — I used to say to my mammy — I had
> difficulty learning it. Twenty (pupils) were doing it ...)

In this extract, the traditional form, *á fhoghlaim*, is followed by the SRC norm,
ag foghlaim é, and by an intermediate structure, *dá dheanamh é*. This example
of flux between forms is indicative of the more systematic shift towards the pronoun-governed structure.

Changes which have completely, or almost completely, replaced standard
forms are much less common than changes which occur sporadically, alternating
with the corresponding norms. Consider, for example, the use of prepositions.
Many of the conservative associations between verbs and prepositions are preserved in the children's Irish, e.g.

eist le; listen to	díol as; pay for
amharc ar; look at	tabhair do; give to
taispeain do; show to	scríobh chuig/ag; write to
tosaigh ar; begin to	tá meas aige air; he respects it
smaoinigh ar; think about	tá grá agam dó; I love it

Similarly, some irregular usages are quite consistent, e.g. 'ag cuartú do leabhar'/searching for a book, which is substituted for the traditional genitive structure, 'ag cuartú leabhair'.

Deviations from norms often reflect the influence of English. These usually
alternate with the traditional usage of prepositions, e.g.

> Fuair se greim de Alastair/He got a grip of Alastair/Fuair se greim ar ...

> Bhí eagla orm, cineál, do na múinteoirí/I was sort of afraid of the teachers/
> Bhí eagla air roimh ...

An bhfuil slághdan agat? Do you have a cold?
An bhfuil slághdan ort?

Alternation between standard and aberrant forms also applies to direct and indirect relative clauses. Some of the older children produce the regular forms quite consistently. More generally, however, individuals produce aberrant forms as well as the orthodox structures, e.g.

(a) standard indirect clauses:

> Daoine a raibh Gaeilge acu/people who had Irish
> Cén sort clár a bhfuil dúil agat ann?/What sort of programme do you like?
> An dóigh a bhfuil an aer .../The way that air is ...

(b) indirect clauses instead of direct clauses:

> Nuair a raibh muid i rang a sé/When we were in primary six
> Rudaí a bhfuil maith duit/Things that are good for you

(c) direct clauses instead of indirect clauses:

> Tá a fhios agat cén clann atá mé ag caint faoi/You know which family I am talking about

The degree of fluctuation between variant forms could be misleading, i.e. suggestive of an *ad hoc*, volatile language system. This assumption would be inaccurate. In fact, the degree of unpredictability characterising many of the linguistic categories is in itself an inevitable feature of a language which races through a series of systematic developments. A slower rate of progression would eradicate much of this fluctuation and afford greater opportunity for consideration of the direction being pursued. However, given the dynamic nature of this bilingual community's rapid growth, traditional variations and non-standard forms contribute to that wider corpus of material from which the children draw. The choice of a form is often unpredictable, but not necessarily random. Various factors influence the speaker's selection from the linguistic repertoire. Formality of situation is one important factor. Others will be discussed later.

Influence of the DL

The influence of English can be discerned in most of the linguistic developments described above. In a language contact situation the dominant language inevitably contributes to the linguistic mould of the lesser used language. The overall processes of simplification, reduction and overgeneralisation are not confined to bilingual contexts, but are globally active in language systems.

Nevertheless, it is clearly the influence of English that is determining the specific configurations which emerge in this particular bilingual environment. One example, already referred to, is the distinctiveness of the two separate verbs 'to be' in Irish which shows some signs of waning in the Irish of the SRC. The intrusion of the 'bí' verb into structures which traditionally demand the copula is not restricted to learners or to urban bilingual areas, e.g. Gaoth Dobhair (Donegal):

> *tá* siad a' dá ó; they are cousins
> *tá* a mháthairsa agus Dónal Mór cousins; his mother and Dónal Mór are cousins (Ó Muiri, 1982)

— and in Antrim:

> dúirt sé go raibh seisean gadaí; he said he was a thief (Doegan record, 1931/1933)

However, the confusion of the two verbs is more intense in the urban situation, in accordance with the more intense exposure to English. SRC examples include:

> Tá sin an fhírinne; that's the truth
> An bhfuil sin gasúr no cailín?; is that a boy or a girl?
> Síleann tusa go bhfuil tusa an fear greannmhar anseo; You think that you're the funny man here.

In a more careful style, where anglicising influences are, to some extent, monitored by the speakers themselves, the two structures are more likely to be distinguished from each other.

It would be an interesting diversion to ponder the results of hypothetical bilingual contact situations. For example, in a hispanico-hiberno contact situation would the two distinct verbs expressing the concept 'to be' (the substantive verb 'bí' and the copula 'is') be better preserved in the Irish? Similarly, would the gender distinctions of nouns show greater tenacity? This temptation to stray into the area of hypothetical questions is duly checked and we return to examine the ways in which English contributes to the Irish in Belfast, today!

Emphasis

One particular area which is more akin to the English system rather than the native Irish concerns the allocation of emphasis. The expression of emphasis in Irish is a subtle process, employing a variety of devices. As in the English language system, the degree of stress may be amplified and the range of intonation extended in order to draw emphasis to a word or sequence of words.

However, in addition, morphological and syntactic changes serve to direct emphasis:

(a) emphatic pronouns
(b) emphatic suffixes to nouns
(c) the use of the copula, either stated or understood.

The SRC make regular use of emphatic pronouns, e.g.

> Bhí *muidinne* ag léamh leabharthaí iontach casta agus muid ar an Bhunscoil.
> *We* (as opposed to children today) were reading very advanced literature when we were at the Bunscoil.

> An cuimhin leat nuair a ba gnách *linne* dramaí agus gach rud a dhéanamh agus ba gnach linn gabhail chuige seo agus siúd.
> Do you remember, when *we* used to perform plays and we used to attend this and that.

However, the principal emphatic techniques employed by the children are the amplification of stress and adjustment of pitch. This reflects the influence of English, most notably where the addition of an emphatic suffix to the noun might have been expected in the Irish. As a consequence, stress is allocated on items which traditionally resist it, e.g. on the possessive adjective:

> Níor scríobh mise chuig *mo* ceann.
> I didn't write to *mine.*
> Bhí máthair Emer, mise, Alastair agus *mo* mhamaí …
> Emer's mammy, me, Alastair and *my* mammy …
> Bhain *mo* mhadadh greim as.
> *My* dog bit him.

In the case of the third person, where 'a' could mean his, her, or their, in Irish, the children avoid ambiguity by widely employing the prepositional pronoun forms. Emphatic suffixes are sometimes added also:

> mála s'aige / s'aigesean; his bag
> mála s'aici / s'aicise; her bag
> mála s'acu / s'acusan; their bag

Also, contrary to the norm, simple prepositions are often stressed by the children. This occurs where the copula would normally be used to draw the significant segment to the fore of the sentence, e.g.

> Tháinig Breandan *ó* Béal Feirste.
> Brendan came *from* Belfast.

(Instead of the traditional '(Is) *ó* Bhéal Feirste a tháinig Bréandan.')

When emphasising a noun, however, the traditional structure is more likely to be used, with the copula understood at the beginning of the phrase, e.g.

Cailín a bhí ann; It was a girl
Fear a bhí ann; It was a man
Coinín deas a bhí ann; It was a nice rabbit

The influence of English idiom can be seen in the following examples, where the emphasised subject is isolated and introduced at the fore of the sentence, before the relevant information is given.

Ach le Micheal, tháinig seisean anseo ...
As for Michael, he came here ...
Ach linne, ní gá duinn ...
As for us, we don't need to ...
You know Aine, dearthair s'aicise, tá leanbh aige.
You know Aine, her brother (he) has a child.
Alastair, ní raibh seisean ag iarraidh uibheacha.
Alastair (he) didn't want eggs.
Bhuel, cailín amhain, tá sí ag déanamh O'level i mbliana, agus tá sí ...
Well, one girl, (she) is doing O'level this year and she is ...

These devices for emphasising a word or phrase are well established in the children's Irish. They do not feature among those aspects of the language repertoire which the children modify or alter in more formal situations.

Syntactic transfers

In a bilingual context, it is usually the influence of idioms and syntactic structures from the DL of which the speaker is least aware. Clyne (1967) observed that fact regarding the language of German migrants to Australia. In the case of learners, the majority of syntactic irregularities can be attributed to the influence of English (Ó Baoill, 1979b) This is true in the case of the SRC also. Naturally, this does not suggest that the children are completely unaware of these deviations from norms; indeed, on occasions they do correct each other's English-based utterances, which diverge from standard Irish. However, whereas a lexical item may be consciously borrowed from English for a variety of reasons, the transference of English syntax or idiom (i.e. semantic transference) is more likely to be unnoticed.

Syntactic transference from English can be seen in many of the examples, already cited, throughout this chapter. Relatively few of them have become fossilised in the Irish (like the 'cionn is' conjunction, or the pronoun-governed verbal structure, 'ag caitheamh iad'; throwing them). Most transfers still show a considerable degree of flux.

One feature of English syntax which is manifesting itself in various Irish structures concerns the isolation of the pronoun. Although this development is not yet firmly established, the pattern does seem to be under way. Examples mentioned, in the SRC Irish, include the movement towards analytic forms of the verb, followed by the pronoun — ithim mé (I eat); glanann mé (I clean). The preference to supply the pronoun after the preposition (where it is traditionally contained within the prepositional pronoun) is also modelled on English syntax — faoi é (under it); roimh tusa (before you); thar iad (over them). This transfer is likely to become more entrenched in the children's Irish (and in modern spoken Irish generally) as the independence and strength of the pronoun grows.

Style does exert some influence upon the tolerance of syntactic transfers. Animated anecdotes are more likely to include these than a more serious dialogue. Consider this lively account of a critical moment in a snooker tournament, by a ten-year-old boy.

Chuaigh sé *istigh* ach tháinig sé *amuigh* arís. Agus i ndiaidh sin chuaigh Steve Davis chuig an tábla agus shíl sé go raibh sé ábalta é a fháil *istigh* agus bhuail sé go crua, ach bhuail sé *na* dhá taobh idir *an* dá poll agus d'fhág sé an shot fa choinne Denis Taylor. Agus shot iontach furast a bhí ann. Nuair a pot Denis e, em, thosaigh gach duine a screadaigh agus da fheicfeá é, Steve Davis — bhí sé cóir a bheith ag caoineadh.

(It (the ball) went in but it came out again. And after that, Steve Davis went to the table and everybody thought that he could get it in, and he struck it hard, but it hit the two sides between the two holes and he left the shot for Denis Taylor. And it was a very easy shot. When Denis potted it everyone began to yell, and if you saw Steve Davis, he was almost crying.)

In this extract, the speaker employs many traditional syntactic structures which are susceptible to transference, e.g. the use of the copula. He fluctuates between the traditional use of the singular form of the article before the number 'two', and the plural form. The adverbs/prepositions 'amuigh' (out) and 'istigh' (in) are used instead of the traditionally required qualifiers which convey the sense of 'motion' rather than 'state' (i.e. amach; isteach).

In the next extract, from a colourful anecdote by an eleven-year-old girl, the speaker hesitates before her selection of the adverb and corrects the first choice, which was irregular;

... I ndiaidh sin, thug sé muid thart, em, istigh, isteach i páirc éigin ...

...After that, he brought us round, em, in, into some field ...

Despite the fact that the children monitor syntactic transference, to some extent, reducing its influence in more formal styles, this aspect of the Irish system still occurs more naturally and unobserved than the incorporation of transferred lexical items. Indeed, sometimes syntactic transference is prompted by the introduction of an item borrowed from English, e.g.

Bhí german measles agam: I had german measles

(where you might otherwise expect the sickness not to be 'agam' (at me) but 'orm' (on me)), or

Tá sé student: He is a student

(where the substantive verb replaces the copula).

Semantic transfers

Similarly, semantic transfers are embedded in the linguistic repertoire, rather than consciously borrowed into it. Examples are abundant and represent the way in which Irish is being adapted to the urban bilingual scene. However, they could easily be matched by a parallel list of examples from the Irish of rural Gaeltacht areas. Semantic and lexical transference in these districts tend to be more advanced than phonological or syntactic transference. The sense of English idiom can be discerned from many of the expressions produced by 'seasoned' Irish speakers as well as the inexperienced learner who seeks to express himself through Irish. Regarding the SRC, some examples from their repertoire hinge on the use of particular adverbs and prepositions.

Cuireann siad daoine suas na ballaí
They send people up the walls (i.e. drive them to distraction)
Thug tú suas
You gave up (stopped playing a musical instrument)
Rith siad amach as
They ran out of
Ta siad siúd air
They are on it (i.e. in a children's game of hide and seek)

Other examples are based on English use of particular verbs:

Théid a aghaigh corcra
His face goes (turns) purple

ag gabháil maol
going (turning) bald
Tá mé briste
I am broke (i.e. penniless)
Chuaigh an guthan
The phone went (i.e. rang)
Chuaigh sé snap!
It went snap!
ag gabháil fa choinne rith sa carr
going for a run in the car

A range of transfers are based on the verb 'to get':

a fháil déanta
to get done
Ta sé ag fáil posta
He is getting married
Ní bhfuair tú buailte aris
You didn't get hit again
Bhí orm fáil suas ar a hocht
I had to get up at eight o'clock
Fuair muid ar shiúl
We got away
Fuair muid as
We got off (school)
Faoin am a fuair muid thart ansin
By the time we got round there
Ní bhfuair mise a codladh
I didn't get to sleep
le fáil ar aghaidh
to get on (i.e. progress)
Faigheann sí é i bhfad i bhfad níos fusa
She finds it much much easier
Nuair a thig sé síos chuig an nitty gritty
When it comes down to the nitty gritty

Lexical transference

The intrusion of English lexical items into Irish is a common feature of the Irish spoken today. The SRC are no less susceptible to the conditions which promote lexical transference; accordingly, in the children's Irish, lexical items are transferred frequently, to meet various needs. These items are not fixed in the

Irish system. Transfers are therefore distinguished from the many loan words and roots of words which have become embedded in the language, e.g. scatáil (to skate); piocadh (to pick); coipeáil (to copy); trampáil (to tramp); réasúnaigh (to reason); rolladh (to roll); votáil (to vote).

In the case of transfers, the same speaker might use a borrowed item and its Irish cognate during the same discourse. Those borrowed elements which are adapted to the Irish system are mainly verbal roots, e.g.

> insisteann sé air: he insists on it
> slamann sé an doras: he slams the door
> thig leis lastadh tamall fada: it can last a long time
> ag nocadh thart leis: knocking around with
> ag bumpail ar an bóthar: bumping on the road
> ag strugladh: struggling
> ag flyáil thart: flying by

Transferred roots are treated as first conjugation verbs. Therefore, no adjustment is required in the past tense; e.g.

> split sé mo ceann: he split my head
> cic sí me: she kicked me

On the other hand, the transferred verb may be in the past tense, e.g.

> knocked mé é out: I knocked him out

In addition, there are some expressions which are conveyed with a single verb in English, but a more complex structure of verb + noun + prepositional pronoun is required in Irish. In these cases a transfer simplifies the business of communication, e.g.

> rinneadh ionsaí air: he was attacked
> atacadh é (transfer)
> Baineadh tuisle asam: I tripped
> trip mé suas (transfer)

English words and phrases incorporated into Irish serve a variety of functions, such as the following.

Stylistic items

Stylistic transfers are sometimes used for their effect in exclamatory expressions, e.g.

> Tá sé crazy! He is crazy

Níl arán maith domsa. I'll tell you that much! Bread isn't good for me. I'll tell you that much!
Meiricea? You must be joking! America? You must be joking!

Over thirty borrowed items function as stylistic links in the dialogue. These items keep the conversation flowing smoothly, e.g.

Má chuaigh tú amach le do thuismitheoirí, *like*, bhí tuismitheoirí eile ann agus labhair tú in Gaeilge leo an t-am uilig. Agus sna siopaí, *just, like*, bhuel, ní chuireann duine ar bith ceisteanna ar páistí óg ón taobh amuigh duit, *you know* ...

If you went out with your parents, like, there were other parents there and you always spoke in Irish to them. And in the shops, just, like, well, nobody from outside asks young children questions, you know ...

English responses, 'aye, yes, no' often replace the Irish verbal responses. Other stylistic link transfers, which keep the conversation flowing, are 'really, alright, sure, exactly, and all, because, even, you know what I mean, now, then, so'.

Stylistic links are also introduced while the speaker searches for the right word or phrase, e.g.

... rudaí, *I mean, just* common knowledge, go fírínneach
... things, I mean, just common knowledge, really

In this context, link words in Irish are often used to introduce a lexical transfer. Not only does this series of 'fillers' allow the speaker to select an appropriate word or phrase, but they also prepare the listener for a transferred item, e.g.

Tusa an *cineál* sore thumb, *you know*.
You are the sort of sore thumb, you know.
Tá siad ag caitheamh, eh, rudaí ar an, eh, *tá a fhios agat*, sign Grange Hill.
They were throwing things at the, you know, the Grange Hill sign.

The older members of the SRC also use the linking term 'mar a deirtear' (as is said). This may be associated with slightly more formal situations, as Dorian observed in Gaelic of South Sutherland (Dorian, 1981: 101). Clyne described 'linking' transfers, in the speech of German/English bilinguals, as 'lexical filled pauses' (1972: 132–44).

The habit of switching from one language to another during informal speech is often viewed critically. In fact, however, the bilingual is usually availing of the two linguistic systems at his disposal in a systematic way, for added effect and colour in his dialogue. Rayfield describes this phenomenon in his analysis of interference in the English and Yiddish of Jewish immigrants in America:

As well as a double lexicon and an almost double stock of constructions
... the bilingual has a double stock of rhetorical devices. He takes full
advantage of them to emphasise and dramatise his speech, and they more
than compensate for any deficiency in expressiveness due to his
unfamiliarity with the full rhetorical resources of the secondary language.
(Rayfield, 1970: 58)

Lexical items

A transferred item is also employed when the Irish cognate is unknown or
temporarily forgotten:

Bhí gach cineál duine close knit.
Everyone was sort of close knit.
Bhí seisean ag gabhail a rá Ár nAthair, em, backwards.
He was going to say the Our Father, em, backwards.

Sometimes circumlocution is preferred to a transfer, such as the ten-year-old
girl's reference to a school uniform as 'cuid éadaigh a dhíth don scoil'. On
another occasion, which was one of the first interviews with these children, this
same group of ten-year-olds were discussing a poster of animals on the wall.
One boy pointed out, 'Sin brown trout' (That's a brown trout). During the same
discourse he made other comments about the 'breac donn' (brown trout). One of
his peers questioned this term and they concluded that 'bradán' might be the
right term. In fact the first boy's choice had been correct. However, his uncertainty had prompted him to use the English term in the first place. Another
member of the group made comments about a crocodile in the picture. Rather
than use the English word she preferred to paraphrase, 'an rud le craiceann iontach iontach tiúbh' (that thing with very very thick skin. These children were
probably conscious of the tape recorder during that first session.

The children sometimes introduce a lexical transfer, in consideration of the
listener. When they estimate that there is a chance the listener will not be familiar with a particular term, the English word prevents any misunderstanding or
hindrance to the flow of the conversation. In the following example, a thirteen-
year-old boy had been asking me about the kind of work I was doing. He knew
that I was involved in some kind of study or project and this reminded him of
some researcher who had been investigating the type of electrical equipment
most popular in the locality. When he introduces a transfer, on my behalf, there
are no link words to prepare me for the switch and confusion results.

Boy: Project éigin. 'S tá a fhios agat, dúirt mo mhamaí liom — bhí an
                 cailin seo agus rinne sí project faoi cad é bhí ag freezers daoine i
                 ceantar s'aici.

Researcher: Freezers? Caidé an rud sin?
Boy: Cuisnitheoir. Fridge freezer. Project mar sin don Ollscoil.
(Boy: Some project. And you know, my mammy told me — there was this girl and she did a project about people's freezers in our area.
Researcher: Freezers? What's that?
Boy: Cuisnitheoir. Fridge freezer. A project like that for the University.)

This sensitivity to the listener's comprehension is one of the extra-linguistic factors which influences the linguistic output. Weinreich stresses the importance of this type of factor, which lies outside the structure of the language itself, influencing the bilingual's speech output (Weinreich, 1974).

Like the stylistic exclamatory transfers, lexical transfers are sometimes considered appropriate because of their fashionable ring, in English, e.g.

Bhí na cailíní uilig *cracked* ar an dhá gasúr seo.
All the girls were cracked on these two boys.

Similarly, onomatopoeic words in English provide an immediate effect when they are left in English. The transfer stands out in the sentence and is, consequently, more striking, e.g.

Whack mé é: I whacked it
nuair a crash tú istigh in sa balla: when you crashed into the wall
Chuaigh sé snap!: It went snap!

Sometimes English words or series of words are incorporated into the Irish conversation, having been triggered by an English proper noun. The dominance of English in the environment means that English proper nouns must enter the Irish frequently, such as references to commercial products and television programmes. In the following examples, the English noun is followed by other English words or phrases with which the children are very familiar in Irish:

Grange Hill an t-ainm atá ar an scoil *in English.*
Grange Hill is the name of the school in English.
Fuair tú coke is *milk* saor, is seven-up.
You got coke and milk and seven-up free.
Chonaic mise agus Una tú ag amharc ar Play School. Tá sé *brilliant — for the younger viewers.*
Una and I saw you watching Play School. It's brilliant — for the younger viewers.

It is clear that the use of lexical items, borrowed from English, serves a variety of functions. On various occasions I observed the children's own ability to distinguish between these, in the Irish of their peers. When they sensed that the speaker could not find the suitable Irish word, they sometimes supplied it. This was always accepted quietly and casually. In the next extract, a ten-year-old boy searches for the right word to replace his friend's transfer.

Boy 1:   Bhí dhá torch ag duine agus bhí siad air.
Boy 2:   Tor- tor-, lochrann
Boy 1:   Lochrann.

(Boy 1:   Someone had two torches and they were turned on.
Boy 2:   Tor- tor-, lochrann. (torch)
Boy 1:   Lochrann.)

When a peer provided the Irish cognate of an English term, it did not cause any interruption in the conversation. The Irish term seemed to be emitted spontaneously and evoked no comment or response. A group of eleven-year-olds chat in the following extract:

Boy 1:   Bhí mise in san Isle of Man.
Boy 2:   Bhí tusa ar an Oilean Manainn.
Researcher: Inis dúinn fa dtaobh dó sin.
Boy 1:   Bhuel, ar dtús tháinig muid ...

(Boy 1:   I was on the Isle of Man.
Boy 2:   You were on the Oilean Manainn.
Researcher: Well, tell us about that.
Boy 1:   Well, at first we came ...)

In the above example, the first boy had chosen the transfer, perhaps for the sake of clarity, or for some other reason. He was familiar with the Irish term. The second boy was intolerant of the transfer. Sometimes the children replaced their own transfers, e.g.

Boy (11 years): Théid muinne a snámh — thíos ag an leisure centre, an sólann.
(We go swimming, down at the leisure centre, 'an solann'.)

The children's tolerance of transferred items was associated with the formality of the situation. I found that they corrected each other's Irish much less frequently after the first few months of meetings and recording sessions. However, a child would provide the Irish term, himself, if he thought it would aid comprehension:

Girl (9 years): Pay sise (She paid)
Researcher: Caidé sin? (What's that?)
Girl: Dhíol sí muid as an tacsai.(She paid our taxi fare.)

Switch to English

Sometimes a more prolonged switch to English is triggered, rather than a few single lexical items. For example, while I was travelling by car with one group of children, everyone was chatting in Irish. As we passed a local hotel, one twelve-year-old girl identified it, 'Greenan Lodge — I heard a lot about it.' A few other comments in English followed before the conversation resumed in Irish.

The fact that lexical items, borrowed from English, trigger a switch to English in the conversation was recognised by the SRC themselves. One sixteen-year-old boy described this process, showing a remarkable understanding of factors influencing their bilingual behaviour.

Boy 1: Má tá tú ag gabhail, you know, eh, rud éigin, political conversation, rud éigin mar sin, a bheith agat. Mar tá mé just i ndiaidh a rá ansin — political conversation. Níl a fhios agam an dóigh le sin a rá in Gaeilge. Tá a fhios agam — dá smaointeoinn air.

Boy 2: Comhrá polaitíocht.

Boy 1: Comhrá polaitíocht. Ach, just thig sé amach mar political conversation. Ach ní stopann tú le smaointiú, just thig, thig, thig amach cad é atá a gabhail a teacht amach. Ach má tá muinne a gabhail a suí ansin agus em, you know, na foclaí móra seo uilig. Agus cuid foclaí — níl siad oiread is ann sa Gaeilge. Ach má tá siad ann, glacfaidh siad, b'fhéidir deich bomaite le rá. You know, I mean, sin an dóigh a thosaíonn an Béarla ag teacht isteach. I ndiaidh sin, tosaíonn tú le just cúpla focal, mise, X agus Y ina shuí anseo san oíche. I ndiaidh deich bomaite tá muid ag caint i mBéarla. Ach i ndiaidh sin — just ar ais ag an Gaeilge arís, like.

(Boy 1: If you are going to have something, eh, a political conversation, something like that. Like I am just after saying — political conversation. I don't know how to say that in Irish. I do know — if I was to think about it.

Boy 2: Comhrá polaitíocht. (political conversation)

Boy 1: Comhrá polaitíocht. But it just comes out as 'political conversation'. But you don't stop to think, just whatever is going to come out comes out! But if we are going to sit there and, you know, all these big words. And some words don't even exist in Irish. But if they do exist, it will take ten minutes to produce them. You know, I mean, that's how the English starts to come in. After that, you start with a couple of words, me and X and Y sitting here at night. After ten minutes we're speaking English. But then, it's just back to Irish again, like.)

Overall Trends

Those influences which bring about change in the spoken language have long been active in the Irish linguistic system, as a natural aspect of its evolution. The tendency to simplify a language, for example, has greatly contributed to the shape of Irish heard today, as it has to other languages. We can see from this chapter that, in a language revival situation, the rate of change is greatly accelerated. In formal situations the speakers' own tolerance of irregular variations is to some extent reduced and the linguistic output adjusted accordingly. However, in casual, everyday speech situations tolerance tends to be high. The sensitivity expressed by the young people of Shaw's Road to linguistic diversity generally is particularly valuable in a society where Irish is so closely associated with the learner. Nothing demoralises a learner more than the fear of being ridiculed or brashly corrected. However, one ironic twist to the linguistic developments which we have considered above, is the fact that the abundance of options which is open to these bilinguals, including regular and irregular features, may in fact be offering a more complex range of choices rather than would a more simplified structure closely adhering to norms.

Conclusions

This book has explored an initiative which drew the Irish language out of the classroom and lodged it firmly in the heart of a Community. As a first step in this process, the language had to be acquired by these young enthusiasts. This meant some years of attending classes, courses, language-related functions and visiting traditional Gaeltacht areas, as well as seeking out every other possible opportunity to practise the language. Irish language learners became accustomed to the fact that availing of existing facilities for using and improving their language skills was not adequate. They had to become adept at creating opportunities.

The commonly perceived interest in the language was already well developed on a community basis. The right personnel existed who had the courage and ingenuity to embark upon an untried course and confront a multitude of obstacles at the outset. In the 1960s the time was ripe for a community enterprise which might repair a deflated confidence and spirit. When this combination of factors interacted, the inevitable outcome was the construction of a social and physical framework wherein such a corporate group could live out their shared objectives. As other speech communities have found, a cohesive social unit was required to create the circumstances wherein their language could survive in everyday usage. An urban Gaeltacht emerged in West Belfast in response to this need.This urban Gaeltacht Community is significant from a series of perspectives:

(1) Firstly, the fact that this small group of Irish language learners succeeded in fulfilling their original goals is a remarkable and revealing feat in itself, considering the weight of factors which militated against the project during the first ten years or so.

(2) The extension of bilingualism throughout the surrounding districts results directly from the Community's introduction of Irish-medium nursery and primary education. Bilingualisation within the Bunscoil families has gained some ground, inspired mainly by a desire to support the children's acquisition of Irish and progress at school. This development adds further dimensions to the Gaeltacht Community itself. The original members created an access for other families to embrace the language in very real terms. The network of Irish speakers, learners and supporters expanded accordingly.

(3) The impact of this urban Gaeltacht Community upon a wider range of projects and initiatives is also relevant. At the most basic level, the existence of the Community instils pride in Irish speakers. People throughout the Six Counties have derived encouragement from the success of the Shaw's Road project. Indeed, many have benefited directly from the expertise and experience of its founder members. The Shaw's Road Community takes a leading role in the Language Movement. This is done quite unintentionally and unobtrusively, by virtue of the model which the Community has come to represent for other individuals and groups who contemplate a language project demanding nerve and commitment.

(4) From the perspective of language revival, this Community managed to introduce the language as the first tongue among its young people. This fact is most significant in view of the concentrated efforts which the parents themselves had to invest initially in order to acquire Irish. The challenge posed by this goal would seem awesome and quite overwhelming if it were considered and pondered fully at the initial stages. However, this has been a 'one day at a time' venture, once the overall objectives were defined and agreed upon. Without dwelling on the various difficulties which would most likely be encountered, each was tackled as it arose. This approach allowed a build-up of self-respect and expertise as objectives were achieved, rather than the depletion of confidence as problems were anticipated.

In Belfast, the language has been proved to be relevant to people in their everyday lives and important to them in a self-fulfilling sense. It can no longer be dismissed amidst ignorance and bias as a language of past times and past territories. Rather, it has been firmly established as a viable medium of communication during everyday interactions in the city. This fact is becoming more widely accepted.

(5) From the linguistic perspective, the Shaw's Road Community has adapted the language to meet its own needs. The children communicate freely, uninhibitedly and happily through Irish. Linguistic trends which are characteristic of their Irish reflect the overall pattern of change to which the language displays a propensity in a much wider sense. However, the accelerated pace of these linguistic developments parallels that of the social emergence and development of the Community itself. Although Irish is the first language of the Community children, a linguistic profile of their Irish shows it to follow the direction of Irish spoken among second language users in the city as a whole.

(6) This Belfast Gaeltacht Community is also significant on a more global level. The experience accumulated, as the Community confronted obstacles to its overall aims and *raison d'être*, could be valuable to other speech groups who seek to assert their own language. As international interest in the welfare of

lesser used languages swelled in recent years, Northern Ireland has emerged as a genuine contributor to that broad cause. This fact has not yet been fully realised and, as a consequence, many books examining the position of minority languages simply make brief comments about the sparsity of official data when dealing with the linguistic profile in Northern Ireland.

Cultural study trips to Northern Ireland — such as those arranged by the European Bureau For Lesser Used-Languages — include visits to the Shaw's Road Community, the Bunscoil and nursery class network. Visitors derive keen insights into the potential achievements of a small group of highly motivated people. In addition to this, it is also interesting and useful for representatives from other speech communities to be aware of the implications which such a community initiative can have upon wider language planning issues. The position of Irish in Northern Ireland has some distance to cover before it will be recognised as a fundamental dimension to the Irish heritage which deserves to be actively and purposefully promoted throughout the Six Counties. Nevertheless, the impression made by Belfast's Gaeltacht Community has already reduced that distance to some extent.

The current climate in Northern Ireland, regarding the Irish language, is one of resolve and optimism. During the early years of the campaign for official recognition and support for the Bunscoil, Department of Education Inspectors commented upon the happy relaxed atmosphere in which the children carried out their school work. This 'natural' and uninhibited way in which the children communicate through Irish has been one influential factor in the promotion of a more enlightened attitude towards Irish. Bunscoil parents reported certain observations about the impact upon adult listeners of hearing young children chat and play through Irish. Prior to the establishment of the Shaw's Road Community and school, people were generally unaware of the feasibility of rearing young bilinguals in the particular sociopolitical context of Belfast. Yet, the opportunity of observing Bunscoil children has, on many occasions, elicited a positive reaction from neutral or even sceptical visitors. A sociolinguistic phenomenon which seemed so idealistic and impractical, less than thirty years earlier, is perceived in its true simplicity and 'matter of factness' today.

The process of language diffusion has spread beyond the local families who send children to the Bunscoil. Other communities in Northern Ireland have been encouraged to take their own initiatives. However, the pattern of permeation of the language across further domains is equally interesting. As the Shaw's Road Community grew it became necessary to extend the social possibilities for using Irish. The quality of the children's lives as Irish speakers would be impaired if the language was restricted to the home and neighbourhood. These principal strongholds for the use of Irish would also be threatened by the dominance of English elsewhere. A social network of Irish language domains had to be built up in order to preserve the children's belief in the value and versatility of their mother tongue. Today, Belfast's Irish speakers may use Irish at school, at religious celebrations, in certain commercial and social centres, in some places of work. Indeed, in some cases a prerequisite for their job is a familiarity with Irish and a love of the language; Irish-medium teachers in the nurseries and primary classes come into this latter category. However, so also do the team working on the Irish language newspaper, in the Irish bookshop, Cultural Officers employed by various Town Councils and BBC personnel associated with Irish language programmes.

This process of diffusion can be considered from two viewpoints. Firstly, it has been implemented across a range of social domains wherein the Irish speakers of the city function during their everyday business. However, it also scales the hierarchical axis of social prestige, whereby the Community engine is also propelling the language upwards into the realm of officialdom. The first striking manifestation of that process was the Government's decision to recognise and finance the Irish-medium project in Belfast and later to introduce some facilities in Derry. Another change which afforded some status to the language was the initiation of Irish language programmes on Northern Ireland radio. A further significant development has been the official recognition of the Irish language as an aspect of the social environment which merits some quantitative analysis (Sweeney, 1988). The representation made by Irish speakers to the recent Planning Appeals Commission reflects a community desire for the language to be taken into account by policy makers. The absence of any provision relevant to proposals made by Irish speakers within the Final Report is regrettable. As the indigenous language, Irish suffered severe blows during the process of colonisation and, later, as a consequence to partition. Even since the pioneering years of the Revival Movement, in the nineteenth century, the language has been guardedly and even suspiciously viewed by many. The broader movement for political independence embraced much of the ideology and personnel of the Language Movement, prior to 1922. Therefore, it was natural for the new government in the Twenty-Six Counties to incorporate a language policy into its new legislature. However, in the remaining Six Counties, the Irish language fell victim to a conflict of economic and political interests.

The Revival Movement in Northern Ireland has always operated from a defensive position. It tries to justify its own attempts to promote the language while remaining nervous about the possibility of giving offence. This dilemma has not yet been resolved. It now seems that Irish language speakers and learners are indeed making some impact on the traditional government indifference to the language. At this very point, however, they must face another, and less expected, threat. The phrase, 'The Irish language has been hijacked by extremists', has now become a fashionable media cliché. Wisely, those who use such clichés do not attempt to justify them. Admittedly, Republican political slogans are often painted on walls using Irish as the medium of expression. Other slogans, both Republican and Unionist, are painted in English, yet no one claims that the English language has been hijacked.

The Shaw's Road founder members did not allow their efforts to be impeded by the social pressure which such claims are intended to assert. Nor did they await a public or official nod of approval. They came to recognise the Irish language as an integral component to their national identity which deserved to be treated candidly and honestly. The alternative of quietly acknowledging the language, within the confines of a library or classroom only, seemed sadly inadequate. When this Community decided to raise their children as Irish speakers and to extend an open invitation to others to share their goals, they boldly confronted that well-worn tradition of simplifying and distorting basic ideologies to suit a contrived set of labels and social stigmas. When the first members of the Community changed their personal names back into Irish from the anglicised versions, it was more than a small degree of courage which was required. The primary motivation for this act was a need to be true to oneself. The likely consequence that this image of self would be misconstrued and misrepresented by others did not dissuade the Shaw's Road members.

This Gaeltacht Community in Belfast has contributed to a more informed view of the Irish language which is gradually evolving in Northern Ireland. During the campaign for official status for the Bunscoil, television crews were frequent visitors to the modest classrooms at Shaw's Road. The media reported favourably upon the Community's achievement and the Irish-speaking youngsters won public acclaim and admiration. The increasing numbers of Irish speakers and learners, together with the mounting interest in the language's welfare at community level, have begun to attract official attention and recognition. This response is manifested in examples outlined above. The significance of these is marked more by their unprecedented nature in the Six Counties than by the degree of progress reached.

The current climate of optimism and conviction in a secure future for the language is generated by that confidence which real achievement brings. However, other plans are being currently negotiated and prepared which should further justify this positive attitude. Several of these projects are directly linked to the success of the Shaw's Road Community and school. Again, the main thrust of these developments emanates from small groups of interested people. Support from the authorities is forthcoming in relation to certain initiatives.

Other proposals are being formulated without any guarantees of official backing, however, in the hope that this may be secured in the future.

The introduction of further Irish-medium facilities for primary school children in the North represents a significant step in the bilingualisation process. The second Bunscoil in Belfast, now in its fourth year, continues to expand its intake and staff. The Irish-medium stream within Steelstown Primary School in Derry is well established. Presently, a group of parents and language enthusiasts are engaged in the work of establishing a third all-Irish school in Newry to receive children attending Irish-medium nursery classes in the town and surrounding districts. These parents, like those who run the second Belfast school, are highly motivated to provide this opportunity for their own children. They have the advantage of knowing that such a project has already succeeded in Belfast and that the prospect of having to involve themselves in as lengthy a campaign for official recognition as that sustained by the Shaw's Road Bunscoil Committee, is unlikely. Newry mothers who recently visited the Shaw's Road Bunscoil were encouraged by seeing the type of project which they envisage in operation. Newry has emerged as an active centre for language-related activities. The establishment of a Bunscoil there reinforces the Language Movement itself, representing a growing commitment to the language in concrete terms.

Plans for providing Irish-medium education at secondary level are also well under way. Research carried out by the Meánscoil (Irish-medium secondary school) Committee indicated that Bunscoil parents strongly favoured an extension to the existing Irish-medium facilities available to their children. A representative from the Rath Carn Gaeltacht, who addressed a meeting of parents, advised against the selection of an Irish-medium stream within an English-medium school as an alternative to setting up a full Meánscoil. In addition, it was recommended that during the initial year or two intake numbers should be restricted in order to allow a gradual build-up of expertise and confidence. These comments were based on his own community's experiences.

It may have been deduced from the various references to projects already in operation or simply being negotiated, that the Irish Revival is being dynamically and diligently promoted by a fragmented Language Movement. An awareness of this fact, as an area of weakness, led to the formation of a central group, comprising representatives from various sources. This core group hopes to resolve some of the difficulties which arise when individual schemes are implemented and managed independently of each other. It is clear that many advantages would be associated with a more integrated approach, in view of the overall unifying aims and ideals of language-related enterprises.

Regarding the area of linguistic competence, interest is currently stirring and some work has been initiated in this respect. The question of language variety has never had a prominent place among the priority questions to be resolved within the context of the diffusion of active bilingualism. During the 1988/89 school year, Bunscoil staff began to thrash out the various questions surrounding this subject with a more organised and co-ordinated vigour. In the spring of that year, an Advisory Committee was set up to meet the requirements by the Minister of Education that a language policy be formulated for instruction through Irish at primary level. This Committee produced an interim report in the autumn, outlining general aims and objectives appropriate to the various age groups. This work has opened the way towards the provision of some clear guidance for teachers, within the Irish-medium network, regarding language skills to be acquired by the children. This type of publication could avail of an opportunity to clarify directions for creating a supportive network of resources and materials to improve the linguistic competence of learners — not only Bunscoil children but their Irish language contacts as well.

Directions for Further Development

During the course of this work, the most striking and impressive fact to emerge was the degree and effectiveness of achievement which could be reached by a small group of highly motivated people. This group lacked political clout and economic backing; nevertheless, they set about realising their own ideal of an Irish-speaking community environment wherein their children could be raised as Irish speakers. This initiative became a springboard for other developments within the Language Movement.

Areas of vulnerability in the current position of the language in Northern Ireland were also identified during the years of fieldwork. It has been shown that this period remains as an exciting and revolutionary one in the story of the Irish Revival. Many needs have already been defined and addressed; others, as we saw above, are currently being tackled. Some of these merit further mention as areas which require the more concentrated attention of enthusiasts, academics, professionals, educationalists, etc.

(1) One such problem was recently confronted by establishing the umbrella group for those involved in Irish-medium education, 'An Comhairle um Oideachas Gaeilge'. This group has drawn together persons interested in Irish-medium education and established contacts with other interested groups in the United States. The aim is to collate and distribute information upon teaching through the medium of Irish and also to monitor and advise upon developments in this field within Northern Ireland. This group was founded in response to the recognition of the disparate, fragmentary nature of the Language Movement. The range of educational ventures was expanding rapidly without any

meaningful integration of objectives and resources. This group has simply taken a first step in correcting that situation. Further development in this area is required to establish a clear structure through which to service efficiently the whole catchment area with nursery, primary and secondary level education through Irish and thereafter to look at strategies for expanding that work.

One of the practical difficulties, which generated an awareness of the need for a co-ordinating group, concerns the swell of Irish-medium nursery classes which guarantee an intake through to the primary sector. A problem arose when it was decided that it was necessary to halt the escalation of pupil numbers at the Shaw's Road Bunscoil. At this point, a new nursery school was due to be completed, which parents had laboured to finance and erect. This building was situated within the immediate catchment area of the Shaw's Road school and considerably further from the second Bunscoil which had not long been in operation, at that time. The subsequent confusion about where children could enrol for primary education was one example of a lack of planned co-operation between various independent units.

Indeed, the various strands of the entire Language Movement, incorporating Irish-medium education as one fundamental aspect, would benefit from a strong co-ordinating initiative which would clearly define the areas of interaction wherein various language projects could share resources as well as their mounting experience. The Comhairle um Oideachas Gaeilge could represent the nucleus of such a group. Its expansion would draw together representatives from every other language-orientated endeavour. Self-interest can so often obviate common interests unless they are all examined within a corporate context wherein the benefits of integrated planning become apparent. Many small groups of dedicated people are engaged in some initiative to serve the cultural needs of their community. They may or may not be members of a cultural organisation. However, in many cases they are relatively uninformed about initiatives taken by other groups, as well as those which are currently being negotiated and planned. The Language Movement in Northern Ireland comprises a multitude of groups and individuals, as well as some larger organisations, who devote themselves to the promotion of the language in accordance with their own interests and areas of expertise. However, the Movement lacks co-ordination and a unifying body of representatives.

During the overview of the Revival Movement in Belfast, reference was made to the key role played by individual Irish speakers who could capture the imagination and motivation of others and channel their efforts along a common path. Another significant factor was the tendency of people to participate in a variety of language-related activities and, thereby, to transfer, from one project to another, the benefit of lessons learned at different stages. This process offered a valuable contribution to the Language Movement. However, as a process, it occurred spontaneously and informally. Today, projects such as the expansion of nursery and primary facilities through Irish have happened on such a scale that a more organised pooling of resources is required. Within the area of formal education, the advantages to this process are obvious. However, the participation of representatives from every other source involved in language-related activities could enhance and assist the pursuit of common goals.

(2) One of the surprising aspects of the emergence of incipient bilingualism in West Belfast, as the area buzzes with language learning activities, has been the spontaneity of the phenomenon. The formulation of an official policy, aimed at maintaining the present momentum of interest in the language and positively encouraging the revival of Irish, is long overdue. Recent years have witnessed some shift away from the lethargy and hostility manifested towards the Irish language in earlier decades. Examples of progress along these lines were cited above. Irish is clearly a pertinent and integral aspect of life for many people in the North; as such, it deserves to be taken into account during the design of policies which affect the lives of its citizens. In addition, it is unfortunate that a significant proportion of its citizens are unfamiliar with the relevance of this language to themselves. Only decisions at the level of official Government policy can correct that situation.

Official approval and support have been won for some initiatives after years of vigorous campaigning. The language has edged its way into the realm of the mass media. Although the language still remains on the periphery in this domain, Irish language programmes have been extended on BBC Northern Ireland radio, since they were first introduced in 1986. The unofficial radio station, operated during various periods by Irish language enthusiasts, which broadcasts entirely through Irish, seeks to provide one of the resources for Irish speakers which does not exist within the official structure.

Similarly, in the area of Irish-medium education, several enterprises have been introduced and proved successful. The demand for further facilities leads to new community initiatives. Government support for language development projects can be achieved in response to tedious campaigning and the production of concrete evidence that both demand and feasibility are real. The recent survey conducted by the Government (Sweeney, 1988) indicated that interest in the Irish language was indeed real. That preliminary Report could represent the start of some basic research upon which policies could be soundly built. As yet, however, the Government has not taken any lead in language planning with regards Irish, on any meaningful scale. Indeed, despite its much acclaimed EMU (Education for Mutual Understanding) policy — a policy which is designed to familiarise each Northern Ireland community with the other community's culture,

Government appears to take the view that this understanding can be achieved without the widespread introduction of well supported Irish language projects. Its recommendation of a cross-curricular programme based on cultural heritage could improve the present situation. However, this can only be seen as a stepping stone towards a strong package aimed not only at educating the public about the relevance of the Irish language in their society, but also at introducing other measures which recognise that relevance.

The time is now ripe for consideration to be given to an overall set of policy measures which would embrace the following ideals:

(a) Educate the wider public about the significance of the Irish language in its immediate environment and counter those negative attitudes towards the Irish language which are endemic among a whole section of the population and for which the Government must accept some responsibility.

(b) Cultivate a co-operative relationship between statutory authorities and non-statutory cultural organisations.

(c) Expand the categories of motivation which encourage the acquisition and usage of Irish. In chapter 7, parents' motives for sending children to the Bunscoil were discussed. A combination of educational and cultural factors dominated in each parent's decision. However, the fact that limited socio-economic advantage or other pragmatic advantages are associated with bilingualism was reflected in the responses. Within the framework of a comprehensive plan for Irish this area could be developed, introducing some social and legal status for the language and creating socio-economic opportunities for Irish speakers. During my own years of studying Irish at second and third level I frequently heard people, with a very limited understanding of the significance of the Irish language, make comments such as, 'Well, maybe you'll get a job in Dublin'. This type of comment does, nevertheless, point to a void in the treatment of Irish in Northern Ireland. Indeed, during discussion of the controversial curriculum reform proposals, prior to the amendment of the position of Irish in the curriculum, much emphasis was placed on the particular advantages of learning European languages, in preparation for 1992. Although the cultural value of Irish was acknowledged, that language was placed, at first, in a less prominent position on the curriculum than French, Spanish and German. Surely it lies within the power of policy makers to create the socio-economic circumstances which favour the acquisition of Irish in Northern Ireland. This type of action at the official level would thereby parallel the rate of development of Irish at community level.

(d) Several existing enterprises greatly enhance the position of Irish in Belfast and, accordingly, the lives of Irish speakers, without the financial

assistance which would enable an expansion of facilities. Official support of
these projects would bolster the status of Irish which the very existence of
these enterprises proves to be well merited. In addition, these organisations
must be encouraged to pursue their linguistic, cultural and social goals with
some degree of security and confidence. The recent withdrawel of funds from
Glór na nGael highlights the vulnerability of cultural and social bodies. At a
whim, funding can be withdrawn without any valid justification. Some
protection for such groups should be built into legislature so that their work
cannot be impeded by prejudice.

(e) Positive action is also required in the area of Irish-medium education.
At present, only the Shaw's Road Bunscoil and the Irish stream in Derry are
funded by the Education Authorities. Yet it is evident that demand for Irish-
medium education is placing strains on existing projects which could be alleviated by official support. However, not only is assistance required to guide and
promote the development of this resource, but special consideration should also
be given to these schools in view of the fact that the education is bilingual. One
of the principal attractions of the Bunscoil, at the time of the fieldwork for this
book, was the relatively low ratio of pupils to teachers. Parents were confident
that their children received concentrated attention in small classes, enhancing
their language development as well as general educational progress. Each year
since then class numbers have risen. The success of this system depends upon
the immersion of the children in an Irish-language environment. Class numbers
over twenty-five pose unfair difficulties for the teacher and, from the children's
point of view, a maximum below this figure is best. Similarly, in light of the
heavier burden of work placed upon staff at an all-Irish school, extra staff should
be made available to assist with the production of Irish language materials.

(f) The establishment of an Irish-medium secondary school is essential.
This fact is recognised by parents and teachers and a Meánscoil will certainly be
founded in the near future. Official support for the project at this stage, rather
than leaving the onus on parents to overcome initial obstacles and to further
prove the school's viability, would be a laudable step by the Department of
Education.

Provisions for studying some subjects through Irish within existing
schools are welcomed. Indeed, they might be well availed of by students who
transfer from English-medium primary schools. However, this service should
not be perceived as a substitute for the opening of a Meánscoil for, as such, it
would be unsatisfactory and inadequate. The numbers of pupils now leaving
the Irish-medium primary sector each year warrants the introduction of a full
and comprehensive system of education through Irish, where the whole school
environment is Irish-speaking and extra-curricular activities will naturally

occur through that language. For two years (1978–1980) a secondary system was operated on primitive resources. Today, the demand exists for a more satisfactory degree of continuity to the Irish-medium education being experienced by ever growing numbers of pupils.

The importance of an Irish-medium secondary school applies to more than the Bunscoil children themselves. Other families would be encouraged to introduce their children to the Irish-medium system if there was evidence of post-primary facilities. The Dublin-based study, referred to in chapter 7, showed that parents did consider the preparation of children for the secondary system when they elected to send them to an Irish-medium primary school. In addition, Bunscoil families themselves would gain much from the establishment of an all-Irish secondary school. This work pointed to the strong links between the attendance of a child at the Bunscoil and the diffusion of Irish through the family network. This process of bilingualisation within the Bunscoil families and among their friends is threatened by the termination of links with the school, i.e. with the children's Irish-medium education and with the central domain associated with their bilingualism.

Irish-speaking teenagers at Shaw's Road described the degree of variety and colour in the social and educational dimensions of life as young Irish-speaking children. Once they transferred to local secondary schools they developed social interests with school friends and other non-Irish-speaking peers. The establishment of an Irish-medium secondary school would have positive implications for the young people's language behavioural patterns, creating wider opportunities outside the school environment for speaking Irish. The various club activities which concentrate on skills developed through sport, culture, music, hobbies, debates, field trips etc. would be associated with the Irish language. This would in turn improve the teenagers' perceptions of the status and functional relevance of their language.

(g) The possible benefits of a Meánscoil to parents' language learning endeavours has been mentioned. However, parents who select Irish-medium education for their children deserve the kind of professional support which is available in other countries. Examples of the kind of facility needed would be similar to that provided by the Center for Educational Advice in Friesland (van der Ley, 1982). Anyone who has observed mothers hovering about the Bunscoil grounds, waiting for the noisy exodus at 3 o'clock may not notice the timidity of many. However, during the interviews conducted in the homes of these parents, many mothers in particular expressed their anxiety about their own lack of competence. They are, naturally, unhappy about using English in the school grounds, yet many who have some grasp of the language lack the confidence to use their Irish in this public setting. Other difficulties encountered by parents who raise bilingual children while struggling to acquire the language themselves also came to light during the interviews. Similarly, methods developed by parents to overcome problems were also discussed. Some clear patterns emerged regarding the language behaviour of children at certain ages, which parents are unaware of as a fairly common and temporary phenomenon. A fair conclusion would be that the communication channels between parents and other sources could be improved.

In some ways this fact concerns parents, the Bunscoil staff and the Committee. Parental involvement in school life at the Bunscoil has shifted into the area of fund-raising. One or two individual mothers have participated in a way that is more meaningful to them, by being present for a few hours each day and offering staff and pupils the benefit of their own particular talents. At the outset their command of Irish was minimal however this improved considerably over quite a short period of time. Bunscoil families, and the school, could gain if this type of relationship was more actively encouraged.

In other ways, the Education Authorities and Educational Institutes could assist the position of parents and their efforts to establish the language in the home domain. For example, a real need exists for the appointment of a professional liaison person or team who could devote more time to the parents, assisting their endeavours to establish home bilingualism and advising on difficulties associated with the bilingualisation of children or families. Such a service could be expanded to monitor and assist the progress of language diffusion and the establishment of stronger social networks wherein families would have the opportunity to use Irish, whatever their levels of competence.

Institutes specialising in Further Education have the scope and resources to encourage the endeavours of parents in the direction of active bilingualism. At this level, some of the difficulties experienced by Bunscoil parents are already being tackled within other fora. For example, teachers in adult language classes are addressing the problem of adults who attend courses for a certain period and reach a particular level of competence but who withdraw from programmes before a real grasp of the language has been achieved. This phenomenon parallels that plateau stage reached by Bunscoil parents regarding competence in Irish, increased use of Irish inside and outside the home, and their involvement in language-related activities. Further research and the subsequent development of special programmes and teaching strategies are required to assist the adult learner overcome this hurdle in the learning process. Some attention is already being given to this question in Further Education Colleges which could benefit Bunscoil parents also.

(h) Colleges of Further Education are not the only educational institutions equipped with resources that have not yet been fully tapped nor developed with respect to the bilingualisation process in Northern Ireland. Teacher Training Colleges have access to the expertise and experience which could make a valuable contribution in this field in a variety of ways.

(1) Firstly, Irish-medium teachers at nursery and primary levels receive no specialised training to prepare them for teaching through that medium. Rather, all training in education, whether at the Training College or at University, concentrates exclusively on teaching through English. Bunscoil and Naiscoil (Irish nursery) teachers learn through experience in the classroom and from the help and advice generously given by colleagues. In consideration of the fact that Irish-medium education is one of the few areas experiencing growth and expansion in education, it is now fitting to introduce suitable modules into basic course work which would equip language students with a certain, well founded degree of confidence when they first enter the Irish-medium classroom.

(2) The incorporation of programmes into general undergraduate and postgraduate education courses would provide the student with some fundamental expertise which would also be of benefit to students who acquired posts as Irish teachers in English-medium schools. In addition, in-service courses for Irish-medium teachers would be very useful. The Irish-medium teacher acquires a mastery of the Irish language while studying at third level. Afterwards, contacts with other Irish speakers are sustained. However, much of the teacher's time is spent communicating with young children. Regular refresher courses on grammatical and phonological aspects of the Irish language would be welcomed as part of a support service for the teachers themselves.

(3) One area of neglect of Irish concerns the lack of support given to adults learning Irish in their spare time. Ways in which this could be corrected have already been suggested. Teacher Training Colleges would make an enormous contribution by responding to the needs of teachers in these classes. Many of the classes offered in local clubs and centres are given by the most competent and willing speaker of Irish in the company. These teachers share their knowledge of the language voluntarily and enthusiastically. They deserve the type of professional back-up service which could be provided to them at the Teacher Training College. Short courses on the teaching methodology suitable for adult learners should be designed and offered to these teachers. In addition, access to the resources of Languages and Education departments within the College should be made available.

(i) At present, Irish may be studied at St Mary's College of Education, which trains teachers for posts in Catholic schools. Teachers in the state schools who have been trained at the Stranmillis College are not offered the option of studying Irish. This position is unfortunate. Curriculum reforms introduced by the Minister of Education refer to the general relevance of an Irish studies course to secondary pupils across religious divides; a general emphasis is placed upon the benefit of educating children about the traditions of others. However, the value of acquiring Irish travels far beyond that level. It is every child's right in Northern Ireland to be offered the opportunity of learning the indigenous language of his country and to be offered this in terms which are encouraging, enlightening and untainted by old misconceptions. However, how serious a possibility is this if the subject has no status in the Teacher Training College which produces many of the language teachers in their schools? A degree course may be taken at University, without any previous familiarity with the language. Nevertheless, the fact that the subject is not offered at Stranmillis nor in most state schools lays foundations for negative assumptions about the relevance of Irish to students in state schools. It is irresponsible to lay blame for these assumptions with those who love the language, as is often done. Policy innovations at government level are necessary to alter the situation and to nurture positive attitudes across the wider community.

(j) Much of the work which is needed in the development of a serious language policy for Irish and in the provision of back-up resources for existing projects would be greatly assisted by the establishment of an Irish Language and Cultural Planning Institute funded by Government. In consideration of this proposal it would be worthwhile examining the range of work carried out at the Frisian Academy in Leowarden. The potential for such an Institute is wide ranging. For example, it could incorporate the work of the co-ordinating group mentioned above. It could also be responsible for carrying out the basic research upon which policy decisions could be soundly based. In addition, this type of Institute or Academy could include units which provide resources and materials for educational programmes related to the promotion of Irish, as a viable and efficient medium in Northern Ireland today. Another aspect to these resources could be the provision of a library service which housed literary and research material on bilingualism as well as on Irish generally. Bunscoil parents would feature among the people who would avail of such a service. A publishing unit might also be included within such a structure, although this could be set up as an independent enterprise which would benefit from the fieldwork and design of materials being carried out in the Institute.

Other possible areas where such an organisation could promote the process of bilingualisation include the encouragement of literary work among young Irish speakers. Recently, the BBC offered an attractive prize for the winning author of an Irish language play. This type of competition adds colour and range to the activities being promoted among Irish speakers.

(k) An Irish Language Institute would be the appropriate place to investigate other research areas which might make a significant contribution to the position of Irish as well as being relevant on an international level. It is hoped that this present work prepares the ground for some further serious research in the evolving patterns of bilingualism in Northern Ireland and the linguistic direction which the Irish language is taking, with a view to developing its functional role in the wider community.

A follow-up survey of Bunscoil parents would surely produce interesting information about the progress made and the difficulties encountered by parents after some years have passed and, in particular, once their children leave the Bunscoil. Illuminating material could also be acquired from comparative studies in Derry, Dublin and urban areas in Scotland and Wales where family and community bilingualism is generated by the children's attendance at primary school. This type of information would be of practical use to parents and to steering committees which are considering the future establishment of such schools.

The whole area of incipient bilingualism deserves immediate attention and Belfast provides a dynamic centre for fieldwork. The impact of community initiatives upon language shift is one question which has been explored in this book, but which could be further examined within a broader social and geographical framework.

The phenomena of language revival and language behavioural patterns within such an exciting sociolinguistic framework as that which has emerged in Belfast warrant further investigation on a more long-term basis. Another phenomenon which will be interesting to observe and examine over the next few years is the linguistic profile of the Irish which is being diffused throughout a growing section of the community. The outline of linguistic developments presented in this book highlighted the accelerated pace of changes being incorporated into the spoken language. Traditionally, the only sources of linguistic controls to check or guide the direction of linguistic developments have been the schools. Schools accept this responsibility within the confines of the classroom. However, the nature of the language shift ongoing in parts of Belfast and other places in Northern Ireland justifies further resources for deciding upon and exercising some controls on linguistic changes occurring as Irish is learnt and bilingualism takes root. Certainly, a monitoring system looking at adult learners as well as school children could be built into the structure of a Language Institute. Follow-up measures and strategies for giving direction to the linguistic system being moulded in Belfast would naturally be based on a comprehensive, ongoing study of the Irish being spoken on the street, in evening classes, in schools and Colleges, at Irish language social events, etc.

This would also necessitate a critical examination of resources available to learners as well as to more proficient speakers.

In chapter 10, it became evident that despite the increased contact with the Irish language in every other respect, no significant proportion of Bunscoil parents established or sought links with traditional Gaeltacht areas. The isolation of Belfast from areas where Irish is spoken on a daily basis must leave its mark on the linguistic shape of the Irish which is emerging there. The consolidation of Irish speakers in the city into a social congregate wherein the language could survive and grow as a functional, relevant medium in their lives also represents one of the social factors influencing the shape of the language itself. This fact deserves some further investigation from the perspective of its implications for the linguistic system. However, it is also worth considering the ways in which closer links with other Irish-speaking areas could be sustained.

Final Comment

Since the early 1970s Northern Ireland has been jolted into a recognition of the reality of bilingualism. A consciousness is evolving of the validity of Irish as a fundamental dimension to the identity of its citizens. Even during the course of writing this book, new developments were occurring regularly. From the point of view of language revival Belfast is, today, a dynamic and exciting place.

The Shaw's Road Gaeltacht Community proved that the Irish language could be brought back into everyday currency in a way that was satisfying, efficient and relevant in their lives. Other groups and communities were inspired by its realisation of an ideal. Within this urban matrix Irish is not perceived by Irish speakers and learners as a cause or issue; rather, it is simply thought of as 'our own language'. The surge of interest in Irish, as a rich cultural resource worth tapping in the most vibrant and meaningful way possible — i.e. by using it in everyday life and passing it on to one's children — is largely attributable to the founder members of the Shaw's Road Community. It was their conviction and commitment which caught the imagination of others and generated the courage needed to accept a challenge.

References

ALCOCK, A., TAYLOR, B. and WELDON, J. (1979) *The Future of Cultural Minorities*. London: Macmillan.

BELL, G. (1976) *The Protestants of Ulster*. London: Pluto Press.

BLOOMFIELD, L. (1933) *Language*. New York: Holt, Rinehart and Winston.

BOAL, W., DOHERTY, P. and PRINGLE, D. G. (1978) *Social Problems in the Belfast Urban Area: An Exploratory Analysis*. Occasional Paper. Dept. of Geography, Queen Mary College, University of London.

BOYD, A. (1969) *Holy War in Belfast*. Republic of Ireland: Anvil Books Ltd.

BREATNACH, R. B. (1964) Characteristics of Irish dialects in the process of extinction. *Communications et rapports du premier congres de dialectologie generale*. Louvain: Centre International de Dialectologie Generale, 141–5.

BRENNAN, M. (Autumn 1964) The Restoration of Irish. *Studies* 53, 263–77.

BRETT, C. (1986) *Housing A Divided Community*. Dublin: Institute of Public Administration, in association with the Institute of Irish Studies, Queens University Belfast.

CAMBRIDGE ECONOMETRICS AND THE NORTHERN IRELAND ECONOMIC RESEARCH CENTRE (December 1988) *Regional Economic Prospects, Analysis and Forecasts to the Year 2000 for the Standard Planning Regions of the U.K. (Abridged version)*. Cambridge: Cambridge Econometrics Ltd.

CLYNE, M. (1967) *Transference and Triggering*. The Hague: Martinus Nijhoff.

— (1972) Language contact at the discourse level. *Studies for Einar Haugen* (pp. 132–44). The Hague: Mouton.

COISTE COMHAIRLEACH PLEANÁLA (1986) *The Irish Language in a Changing Society: Shaping the Future*. Dublin: Bord na Gaeilge.

COMHAR MHÚINTEOIRÍ GAEILGE AN TUAISCIRT (1988) In P. O LABHRADHA and C. de BURCA (eds) *A Response from Craobh Bheal Feirste (Belfast Branch) to the discussion paper 'Education in Northern Ireland: Proposals for Reform'*. Unpublished document.

COMMISSION OF THE EUROPEAN COMMUNITIES (1986) *Linguistic Minorities in Countries belonging to the European Community*. Summary Report prepared by the Instituto Della Enciclopedia Italiana, Rome.

COMMITTEE ON IRISH LANGUAGE ATTITUDES RESEARCH (CLAR) (1975) *Report*. Dublin: Stationery Office.

CORKERY, D. (1968) *Fortunes of the Irish Language*. First published 1954. Dublin: Mercier Press.

DE BHALDRAITHE, T. (1979) *The Diary of Humphrey O Sullivan*. Translated from 'Cin Lae Amhlaoibh'. Dublin: Mercier Press.

DE FREINE, S. (1978) *The Great Silence*. Dublin: Mercier Press.

DEPARTMENT OF EDUCATION FOR NORTHERN IRELAND (1974) *Primary Education — Teachers' Guide*. Belfast: HMSO.

— (1988) *Education Reform in Northern Ireland: The Way Forward*. Bangor: DENI.
DEPARTMENT OF EDUCATION AND SCIENCE (1988) *Modern Languages in the Curriculum —
A Statement of Policies*. London: DES.
DOEGAN RECORD (1931/3) *Cogadh na nGaiscidheach*. Doegan record, number LA1204.
Transcript unpublished. For general information, refer to Royal Irish Academy
Minutes of Proceedings, Session 1931/33, Appendix, p. 26.
DORIAN, N. (1981) *Language Death*. Philadelphia: University of Pennsylvania Press.
FARRELL, M. (1976) *Northern Ireland: The Orange State*. London: Pluto Press Ltd.
FASOLD, W. (1984) *The Sociolinguistics of Society*. Oxford: Basil Blackwell.
FENNELL, D. (1983) *The State of the Nation: Ireland in the Sixties*. Dublin: Ward River
Press Ltd.
FISHMAN, J. (1967) Bilingualism with and without diglossia; diglossia with and without
bilingualism. *Journal of Social Issues* 23 (2), 29–37.
FERGUSON, C. (1959) Diglossia. *Word* 15, 325–40.
FILE ED. 13/1/156. Public Records Office, N.I.
FILE ED. 13/1/516. Public Records Office, N.I.
FILE ED. 13/1/878. *Instruction in Irish in Public Elementary Schools in N.I.* Public
Records Office, N.I.
GREGG, R. (1964) Scotch-Irish Urban Speech in Ulster. *Ulster Dialects*. Holywood:
Ulster Folk Museum.
HAMILTON, N. (1974) *The Irish of Tory Island*. Belfast: Institute of Irish Studies, Queens
University Belfast.
HAUGEN, E. (1956) *Bilingualism in the Americas: A Bibliography and a Research Guide*.
Montgomery: University of Alabama Press.
— (1969) *The Norwegian Language in America*. Bloomington: Indiana University Press.
— (1977) Norm and deviation in bilingual communities. In P. HORNBY (ed.)
Bilingualism: Psychological, Social and Educational Implications. New York:
Academic Press, pp. 91–102.
HOLMER, N. (1940) *On Some Relics of the Irish Dialect Spoken in the Glens of Antrim
(with an Attempt toward the Reconstruction of North-Eastern Irish)*. Uppsala:
Lundequist.
— (1942) *The Irish Language in Rathlin Island, Co. Antrim*. Todd Lecture Series, XVIII.
Dublin: Royal Irish Academy.
LAMBERT, W. (1977) The effects of bilingualism on the individual: cognitive and socio-
cultural consequences. In P. HORNBY (ed.) *Bilingualism: Psychological, Social and
Educational Implications*. New York: Academic Press.
LEY, L. VAN DER (1982) Role and function of a center for educational advice in a bilingual
province. In K. ZONDAG (ed.) *Bilingual Education in Friesland*. Franeker, The
Netherlands: Uitgeverij T. Wever B.V., pp. 132–48.
LUCAS, L. (1979) *Grammar of Ros Goill Irish*. Belfast: Institute of Irish Studies, Queens
University Belfast.
MAC ÉINRÍ, E. (1981) Muineadh na Gaeilge i mBunscoileanna an Tuaiscirt. In L. MAC
MATHUNA (ed.) *Teagasc na Gaeilge 2*. Dublin: Comhar na Múinteoirí Gaeilge.
MACNAMARA, J. (1967) The bilingual's linguistic performance — A psychological
overview. *Journal of Social Issues* 23 (2), 121–35.
— (1971) Successes and failures in the movement for the restoration of Irish. In J. RUBIN
and H. J. BJORN (eds) *Can Language be Planned?* Hawaii: University Press, 65–94.
MC KENDRY, E. (1988) *'The Way Forward' And Some Comments*. Unpublished document.
MILROY, J. (1981) *Regional Accents of English: Belfast*. Belfast: Blackstaff.

MORTON, D. (1956) Saol Culturtha Bhéal Feirste Roimh 1850. *Fearsaid*. Cumann Gaelach, Queens University, Belfast.

N.I. HOUSING EXECUTIVE (1985) *Belfast Household Survey*. Belfast: N.I.H.E.

N.I. PARLIAMENTARY DEBATES, Commons, vol. XV, c.1084–5, 25th April 1933.

— Commons, vol. XVIII, c.640–2, 24th March 1936.

— Commons, vol. XVIII, c.646, 24th March 1936.

— Commons, vol. XXX, c.4641, 5th March 1947.

— Commons, vol. XXXIII, c.1546–7, 19th October 1949.

Ó HADHMAILL, F. (1985) *Report of a Survey carried out on the Irish Language in the Winter of '84/85*. Belfast: Glor na nGael.

Ó HAILÍN, T. (1969) Irish Revival Movements. In B. Ó CUIV (ed.) *A View of the Irish Language*. Dublin: Stationery Office.

Ó BAOILL, D. (1979a) The study of interlanguage. *Teanga* 1, 3–16.

— (1979b) Error tendencies in learners of Irish. *International Journal of Human Communication* 12, 3–4, 415–39.

— (1981a) Cad é an ní earraid? In L. Mac Mathuna (ed.) *Teagasc na Gaeilge 2*. Dublin: Comhar Na Múinteoirí Gaeilge.

— (1981b) The reality of learning another language. *ISLF Journal* 7, 38–47.

Ó BUACHALLA, B. (1968) *I mBéal Feirste Cois Cuain*. Dublin: An Clochomhar Teo.

Ó BYRNE, C. (1946) *As I Roved Out*. The Irish News Ltd. (Belfast: Blackstaff Press, 1982).

Ó CADHAIN, M. (1964) Mr. Hill: Mr. Tara. Essay. *Áistí Éireannacha I*. Dublin.

Ó CEIRÍN, C. (1970) Translation, 'My Story' by Peter O Leary. Cork: Mercier Press.

Ó CUIV, B. (1971) *Irish Dialects and Irish Speaking Districts*. Dublin: Institute For Advanced Studies.

Ó DOCHAIRTAIGH, C. (1982) Generational differences in Donegal Irish. *Belfast Working Papers in Language and Linguistics* 6, 67–103.

Ó DOMHNALLÁIN, T. and Ó BAOILL, D. (1978) *Earaidí Scríofa Gaeilge. Cuid 1, 2, 3*. Dublin: Institiúid Teangeolaíochta Éireann.

Ó DROIGHNEÁIN, M. (1936) *Taighde i gcomhair Stair Litríocht na Nua Ghaeilge*. Dublin: Oifig Díolta Foilseacháin Rialtais.

Ó FIAICH, T. (1969) The language and political history. In B. Ó CUIV (ed.) *A View of the Irish Language*. Dublin: Stationery Office.

— (1972) The great controversy. In S. Ó TUAMA (ed.) *The Gaelic League Idea*. Dublin: Mercier Press.

Ó GALLACHÓIR, C. (1981) Diglossic bilingualism — domain usage and its implications for Irish and English in one community. *ISLF Journal* 7, 48–56.

Ó GRIANNA, S. (1976) *Caisleáin Oir*. Dublin: Mercier Press.

OMNIBUS SURVEY (1985) *Irish Language — Potential for Educational Programmes*. Unpublished survey. Prepared for Ulster Television Ltd. by Ulster Marketing Surveys Ltd.

Ó MUIMHNEACHÁIN, A. (1974) *Dóchas agus Duaineis*. Dublin: Mercier Press.

Ó MUIRÍ, D. (1982) *Coimhréir Ghaeilge Ghaoth Dobhair*. Dublin: Coisceim.

Ó RAHILLY, T. F. (1972) *Irish Dialects Past and Present*. Dublin: Institute For Advanced Studies.

Ó RIAGÁIN, P. (1988) Bilingualism in Ireland 1973–1983. In J. FISHMAN (General ed.) *International Journal of the Sociology of Ireland* 70, 29–51.

Ó RIAGÁIN, P. and Ó GLIASÁIN, M. (1979) *All-Irish Primary Schools in the Dublin Area*. Dublin: Institiúid Teangeolaíochta Éireann.

Ó SEARCAIGH, S. (1925) *Foghraidheacht Ghaeilge an Tuaiscirt*. Dublin: Brún agus Ó Nuallain, Teo.

Ó SNODAIGH, P. (1973) *Hidden Ulster*. Dublin: Clodhanna Teo.

Ó HUIGINN, R. and Ó MAIRTÍN, M. (eds) (1988) *Irish in the Education System*. Belfast: Comhaltas Uladh.

PEARSE, P. (1976) *The Murder Machine and Other Essays*. Dublin: Mercier Press.

PICKVANCE T. (1975) *Peace through Equity: Proposals for a Permanent Settlement of the N.I. Conflict*. Birmingham: The author.

POOLE, M. A. and BOAL, W. (1973) Religious segregation in Belfast in mid-1969: a multi-level analysis. In B. D. CLARK and M. B. GLEAVE (eds) *Social Patterns in Cities*. London: Institute of British Geographers. Special publication, no. 5, 1–40.

RAYFIELD, J. R. (1970) *The Languages of a Bilingual Community*. The Hague: Mouton.

SAUNDERS, G. (1982) *Bilingual Children: Guidance for the Family*. Clevedon: Multilingual Matters Ltd.

STOCKMAN, G. (1988) Linguistic trends in the terminal stage of Q-Celtic dialects. In G. MAC LENNAN (ed.) *Proceedings of the First North American Congress Of Celtic Studies. 26–30 March 1986*. University of Ottawa, pp. 387–96. (ISPN 0-9693260-0)

SWEENEY, K. (1988) *The Irish Language in Northern Ireland 1987. Preliminary Report of a Survey of Knowledge, Interest and Ability*. Belfast: A Government Statistical Publication, Policy Planning and Research Unit. Occasional Paper no. 17.

WAGNER, H. (1959) *Gaeilge Theilinn*. Dublin: Institiúid Ard Léinn.

WAGNER, H. and STOCKMAN, G. (1965) Contributions to a study of Tyrone Irish. *Lochrann III*.

WALL, M. (1969) The decline of the Irish language. In B. Ó CUIV (ed.) *A View of the Irish Language*. Dublin: Stationery Office.

WEINRICH, U. (1974) *Languages in Contact*. The Hague: Mouton, pp. 99–102.

Index

Page references in italics indicate tables and figures.